SELECTIONS FROM
JAPANESE LITERATURE

Selections from Japanese Literature

(12TH TO 19TH CENTURIES)

Texts with notes, transcriptions

and translations by

Members of the Japanese Seminar

School of Oriental and African Studies

GENERAL EDITOR

F. J. DANIELS

Reader in Japanese in the University of London

LUND HUMPHRIES
12 BEDFORD SQUARE, LONDON WC1

MADE AND PRINTED IN GREAT BRITAIN BY

PERCY LUND, HUMPHRIES AND COMPANY LIMITED

LONDON AND BRADFORD

(JAPANESE TEXT SET UP BY
HUSOO-INSATU-KABUSIKI-GAISYA, TOOKYOO)

The Editor wishes to express his gratitude to the School of Oriental and African Studies, University of London, for having met the cost of publication of this book.

LIST OF CONTENTS

GENERAL INTRODUCTION

This work is intended primarily for students who are working for an Honours degree in Japanese. Such students are presumed to have a fair competence in the modern language and a knowledge in outline of the grammar of Classical Literary style. The work may also be found useful by students with rather less knowledge of the language, or even by those with none, who wish to enlarge their understanding of Japanese literature chiefly through the reading of descriptions and translations.

The pieces have been selected to illustrate a wide variety of Japanese literary styles, as well as with an eye to their intrinsic interest. So far as is known, only two of them have been published in an English translation before. These are the story from *Tutumi-tyuunagon-monogatari*, 'The Minor Captain who plucked the cherry-blossom', which is included in the full translation of the work, with an introduction, by Edwin O. Reischauer and Joseph K. Yamagiwa in *Translations from early Japanese literature*, Cambridge, Mass., 1951; and the chapters from *Gozyuu-no-too* ('The pagoda'), a translation of the whole of which by Sakae Shioya was published in Tookyoo in 1909, our two chapters, in her translation, being included also in *The Treasury of Japanese Literature* (editor, T. Watanabe), Tookyoo, 1933. The special feature of the present work is its very detailed notes.

Since the primary purpose of the work is to help students at the undergraduate level, a modern printed text has in each case been chosen and taken as it stands. That is to say, no attempt has been made to establish a better text than that of the version chosen, even where it is known, as regards some of the older pieces, that variants exist.

The work has been done over a number of years by members of the Japanese seminar of the School of Oriental and African Studies. The usual procedure was for the notes to a piece, with a translation, to be presented to the seminar by one of its members for discussion, often over a number of sessions; then, in the light of the criticisms made, for a revision to be undertaken, most often by some other member. All the pieces have been discussed in detail by the seminar at least once, and the notes and translations are in the main substantially in the form which emerged from the final discussion, although in some cases additions and amendments were made subsequently by the editor or other members of the teaching staff. For the final form in all cases the editor takes general responsibility.

The members of the seminar who prepared or revised one or more of the pieces in whole or in part were the following. Not all were present at all the discussions.

JOHN BESTER, research student.

CARMEN BLACKER, research student (now Lecturer in Japanese at Cambridge).

F. J. DANIELS, Reader in Japanese.

R. P. DORE, Lecturer in Japanese Institutions (now Associate Professor, University of British Columbia).

C. J. DUNN, Lecturer in Modern Japanese.

K. B. GARDNER, Assistant Librarian and research student (now Keeper of Oriental Books and Manuscripts, British Museum).

B. MATSUKAWA, Lecturer in Japanese (now retired).

D. E. MILLS, Lecturer in Ancient Japanese.

P. G. O'NEILL, Lecturer in Classical Japanese.

W. E. SKILLEND, at first research student, later Lecturer in Korean.

S. YANADA, Lecturer in Japanese.

Initials at the end of the various introductions indicate those who took a major part in the work on each piece.

Every reader will of course make use of the work in whatever way he finds most useful. But those more serious students who are training themselves to read Japanese literature in the original, perhaps in the first place for the purpose of tackling 'unseens' in an examination, are recommended to try to understand some of the texts at least with the help of the notes before turning to the transcription and translation of the text in question in the second part of the book. They will do well, too, to attempt their own translation on paper of some passages from a text, so that they may then compare their attempts with the translations given here. These translations are offered as models, but that of course does not mean that another equally competent translator might not have used other words.

The order of the pieces in the book is that of their date of composition or publication, so far as these can be ascertained – with the one exception that *Tuuhuu-Ise-monogatari*, published six years after *Ugetu-monogatari*, is placed before the story from the latter collection because it represents an earlier type. The student may take the pieces in any order, according to his special requirements and interests. The notes to any piece are self-sufficient and independent.

Superscript numbers before words in the transcriptions are intended to facilitate reference to the numbered columns of the texts.

F.J.D.

PART I

INTRODUCTIONS
TEXTS AND NOTES

FROM

KONZYAKU-MONOGATARI

Two stories: *Seimei o yobarete kusainagi o iarawasu monogatari;*
and *Oomi no kuni no Sinohara no tukaana ni iru otoko no monogatari*

THE stream of *setuwa-bungaku*, tale literature, to which the *Konzyaku-monogatari* 今昔物語 belongs, began in the early ninth century with the collection of Buddhist tales known as the *Nihon-reiiki* 日本靈異記. This, like almost all such collections made during the next two or three centuries, was written in *kanbun* 漢文, but the *Konzyaku-monogatari*, compiled in the last third of the Heian 平安 period (794–1191), is one of the earliest, though not the first, of these tale collections to be written in Japanese. It is therefore a most interesting example of the transitional language, greatly under the influence of Chinese, which developed eventually into the language of the *gunki-mono* 軍記物 of the Kamakura 鎌倉 period (1192–1333). But the most important respect in which it differs from its Buddhist precursors is that it contains not only Buddhist but also a great number of secular tales. It is in fact the largest and most varied collection of its kind in the whole of Japanese literature, numbering some 1100 tales in all.

It is divided into thirty-one *maki* 卷, of which numbers 8, 18, and 21 (and also a few individual stories in other *maki*) are no longer extant, and into three sections, the first five *maki* being called *Tenziku no bu* 天竺の部, the next five *Sintan* (震旦) *no bu*, and the remainder *Hontyoo* (本朝) *no bu*. Of these three sections, the first consists of Indian stories (nearly all Buddhist), the second of Chinese stories (the majority Buddhist), and the last of Japanese stories, *maki* 11–20 being exclusively Buddhist and the rest almost entirely secular. It is clear that the main purpose of the collection was the making of Buddhist propaganda, for the Buddhist *maki* are full of stories telling of the rewards of faith, the miracles worked by Kannon 觀音, Zizoo 地藏, and other Buddhist divinities, and the awful retribution to be exacted for sin. It seems most likely that it was designed for popular consumption; it may well have been read aloud to illiterate audiences by educated persons, such as priests. Its language appears well suited for such a purpose, being plain to the point of crudeness, without any pretensions to elegance. The foreign reader will undoubtedly find it less troublesome to understand than the style of most works of Heian literature, with their notorious vagueness and sometimes economy of language; the narrative method of the *Konzyaku-monogatari* is almost over-explicit.

The most interesting parts of the work are the non-Buddhist ones, for the Buddhist stories tend to follow stereotyped formulas, with often a whole group of stories being little more than variations on a single theme. Since many of the Buddhist tales are miracle tales, it is perhaps not surprising that the supernatural should loom large in the non-Buddhist tales too, in the

2

shape of foxes, demons, and ghostly manifestations of various kinds. Besides
these stories, however, there are many others, such as tales of prodigious
feats of strength, tales about notable figures in history, tales about courtiers
and scholars, tales explaining the genesis of famous poems or the derivation
of place-names, tales of evil deeds, love stories, humorous anecdotes, etc. The
first story translated here is taken from *maki* 27, which consists of tales of
the supernatural, under the general title *reiki* 靈鬼, while the second is from
maki 28, which largely contains humorous stories, under the general title
sezoku 世俗.

The oldest extant manuscript of the *Konzyaku-monogatari* is thought to
date from the Kamakura period; it is not known exactly when the work was
written, nor indeed by whom. Traditionally it was always attributed to
Minamoto-Takakuni 源隆國, who died in 1077; he was supposed to have
compiled it while in summer retreat at his villa in Uzi 宇治, entertaining
passers-by and persuading them to tell stories, which he then wrote down.
There is no need for any detailed discussion here of the problem of the
authorship and date of compilation, and it must suffice to say that modern
Japanese scholarship has on the whole tended to reject Takakuni as author,
and would place the date of compilation several decades later than the date of
Takakuni's death. Whatever may be the truth in these matters it is clear that
the *Konzyaku-monogatari* does not consist of stories previously transmitted
only by word of mouth; some of the stories in the *Hontyoo* section may well be
of this nature, but for the great majority of the stories in the collection, literary
sources have been established, ranging from Buddhist sutras and Chinese
collections of Buddhist tales to Japanese *monogatari* of the Heian period. In
many cases the sources have been followed almost word for word. Thus most
of the *Konzyaku-monogatari* is not work of original creation, and indeed little
of it can lay claim to any real literary merit. Much of its value today lies in the
rich fund of material it affords to specialists in fields of study such as social
history, popular religion, etc. Yet though it is certainly not great literature, it
nevertheless has an attraction all its own, at least in the non-Buddhist stories
of the Japanese section. These often show very skilful touches, and they give
us a picture of the times which is not only wide in range—for the characters
include all ranks of society and the stories are set in many different parts of
Japan, not limited to Kyooto 京都 and the Court—but very lively. Even the
stories about Court nobles often show us a very human and comic side of their
life, far removed from the artificial elegance and sentimentality of the
romances written by Court ladies.

It will be noted that the stories included here both begin with *ima wa
mukasi* and end with . . . *to namu kataritutaetaru to ya*, while almost all of the
intermediate paragraphs begin with some formula such as *sikaru aida*, *sono
toki ni*, *sareba* or *sate*. The same pattern is in fact followed by all the stories in
the collection; and it is from the *on* readings of the Chinese characters used in
the opening formula that the word *Konzyaku* in the title is derived.

The text used is that of the NIHON-BUNGAKU-TAIKEI, vol. 9, pp. 715–17 and
828–30. This is written out in modern form. It may be noted that the text of,
say, *Koosyoo-Konzyaku-monogatari-syuu* by Haga-Yaiti 芳賀矢一. which
reproduces the form of the manuscript on which it is based, includes not only

3

combinations of Chinese characters which must be read in inverted order, but also a development of the *senmyoo* 宣命 style of writing, in which the *kana* are written small and verb-endings requiring several *kana* are arranged in two columns. Summaries of nine tales from *Konzyaku-monogatari* are given in the Kokusai Bunka Shinkokai *Introduction to Classic Japanese Literature*.

D.E.M.

---

6 *tomosi*—also written 照射. A method of hunting on moonless nights in summer and autumn, the deer being attracted by the light of bonfires or of a flare or torch (*taimatu*). The gleam reflected from the eyes apparently served as a mark for the hunter to aim at.

8 *karabitaru koe:* a gruff (hoarse) voice. *cf. syagaregoe.*

10 *uma o osi-kaesite:* turning his horse round.

10 *yunde-zama ni nasite:* putting (the voice) on his left. *Yunde* (<*yumite*) is the bow hand, i.e. the left hand. *Zama* here means direction.

11 *hogusi:* a holder for a flare. This story does not state where the holder was, and it might be thought that it was fixed on the horse. It should be noted that, according to *Daigenkai*, in its explanation of *tomosi*, these holders were set up at several points near a junction of roads or paths in the mountains, one path being left unlit to provide cover for the hunter; however, this was evidently not always the case, for in a story in the *Kozidan* 古事談 and the *Uzi-syuui-monogatari* 宇治拾遺物語 (*maki* 1, No.7), a man engaged in *tomosi* is described as wandering about with a flare until he sees the gleam from it reflected in what he takes to be a deer's eyes, and then putting his flare into a holder in order to be able to shoot.

12 *mete:* the 'horse hand', i.e. the right hand, with which a horseman holds the reins. It is usually written 馬手.

13–14 *kamaete＝kanarazu:* I must find some way to shoot this thing.

15 *irubeki yoo mo nakute:* there was no way (means) of shooting.

15 *yogoro*—usually written 夜頃. It may mean either 'a period of several nights' (as here), or 'the last few nights'.

姓名を呼ばれて野猪を射顯はす語

今は昔、□の國□の郡に兄弟二人の男住
みけり、兄は本國に有りて朝夕に狩するを役
としけり。弟は京に上りて宮仕して、時々ぞ本
國には來ける。
而る間其の兄九月の下つ暗の比、燈と云ふ
事をして、大きなる林の當りを過ぎけるに、林
の中に辛びたる音の氣色異なるを以て、此の
燈爲る者の姓名を呼びければ、怪しと思ひて
馬を押返して、其の呼ぶ音を弓手樣に成して、
火を焰串に懸けて行きければ、其の時には呼
ばざりけり。本の如く女手に成して火を手に
取りて行く時には必らず呼びけり。然れば構
へてこれを射ばやと思ひけれども、女手なれ
ば射るべき樣もなくて、此樣にしつゝ夜來を
過ぎける程に、此の事を人にも語らざりけり。

Seimei o yobarete kusainagi o iarawasu monogatari
(*Konzyaku-monogatari* XXVII, 34)

1 *kusainagi:* wild boar. The *Nihon-bungaku-taikei* edition of the *Konzyaku-monogatari* regularly gives the last syllable of the *hurigana* reading of this word as *gi*. Whether this is a misprint or not is uncertain, but it should be noted that the word appears in dictionaries as *kusainaki*. According to one theory, it is a compound of *kusa* (grass) + *i* (be, live) + *naki* (grunt), *i.e.* it means 'the thing which lives in the grass and grunts'; but the true derivation is obscure.

1 *iarawasu:* show up a thing for what it is by shooting it, expose the trickery of something (or someone) by shooting it (or him).

2 [　]-*no-kuni* [　]-*no-koori*. Here, as in a number of passages in the *Konzyaku-monogatari*, there are lacunae in the text.

3–4 . . . *o yaku to sikeri:* made . . . his usual occupation, spent his time . . . -ing, made his living by . . . -ing.

4 *miyazukae:* serving in a nobleman's house. Note that this word is not restricted to service at Court.

6 *simotuyami:* the period towards the end (*simo*) of the lunar month when the nights are dark because the moon rises late. *Tu* is the genitive particle. (*continued on p.4*).

而る間其の弟京より下りたりけるに、兄然

々の事なむ有ると語りければ、弟、「いと布有

なる事にこそ侍るなれ、己罷りて試みむ。」と

20　云ひて燈に行きにけり。彼の林の當りを過ぎ

けるに、其の弟の名をば呼ばずして、本の兄が

名を呼びければ、弟其の夜は其の音を聞きつ

る許りにて返りにけり。兄、「何にぞ聞き給ひ

つや。」と問ひければ、弟、「實に候ひけり、但し

25　えせ者にこそ候めれ。その故は實の鬼神なら

ば己が名こそ呼ぶべきに、其の御名をこそ呼

び候ひつれ、其れを悟らぬ許りの者なれば、

明日の夜罷りて必ず射顕は・して見せ奉らむ。」

と云ひて其の夜は明しぬ。亦の夜、夜前の如く

30　行きて火を燈して其を通りけるに、女手なる

時には呼び、弓手なる時には呼ばざりければ、

馬より下りて鞍を下して、馬に逆様に置きて

17–18 *sikazika no koto:* literally, such and such a thing; when his brother told him what had happened (or: about the affair).

19 *ni . . . haberu*—deferential substitute for *ni . . . aru* (=*naru*).

22–23 *kikituru . . . kaerinikeri:* . . . having just heard (the voice), went home, i.e. having heard the voice, he did nothing else, but went home.

23 *ika ni zo:* 'Well?', 'How was it?'

24 *sooraikeri. Sooroo* is here and in col. 25 a deferential substitute for *aru*. It may also be used as a deferential auxiliary, as in col. 27, *yobisooraiture*.

26 *soko no:* your. Note the unusual reading here of 其 alone.

29 *sono yo wa akasinu:* literally, let that night pass, i.e. did nothing that night.

29 *yoobe*—the accepted reading here of 夜前. It would normally be written 昨夜.

6

逆様に乗りて、呼ぶ者には女手と思はせて、我

は弓手に成して火を焔串に懸けて、箭を番ひ

儲けて過ぎける時に、女手と思ひけるにや、前

の如く兄が名を呼びけるを、音を押量りて射

たりければ、尻答へつと思えて、其の後鞍を例

の様に置き直して馬に乗りて、女手にて過ぎ

けれども音も為ざりければ、家に返りにけり。

兄、「何にか。」と問ひければ、弟、「音に付けて

射候ひつれば尻答ふる心地しつ、明けてこそ

は当り当らずは行きて見む。」と云ひて、夜明

けける儘に兄弟搔烈れて行きて見ければ、林

の中に大きなる野猪木に射付けられてぞ死

して有りける。此様の者の人謀らむと為る程

に、由なき命を亡ぼすなり。これ弟の思量の有

りて射顕はかしたるなりとてぞ人讃めける

となむ、語り傳へたるとや。

36　*koe o osi-hakarite:* judging where the voice was coming from.

37　*sirikotaetu:* sensed that it had hit the mark. *Sirikotoo* refers to the sensation which, according to the Japanese, one experiences in the hand when a hit has been scored.

40　*ni tukete = ni yotte.*

43　*mama ni:* as soon as.

43　*kaki-turete = issyo ni.* 烈 is here an *ate-zi* for 列. *Kaki* is a 'forceful' prefix.

45　*kayoo no mono no. Mono* is the subject of the sentence.

46　*yosi naki inoti o horobosu nari. Yosi naki* is a kind of transferred epithet. The sentence must be translated as if it read *yosi naku . . . nari*— . . . lose their lives in vain, . . . throw away their lives.

近江國の篠原の墓穴に入る男の語

今は昔、美濃國の方へ行きける下衆男の、近
江國の篠原と云ふ所を通りけるほどに、空暗
くて雨降りければ、立ち宿りぬべき所や有る
と見廻しけるに、人氣遠き野中なれば立ち寄
るべき所無かりけるに、墓穴の有りけるを見
付けて、それに這ひ入りて暫く有りける程に、
日も暮れて暗くなりにけり。雨は止まず降り
ければ、今夜許りは此の墓穴にて夜を明さむ
と思ひて、奥様を見るに廣かりければ、いと吉
く打息みて寄り居たるに、夜打更くる程に聞
くに、物の入り來る音す。暗ければ何物とも見
えず、只音ばかりなればこれは鬼にこそはあ
らめ、はやう鬼の住みける墓穴を知らずして
立ち入りて、今夜命を亡ひてむずる事を心に
思ひ歎きける程に、此の來る物只來りに入り

Oomi-no-kuni no Sinohara no tukaana ni iru otoko no monogatari
(*Konzyaku-monogatari* XXVIII, 44)

1 *tukaana*: burial-cave. This appears to be the accepted reading of the characters 墓穴 here, though they would normally be read *hakaana*. *Tukaana* is usually written 塚穴.
2 *gesu-otoko*: man of the lower classes, man of humble station.
4 *tati-yadorinubeki tokoro*: a place where he might shelter.
10 *oku-zama = oku no hoo*.
11 *yoriitaru*. *Yoru* seems to mean lean (back). It is possible that *itaru* here is an auxiliary, but it is probably best to interpret it as having its meaning of sit down (see 21 *inuru*; but *cf*. 30–31 *kikiitaru*).
14–15 *hayoo . . . tati-irite*: I have rushed into this cave not knowing that a demon lived here. *Hayoo* (< *hayaku*) is to be taken with *tati-irete*.
15 *usinaitemuzuru = usinaiten to suru* (*usinatte simaoo to suru*).
16–17 *kitari ni irikitareba*: came further and further in. This reduplication for emphasis is a common feature of *Konzyaku-monogatari* style.

來れば、男怖ろしと思ふ事限りなし。然れども

遁るべき方無ければ、傍に寄りて音も爲で曲

まり居たれば、此のもの近く來て、先づ物をば

たと下し置くなり。次にさやさやと鳴る物を

置く、其の後に居ぬる音す。これ人の氣色な

り。

此の男下衆なれども思量有り心賢かりけ

る奴にて、これを思ひ廻らすに、これは人の物

へ行きけるが、雨も降る日暮我が入りつる樣

に、此の墓穴に入りて前に置きつるは持ちた

りける物をはたと置きつる音なめり。次には

蓑を脱ぎて置く音のさらさらと聞えつるなめ

りと思へども、尙これは此の墓穴に住む鬼な

めりと思へば、只音も爲で耳を立てて聞き居

たるに、此の今來たる者男にや有らむ、法師に

や有らむ、童にや有らむ、知らず。人の音にて

20 *sayasaya = sarasara*: rustling.
21 *inuru. Iru* here = sit down.
24 *omoimegurasu*: ponder on.
24 *mono = dokoka.*
25 *ame mo huru higure*—adverbial—on this rainy night; as it was a wet night.
26–27 *saki ni okituru wa . . . oto nameri.* This sentence is loosely constructed, though the meaning is clear. *Saki ni okituru* must be interpreted as 'the noise which he had heard of something being put down'. *Nameri = narumeri.*
30–31 *kikiitaru.* Here *itaru* is almost certainly an auxiliary (but *cf.*11 *yoriitaru*).
31 *ima kitaru mono:* the man who had just come, the newcomer.
32 *sirazu.* There is no real break in the sense here, and a *tyon* would seem to be more appropriate than the *maru* given in the text. *Otoko ni ya . . . sirazu* is a parenthesis between *ima kitaru mono* and the verb of which this is the subject.

云ふ様、「此の墓穴には若し住み給ふ神などや

御する、然ればこれ聞しめせ、己は物へ罷りつ

る者の此を通りつる間に、雨は痛う降る、夜は

深更けぬれば、今夜許りと思ひて、此の墓穴に

入りて候なり。」と云ひて、物を祭る様にして

置けば、本の男其の時にぞ少し心落ち居て、さ

ればこそと思ひ合はせける。

然て其の置きつる物を近き程なれば、竊か

に何ぞと思ひて手を指遣りて捜れば、小さき

餅を三枚置きたり。然れば本の男實の人の道

を行きけるが、持ちたる物を祭るにこそ有り

けれと心得て、道は行き極じて物の欲しかり

けるまゝに、此の餅を取りて竊かに食ひつ。今

の者暫し有りて此の置きつる餅を捜りける

に無し。

其の時に實に鬼の有りて食ひてけるなめ

---

34 *kikosimese:* deign to eat.

35 *koko.* The reading here (though not the meaning) of 此 is parallel to that of *soko* in col. 26 of the other *Konzyaku-monogatari* story.

35 *itoo* (< *itaku*): very.

37 *sooroo*—here a deferential auxiliary.

37 *maturu:* offer to a deity.

38 *kokoro otiite* = *otituite*.

38–39 *sareba koso:* just as I thought.

40–41 *sono okituru mono o . . . sagureba. Okituru mono* is the object of *sagureba.*

44 *miti wa yuki-koo-zite:* tired after his journey. *Koo-zite* is usually written 困 じ て.

44 *mono:* something to eat.

りと思ひけるにや、男俄に立ち走るま丶に、持

ちたりつる物をも取らず、蓑笠をも棄てて走

り出で去にぬ。身の成らむ様も知らず逃げて

去にければ、本の男然はこそ人の來りけるが、

餅を食ひたるに恐れて逃げぬるなりけり。吉

く食ひてけると思ひて、此の棄て去りぬる物

を捜れば、物一物入りたる袋を鹿の皮を以て

裏みたり、亦蓑笠有り。美濃邊より上りける奴

なりけりと思ひて、若し伺ひもぞ爲ると思ひ

ければ、未だ夜の内に其の袋掻き負ひて、其の

蓑笠を打著て墓穴を出でて行きける程に、若

し有りつる奴や人郷に行きて、此の事を語り

て人などを具して來ぬらむと思ひければ、遙

かに人離れたる所に山の中に行きて、暫く有

りける程に夜も明けにけり。

其の時に其の袋を開けて見ければ、絹布、綿

49–50 *tatihasiru mama ni . . . sutete.* The man got up and ran, not stopping as he did so to pick up . . . (*mama ni = to doozi ni*).
51 *mi no . . . sirazu:* not knowing what would happen to him, blindly.
52 *sa wa koso = sareba koso* (see 38–39 *sareba koso*).
53 *moti o kuitaru ni osorete:* frightened when someone ate his rice-cakes, frightened at having his rice-cakes eaten.
53–54 *yoku kuitekeru:* (exclamatory) 'What a good thing I ate them!'
55 *hitamono = ippai.*
56–57 *Mino no atari . . . to omoite.* It is not clear why he thought the man had come up from Mino.
57 *ukagai:* investigation.
60 *arituru yatu:* i.e. the man who had run away from the cave.
61 *o gu-site:* accompanied by, together with.
64 *kinumono.* This is the accepted reading of 絹布 here.

たるとや。

思ひけむ。希有の事なれば、かくなむ語り傳へ

食ひて、今の奴の逃げにけるを、何に可咲しと

得をも爲るなりけり。然るにても本の男餅を

時にも萬を心得て、吉く翔ひて思ひ懸けぬ所

然れば心賢しき奴は下衆なれども、かかる

に誰とも知らで止みにけり。

に語りけるを聞き傳へたるなり。今の奴は遂

此の事は本の男の老いの畢てに、妻子の前

蠢付けし。

なりかし。現に誰も逃げなむ。本の男の心いと

ぬ所得したる奴かな。今の奴は逃ぐる尤も理

れよりなむ行きける所へは行きにける。思は

ば、天の然るべくて給へると思ひて、喜びてそ

などを一物入れたりけり。思ひ懸けぬ事なれ

---

66 *ten . . . tamaeru. Ten* is the subject of *tamaeru*, which is used here not as an auxiliary but in its original meaning of 'bestow'. *Sarubekute* is adverbial, meaning literally 'it being right that it should be so', 'it being destined to be so'.

66–67 *sore yori namu.* This must be taken not with the verb *yukikeru* immediately following but with the final verb *yukinikeru.*

67–68 *omowanu syotoku:* a windfall.

68–69 *niguru . . . nari kasi. Niguru* is the subject of *nari. Kasi* is emphatic. *Mottomo* and *kotowari* here mean much the same—'what one might expect'.

69 *ge ni*—usually written 實に.

70 *mukutukesi:* unpleasant, despicable.

71 *hate*—an unusual reading of the character 畢.

72–73 *ima . . . yaminikeri:* No-one ever found out who the second man was.

75 *yorozu o kokoroete:* knows what's what.

77 *ika ni okasi:* how funny.

TUTUMI-TYUUNAGON-MONOGATARI

One story: *Hanazakura oru syoosyoo*

ONE of the categories of novels in the Heian 平安 period (794–1191) is concerned with life at the capital, the modern Kyooto 京都, and in particular with the love affairs and marriages of the characters. It can be thought of as starting with *Otikubo-monogatari* 落窪物語 in the middle of the tenth century and as reaching its highest level in *Genzi-monogatari* 源氏物語 at the beginning of the eleventh century. *Tutumi-tyuunagon-monogatari* 堤中納言物語 is a collection of stories largely of this same type, and represents its final stage. From internal evidence these ten stories are assigned to the end of the Heian period or later, that is, something like two centuries after *Genzi-monogatari*.

The author of these stories is not known. They were once attributed to Huziwara-Kanesuke 藤原兼輔 who was called Tutumi-tyuunagon (Middle Counsellor of the Embankment) from his living near the River Kamo 加茂川, but he died in 933 and is thus far too early. Whether the title of the work arises from this attribution is not known; at any rate, no other satisfactory explanation has appeared, and it remains a mystery. We do not know when the compilation was made, but two seventeenth century MSS. bear a note that they are copied from texts of the thirteenth and fourteenth centuries. From this we may gather that the collection existed under its present title (or simply that of *Tutumi-tyuunagon*) by that time.

It consists of ten stories (and a fragment) arranged in order of the seasons in which they are set. Most of them have a flavour of humour or irony; for example, the tale translated here deals with a young courtier who planned to abduct a beautiful girl but seized instead her aunt, a nun and too old to be a victim of such an adventure. In other stories there is a young man of little self-confidence who fails to persuade his lady to submit to him, a young woman who applies blackening to her face thinking it to be powder, and ten sisters, all maids to separate concubines of the Emperor, who have concealed their relationship and meet in secret to discuss their mistresses. It is possible that the humorous element was added to make interesting a type of story that was beginning to pall.

We have translated the first of these stories, *Hanazakura oru syoosyoo*, 花櫻折る少將, 'The Minor Captain who plucked the cherry-blossom'. It owes its position in the collection to the fact that its period is spring, with the cherry-trees in flower, though the *susuki* grass in which the hero hides is unseasonable, for it would not be high enough to conceal anyone in spring, unless perhaps the previous year's dead growth had not been cut.

The background of this story, and indeed of the whole collection, with the possible exception of the last of them, *Yosinasigoto*, which is thought to be of early Kamakura 鎌倉 date (Kamakura period, 1192–1333), is the Imperial court. The Heian period was generally one of peace and stability, with the whole artistic interest centred in the capital. The main occupations of the court folk were what they have been in many courts later, namely, intrigue, both for the favour of superiors and of the amatory kind, participation in polite recreation and amusement, and the carrying out of ceremonial.

Polite entertainments were what one might expect—ability to compose poems, to write them beautifully on appropriately decorated paper and to know what tree twig to tie them to to symbolize one's meaning, ability to play musical instruments, and participation in various games such as shell-matching and identifying incense. Ceremonials were religious or traditional, and often involved stately dancing.

Intrigue of the first kind went on by the usual weapons of back-biting, flattery and gossip, but amorous intrigue in the period has a character of its own, which, since it is the theme of our story, and indeed of much of the other literature of the time, requires a fairly full description.

Love has rarely been so free in a civilized society as it seems to have been in the Heian court. The physical conditions were well adapted. Ladies usually had separate quarters, generally secluded, for it was their aim to hide themselves from prying male eyes, and they were as jealous of being seen as any inmate of a harem. Thus once a man could reach his lady's chamber he could feel safe from interruption. And though the ladies tried to hide themselves they were often betrayed by their servants, or by the architecture, which afforded so many shutters and doors for entrance. Marriage was a matter of the man choosing a girl, arranging, by exchange of letters and poems, to visit her one night, sending her next day, if she had pleased, a further letter, visiting her on the next two nights and remaining in her bed on the third, whereas he had crept away at dawn on the first two. Then rice-cakes were eaten and there was a formal interview with her parents. Naturally, in many cases, these marriages were arranged between parents. The bride often stayed at her father's house, though she might be taken to her husband's when, for example, she became pregnant. Among the ladies-in-waiting and the male courtiers lasting marriages seem to have been rare, and affairs commonplace, the men regularly leaving their mistresses at dawn. Both men and women could have more than one lover at a time, though this appears to have been unusual. It was not unknown for a man to abduct a woman he fancied or to use force to win one over, though a woman was usually allowed to refuse admittance or her favours to a man, or to send him away early if she wished. Whatever happened, a well-conducted love affair had a necessary accompaniment of poetry.

In our story, the young woman in the desolate dwelling, the hiding in the *susuki* grass to watch without being seen, and the poems exchanged with the mistress in the early part are all typical elements of Heian love stories. Young women in almost derelict houses seem to have been attractive to Heian gallants. This is partly an aspect of the Heian liking for melancholy, and partly because such women would almost always be orphans, with no father to keep the house in repair, and thus would be less protected and easier to lead into transitory unions, as were widows and girls turned down after one night

14

by intended bridegrooms. The originality of this story is in the laughable situation of the young gallant who examines his capture only to find a woman of some age, and a nun to boot.

The language of the story is fairly straightforward literary Japanese typical of the Heian period, as far as conjugation of verbs and use of particles is concerned. The style, however, is remarkable for the looseness of its sentence structure and for its economy. So much is left unsaid that a detailed commentary is now necessary for comprehension. It is a matter of doubt whether this economy is evidence of lack of skill, or whether the whole range of court life was so familiar to the author's reader that a few virtually disconnected suggestions were enough to evoke a complete picture.

The earliest extant MSS. date only from the seventeenth century, perhaps five hundred years after the date of composition, and are rather corrupt. The first printed edition was in 1890. The text used for this translation is that prepared by Simizu-Yutaka 清水泰 in his *Zootei Tutumi-tyuunagon-mono-gatari-hyoosyaku*, Kyooto, 1938.

The complete set of stories has been translated by Professors Reischauer and Yamagiwa, *Translations from Early Japanese Literature*, Harvard University Press, 1951, where there is also an excellent introduction. Dr. Arthur Waley has translated one story as *The Lady who loved insects* (London, 1929; reprinted in *The real Tripitaka and other pieces*, London, 1952).

C.J.D.
K.B.G.
D.E.M.

月にはかられて、夜深く起きにけるも、思ふ
らむ所いとほしけれど、立ち歸らむも遠きほ
どなれば、やう〳〵行くに、小家などに例音な
ふものも聞えず、隈なき月に、所々の花の木ど
もも、ひとへに混ひぬべく霞みたり。今少し過
ぎて見つる所よりも、おもしろく過ぎがたき
心地して、

そなたへと行きもやられず花櫻
にほふ木かげに立ちよられつ、

とうち誦じて、早くこゝに物言ひし人ありと、
思ひ出でて立ち休らふに、築地の崩より、白き
ものの、いたう咳きつゝ出づめり。哀れげに荒
れ、人氣なき處なれば、此所彼所のぞけど咎む
る人なし。このありつる者を喚びて、「此所に
住み給ひし人はいまだおはすや、やま人に物

Hanazakura oru syoosyoo

1 *hanazakura oru syoosyoo*. Whether there is a precise allusion in the title remains undisclosed, but one can at least see in it a figurative reference to the abduction of the lady. It is not known whether *hanazakura* is a particular variety of cherry or a synonym of *sakurabana*, but the point appears to be of no great importance. *Syoosyoo*: the third highest rank in the Imperial Bodyguards, the *kon-e* 近衛. On the possibility that the word *syoosyoo* here may be a mistake, see 62 *tyuuzyoo-no-kimi*.

2 *hakararete*. *Hakaru* = *damasu* (cf. *hakarigoto, tabakaru*).

2 *okinikeru mo*. The subject of *okinikeru* is to be taken as the *syoosyoo* mentioned in the title; *mo* has a slight adversative meaning, very similar to a modern *ga*. The verb in what may be considered the co-ordinate clause to this is *yuku*, col. 4. Thus the structure of the sentence is: 'He got up . . . but nevertheless went on (even after he had discovered that it was not yet daylight) . . . because (*nareba*) . . . , although he felt sorry (*itoosikeredo*) . . . , it would have been a long way . . .' The contemporary reader would require no more than the first few words to see the whole scene clearly—the *syoosyoo* is visiting a lady and it is her bed he leaves. If he were in his own bed, he would not have to rise at daybreak, which the brightness of the moon makes him think has come.

2–3 *omooramu tokoro*. The subject of *omooramu* is to be taken as some lady whose presence the *syoosyoo* has thus left. *Tokoro* corresponds to English 'what'—'what she would be thinking'. The *syoosyoo* would naturally imagine that the lady would be in despair at his untimely departure.

3 *tati-kaeramu mo* indicates one of the courses of action open to him—'were he to go back'
It is possibly from some such construction that the adversative *mo* arose.

3–4 *tooki hodo*. This 'great distance' was possibly the corridors, etc. that he would have to
go through.

4 *yuku ni*. *Ni* = as, when; in translation it can often be replaced by a full stop.

4 *koie*—where the common folk lived.

4 *rei*—here an adverb (= *itumo*) modifying *otonoo*.

4–5 *otonoo mono mo*. *Otonoo* = *oto ga suru*. *Mo* seems to be used here in two ways (*i*)
followed by the negative *kikoezu*—'not *even* the usual noises were to be heard', and (*ii*)
connected with the *mo* of the next clause (... *mo* ... *mo* = both ... and ...), detailing
points descriptive of the solitary moonlit scene.

5 *kumanaki tuki:* moonlight leaving nothing unlit, pervasive moonlight.

5 *hana* refers to the cherry.

6 *hitoe ni:* altogether, completely.

6 *magainubeku*. *Magoo* = to resemble in such a way as to cause anyone to make a mistake,
to take it for something else. The construction NU form (past tense) + *beku* is very like
a modern 'dictionary form' + *hodo*.

6 *kasumitari*. *Kasumu* is often applied to cherries in bloom. *Magainubeku kasumitari*—were
so like a mist as to deceive the eye.

6 *ima sukosi:* just now. Note, however, that *sukosi* refers here to distance and not time.

6–7 *sugite:* going by, passing.

7 *yori:* than.

9 *sonata ... yararezu*. *Sonata e* = *atira e*, i.e. somewhere else, away. *Yuki mo yararezu*
corresponds to modern *iku koto mo dekinai* (or *dekinakute*).

10 *nioo* here = be bright.

10 *tati-yorare-tutu:* being drawn towards. *Yoru* here seems to have a transitive force (*cf.*
12 *omoiidete*).

11 *uti-zunzite*. *Uti* is a very common first component of compound verbs, and in many cases
adds a meaning of speed or violence, but in others seems to add nothing to the total
signification. Here it may hint at the ease with which the *syoosyoo* recited the *waka*.

11 *hayaku:* some time ago, earlier.

11 *monoiisi hito:* a person with whom he had conversed (at night), a lover.

12 *omoiidete*. This and *uti-zunzite* above are parallel constructions, connected with *tati-yasuroo*. The verb *omoiizuru* (*omoideru*, *cf. omoide*) = *omoidasu*. This is another case of
different uses with regard to transitive and intransitive, at the time of the story and today.

12 *tati-yasuroo:* linger.

12 *tuizi:* earth-bank.

12–13 *siroki mono:* person clothed in white, 'a white figure'; apparently a servant in this
house where the *syoosyoo's* former lover had lived.

13 *itoo* < *itaku*—very; very much.

13 *siwabuki-tutu:* coughing.

13 *izumeri*. The use of *meri* is difficult here. Since the figure did appear, one cannot translate
'seemed to appear'; *meri* would seem to put the meaning of the verb into relation with the
watcher, i.e. the *syoosyoo*. Perhaps 'he saw a white figure appear' gives a fair idea of the
nuance intended.

14 *hitoge naki:* devoid of any sign of humanity, deserted.

14 *nozokedo* probably through the screens of the house, in the manner of most lovers of the
time. He would, however, not go inside without making sure the lady was not otherwise
engaged, hence his desire to be challenged. He would also probably want to send in a
poem.

15 *kono* qualifies *mono*.

15 *arituru mono*. *Aru* here = appear; 'this man who had appeared just now'.

16 *owasu*—honorific substitute for *iru*.

16 *yamabito:* hermit; used jocularly for the lady in the fastnesses of her house.

聞えむといふ人あり、とものせよ。」といへば、

「その御方は此所にもおはしまさず、何とかい

ふ處になむ住ませ給ふ。」と聞えつれば、あは

れの事や、尼などにやなりたるらむと、後めた

くて、「かのみつとをに逢はじや。」など、ほゝゑ

みての給ふほどに、妻戸をやはら搔放つ音す

なり。男ども少しやりて、透垣のつらなる群薄

の繁き下に隠れて見れば、「少納言の君こそあ

けやしぬらめ、出で、見給へ。」といふ。よき程

なる童の、容體をかしげなる、いたう萎え過ぎ

て、宿直姿なる蘇芳にやあらむ、艶やかなる袙

に、うちすきたる髪の裾、小袿に映えてなまめ

かし。月の明き方に、扇をさしかくして、「月と

花とを。」と口ずさみて、花の方へ歩み來るに

驚かさまほしけれど、暫し見れば、おとなしき

人の、「すゑみつはなどか今まで起きぬぞ、辨

17 *kikoemu* = *moosamu*.

17 *mono seyo*. *Mono suru* is a verb of very general and imprecise sense; here = say.

18 *on-kata*: the lady.

18 *koko ni mo*. This *mo*, connected with the negative *owasimasazu*, seems to be equivalent to a modern *wa* in the same position, and thus lays stress on *koko ni*.

18 *owasimasazu*. In Heian Japanese the suffix *masu* was more frequently conjugated according to the *yodan katuyoo* (. . . *masazu*) than to the *simo-nidan katuyoo* (*cf*. modern . . . *masen*).

18–19 *nani to ka yuu tokoro*. It is not clear whether these are supposed to be the speaker's actual words.

19 *kikoetureba*. See 17 *kikoemu*.

20 *ama nado ni* = *ama ka nanika ni*.

20–21 *usirometakute*: with a feeling of uneasiness. (May not his having left her on the previous occasion have been the cause of her shaving her head?)

21 *Mitutoo*: presumably a man's name; possibly another suitor when the *syoosyoo* was visiting the lady, or a figure in a novel popular at the time.

21 *nado* gives an idea of indefiniteness (*cf*. 20 *ama nado ni*). When used with verbs like *notamoo* or *yuu* it implies that what precedes is not necessarily all that is said, nor necessarily the actual words used. This *nado* may sometimes (as here and in col. 63) be translated by avoiding the use of direct speech, and sometimes by 'with more to the same effect'. Note that it can be used with verbs of saying and thinking without an intervening *to*.

22 *hodo:* when, as.

22 *tumado:* a door with hinges, opening onto the veranda.

22 *yawara:* gently.

22 *kai-hanatu* refers to the creaking of the door as it opens. *Kai < kaki.*

22–23 *oto su nari.* This *SYUUSIKEI* (*su*) followed by *nari* is an unusual construction. The *RENTAIKEI* (*suru*) + *nari* is equivalent to a modern *suru no desu;* the construction used here may be to add further vividness to the narrative.

23 *otokodomo sukosi yarite:* sending his men a little way off. The subject of the sentence is the *syoosyoo.*

23 *suigai no turanaru. Suigai:* a type of fence with spaces between the palings. Note the phonetic change in both parts of the word—*sui < suki, gai < gaki (kaki). Suigai* is the subject of *turanaru;* it seems more natural in English, however, to say 'beside the open-work fence', as if the Japanese were *suigai ni turanaru.*

24–25 *Syoonagon-no-kimi . . . sinurame:* Mistress Syoonagon! Is it daylight yet? *Kimi* is properly an honorific word, as in *tyuuzyoo-no-kimi,* col. 62, and in some contexts approximates to 'Lord' or 'Lady'. While *Syoonagon-no-kimi* and *Ben-no-kimi,* col. 32–3, would be by no means of humble birth, since their names indicate that they had male relatives of sufficient rank to hold the offices of *syoonagon* and *ben,* they are in this household only unimportant attendants, and thus *kimi* can here have little more honorific sense than modern *san.* It might almost be regarded as forming part of the names. Note *koso* (as later in col. 33) used in calling someone; the later example shows that with this use of *koso,* the *IZENKEI* is not always found.

25–26 *yoki hodo . . . okasige naru.* This phrase shows a common construction used when a noun is qualified by more than one adjective or adjectival phrase. A parallel may be found in modern colloquial phrases like *akai enpitu no ii no. Yoki hodo naru* means young but not too young, i.e. of marriageable age. Note that *okasi* means pleasant and not, as in modern colloquial, funny or peculiar. *Warawa* is the subject of the whole sentence, which is very loosely constructed. *Namamekasi* at the end characterizes the total effect made by the girl whose appearance is described in detail, or, what comes to the same thing, the *syoosyoo's* reaction to this effect.

26–27 *naesugite* means that the *akome* has lost its stiffness and become soft through being worn.

27 *tonoi-sugata:* one's dress when on *tonoi,* i.e. when in attendance at night.

27 *suoo:* a dark red colour. The dye is made from the *suoo no ki,* sapan wood.

27 *tuyayaka:* literally 'glossy', but here rather 'beautiful'.

27 *akome:* a short under-garment like the *kosode* of later times, worn by men and women.

28 *uti-sukitaru. Suku =* to comb; for *uti,* see 11 *uti-zunzite.*

28 *koutigi:* an outer garment worn by women only.

28 *haete:* contrasted with, set off by.

29 *akaki = akaruki.*

29 *oogi o sasikakusite:* holding up her fan to cover her face. The phrase seems to be a combination of two ideas, *oogi o sasu* and *kao o kakusu.*

29–30 *tuki to hana to o:* a quotation from a poem (*Gosen-syuu* 後 撰 集 vol.3) by Minamoto-Saneakira 源 信 明 : *Atara yo no / tuki to hana to o / onazikuba / kokoro sireramu / hito ni miseba ya*—'Oh, the precious moonlight and the flowers! Would that I could show them to one who knew the meaning of their beauty!' As always in this story, *hana* means specifically cherry-blossom.

30–31 *hana no kata . . . odorokasamahosikeredo:* as she walked up to the flowers, he (the *syoosyoo*) felt a desire to surprise her but . . .

31 *sibasi mireba.* The subject is the *syoosyoo.*

31 *otonasiki = otonarasiki.*

32 *Suemitu*—a male servant, perhaps.

32 *nado ka:* why.

の君こそ此所なりつる、參り給へ。」といふは、

物へ詣づるなるべし。ありつる童は留るなる

べし。「侘しくこそ覺ゆれ。さばれ唯御供に参

りて、近からむ所に居て、御社へは參らじ。」な

どいへば、「物ぐるほしや。」などいふ。皆仕立て

、五六人ぞある。下るゝ程もいと惱しげに、こ

れぞ主なるらむと見ゆるを、よく見れば、衣脱

ぎかけたる容體、さゝやかにいみじうこめい

たり。物言ひたるも、らうたきものゝゆゑ〳〵

しく聞ゆ。嬉しくも見つるかなと思ふに、やう

〳〵明くれば歸り給ひぬ。日ざしあがるほど

に起き給ひて、昨夜の所に文書き給ふ。「いみ

じう深う侍りつるも、道理なるべき御氣色に

出で侍りぬるは、つらさもいかばかり。」など、

青き薄樣に柳につけて、

知らざりし古よりも青柳の

32–33 *Ben-no-kimi*. Mistress Ben is a woman of the household. For *kimi* and *koso* see 24 *Syoonagon-no-kimi . . . sinurame*.

33 *koko narituru = koko ni arituru (koko ni ita no desu ka)*.

33 *mairi-tamae*. *Mairu* here means to visit a shrine (詣).

33–35 *. . . yuu wa, mono . . . narubesi. Arituru . . . narubesi*. Both these sentences show what the *syoosyoo* presumed (hence *besi*). *Mono e moozuru* means the same as *mairu* above. *Mono e = dokoka e. Arituru warawa*: the girl who came out into the garden, who is presumably Mistress Syoonagon.

35–36 *sabare . . . mairazi*. This is said by Mistress Syoonagon, who is to stay behind, presumably because of some ritual defilement, probably the menses. *Sabare = sa mo araba are*, i.e. be that as it may, all the same. *On-tomo*: with her ladyship (the mistress of the house, who has not yet appeared in the story).

37 *monoguruosi ya*: Nonsense! This is said by the *otonasiki hito*.

38 *oruru hodo mo*. *Oruru* means coming down the steps in front of the house. *Hodo = yoosu*.

38 *nayamasige ni*. *Ni* here has the force of *nite* or modern colloquial *de, de atte*. *Nayamasi* may mean ailing, referring to physical as well as mental distress. Perhaps it is best translated here as 'frail'. [It is instructive to compare the Victorian use of 'delicate' to make the covert assertion, according to W. Empson (*The structure of complex words*, pp.44 ff.), that 'refined (= delicate) girls are sickly (= delicate)'.]

39 *. . . miyuru o, yoku mireba*. The clause ending in *miyuru* refers to one of the five or six people. The subject of *mireba* is the *syoosyoo*. 'Looking carefully at one of them who seemed . . .'

39–40 *kinu nugikaketaru*: the collar of her coat was set well back from the nape of her neck.

40 *sasayaka* expresses the idea of smallness or daintiness. The *ni* following it has the same force as that after *nayamasige* in col. 38.

40 *imizyuu (< imiziku) = taihen*.

40–41 *komeitari* < *komekitari*. Smallness and daintiness were clearly features of importance in the contemporary conception of female beauty.

41–42 *mono iitaru . . . kikoyu:* her voice, too, was charming yet with a note of dignity. *Rootaki* = *kawairasii*. *Mono no* is adversative. *Yueyuesiku:* dignified.

42–43 *uresiku mo . . . kaeri-tamainu* again refers to the *syoosyoo*. *Uresiku mo mituru kana* means 'With what delight I have seen (her)!'

44 *yobe no tokoro* refers back to the beginning, i.e. to the lady whom the *syoosyoo* left because he thought it was already daylight. It seems that he gallantly refrains from suggesting that her charms had not been enough to keep him from mistaking the moonlight for the dawn, and pretends that he was only obeying what he took to be her hint.

44–46 *imizyuu hukoo . . . ika bakari:* 'Though it was still dead of night your manner told me (I should go), and so I left you, but oh! with what an ache in my heart!' *Haberu* is here a deferential auxiliary verb. *Kotowari* 道理 *narubeki on-kesiki ni:* literally, in view of your manner (which hinted) that it would be right (for me to go) . . .' This is the interpretation given by Japanese editors, and seems most likely to be correct, though another possible interpretation would be: 'in view of your manner, for which you doubtless had reason . . .' Note that women had the right to indicate in this indirect way when they wished their nocturnal visitor to leave.

47–50 *aoki usu-yoo . . . tote yari-tamaeri:* the poem was written on green *torinoko*, and attached to a willow branch, and sent . . .

47 *usu-yoo:* the thinnest of three varieties of *torinoko* 鳥子 writing-paper.

48–49 *sirazarisi . . . omoimidaruru*. The poem compares the *syoosyoo*'s thoughts, distraught as he is with love, to the tangled tresses of the willow. The colour of the paper and the method of sending reinforce the conceit. *Sirazarisi inisie* means 'when I knew (you) not'. Note the puns on (1) *ito—aoyagi no ito* (where *aoyagi no* is a *makurakotoba* 枕詞) and *itodo* (= more and more); and (2) *midaruru*, to be tangled (literal), and *omoimidaruru*, to be distraught. The plain sense of the poem can be obtained by omitting the words *aoyagi no*.

21

いとゞぞ今朝はおもひみだる、

とて遣り給へり。返事めやすく見ゆ。

かけざりしかたにぞはへし絲なれば

解くと見し間にまた亂れつゝ

とあるを見給ふほどに、源中將・兵衞佐、小弓

持たせておはしたり。「昨夜は何所に隠れ給へ

りしぞ、内裏に御遊ありて召ししかども、見つ

け奉らでこそ、」との給へば、「此所にこそ侍り

しか、怪しかりける事かな。」との給ふ。花の木

どもの咲きみだれたる、いと多く散るを見て、

あかで散る花みる折はひたみちに

とあれば、佐、

わが身にかつはよわりにしかな

との給ふ。中將の君、「さらば甲斐なくや。」とて、

散る花を惜しみとめても君なくば

誰にか見せむ宿のさくらを

50 *kaerigoto meyasuku miyu:* her reply was written so that it looked 'easy on the eye', i.e. in a beautiful hand.

51–52 *kakezarisi ... midare-tutu.* This poem continues the play on the word *ito*, tresses. Those tresses had grown, she says, where he had not really set his heart, and so no sooner did she think them untwined than they became entangled (i.e. he and she fell in love and she thought he would be true to her, not realizing that he was fickle and would form other attachments). *Kakezarisi* = *omoikakenakatta* (*omoi o kakenakatta*), i.e. you had not set your heart, you did not really love. The subject is the *syoosyoo*. *Kata* = direction. There are puns on both *toku* and *midare-tutu*. *Toku* means (1) to untangle (untangled tresses being a symbol of love whose path is smooth), and (2) to be on terms of intimate friendship, to 'melt' towards each other (*cf. tokeau*), while *midare-tutu*, in addition to the literal meaning of becoming entangled, has also the figurative sense of becoming 'entangled' with other women. The tense idea in *midare-tutu* is very vague, and it could be interpreted as past, present or future.

53 *mi-tamoo hodo ni.* The subject is the *syoosyoo*.

53 *(Gen)-tyuuzyoo:* the second highest rank in the Imperial Bodyguards, the *kon-e*.

53 *hyooe-no-suke:* the second highest rank in the *hyooe*, Military Guards. The *kon-e* and the *hyooe* were two of the three groups of Palace Guards, the other being the *emon* 衛門, Gate Guards. There were in all six units of guards, each of the above groups being divided into two, Left and Right.

53–54 *koyumi motasete owasitari*—literally, 'came in, causing (someone) to carry their bows', i.e. their bows were carried by servants. *Koyumi* were small bows used in competitions.

55 *uti:* the Imperial Palace. This is a common reading of the characters 内裏, also read *dairi*, with the same meaning.

55–56 *mesisikado mo, mituke-tatematurade koso:* 'You were sent for but we didn't find you.' A rough (colloquial) equivalent for *mituke-tatematurade koso* would be *o-mituke sinakute ne.*

57–58 *hana no kidomo no sakimidaretaru.* For the construction, see 25–26 *yoki hodo . . . okasige naru.*

59 *akade . . . hitamiti ni.* One of them, probably Gen-tyuuzyoo, composes the first part of the poem, leaving the second to be added by Hyooe-no-suke: 'When I see the flowers falling before I have gazed my fill at them . . .' *Akade = akazu ni, akanaide.* Nowadays 'to have had enough of' is more usually expressed by *akiru,* though *aku* survives in the phrase *aku made,* 'to the bitter end'. *Hitamiti ni = hitasura ni,* i.e. 'earnestly, keenly'.

61 *waga mi . . . kana. Ni* and *katu* in this poem are usually considered to be copyists' errors for *mo* and *kaku,* so that the meaning is taken to be ' . . . (how keenly I feel that) in the same way I too have withered and faded.' It is possible, however, that *katu wa* may have been used in the sense of *mata,* and that only one emendation (*mo* for *ni*) is necessary.

62 *tyuuzyoo-no-kimi.* As the text stands, this must be Gen-tyuuzyoo. However, the poem which follows is reproduced in the *Huuyoo-syuu* 風 葉 集, with the title of this story given as *Hanazakura oru tyuuzyoo.* The word *syoosyoo* in our title then may be a mistake, and the author of this poem may be the hero of our story. *Kimi* here is honorific, but no specific equivalent seems called for in English, since it follows a rank (*cf. taisyoo-dono,* col. 89).

62 *saraba kai naku ya.* This may be translated as 'That won't do', but note that two different interpretations of the sense are possible (1) 'You mustn't say such despairing things' (*kai naku = sikata ga arimasen*), and (2) 'The flowers will bloom in vain', 'flowers' being really a reference to women. *Ya* is here exclamatory and not interrogative, *cf. mono-guruosi ya,* col. 37.

63 *tiru hana o osimitomete mo:* Though I should try to keep the flowers from falling. For the double reference in *hana,* see the preceding note.

とのたまふ。戯れつゝ諸共に出づ。かの見つる

處尋ねばやとおぼす。夕方殿にまうで給ひて、

暮れゆくほどの空、いたうかすみこめて、花の

いとおもしろく散り亂るゝ夕ばえを、御簾卷

き上げてながめ出で給へる御容貌いはむか

たなく、光みちて、花のにほひも無下にけおさ

るゝ心地ぞする。琵琶を黄鐘調にしらべて、い

とのどやかにをかしく彈きたまふ御手つき

など、限なき女も斯くはえあらじと見ゆ。この

方の人々召し出でゝ、さまぐ うち合せつゝ

遊び給ふ。みつすゑ、「いかゞ女のめで奉らざ

らむ。近衞の御門わたりにてこそ、めでたくひ

く人あれ。何事にもいとゆゑづきてぞ見ゆる。」

と、おのがどち言ふを聞き給ひて、「いづれ、こ

65–66 *kano . . . obosu.* The subject is the *syoosyoo.*
66 *tono*—used of the dwelling of an exalted person: Hall.
67 *kasumikomete:* covered by haze.
69 *nagameide.* The force of *ide* here is not clear, but the expression probably means *soto o nagamete.*
70 *hikarimitite:* filled with light, so beautiful that it seemed radiant.
70 *hana no nioi*—not 'scent'. See 10 *nioo,* above.
70 *muge ni:* completely.
70–71 *keosaruru:* be overpowered, outshone.
71 *kokoti zo suru* refers to the feeling awakened in the onlooker. *Kokoti* is the subject of *suru.*
71 *ooziki*—one of the twelve musical 'modes'.
71 *sirabete:* tuning.
72 *nodoyaka = nodoka*—quiet, peaceful.
73 *kagiri naki onna:* a woman whose beauty is unbounded.
73 *kaku wa e-arazi = modern Japanese kore hodo arienai.*
73–74 *konokata no hitobito:* people who excelled in this art (music).
74 *uti-awase-tutu:* (playing instruments) in concert together. *Uti* perhaps suggests the ease with which they, or rather the *syoosyoo,* performed.
75 *Mitusue*—probably a serving-man at the Hall.
75–76 *ikaga . . . mede-tatematurazaramu:* How could a woman fail to find him (the *syoosyoo*) attractive?
77 *yuezukite:* being skilful, accomplished.
78 *onogadoti yuu = zibun-doosi de yuu:* say in conversation with one's fellows.
78 *kiki-tamaite.* The subject is the *syoosyoo.*

85　　　　　　80

の櫻多くて、荒れたるやど、わらはいかでか見

し、我に聞かせよ。」とのたまへば、「猶便あり

て、罷りたりしになむ。」と申せば、「さる所は見

しぞ、細に語れ。」との給ふ。かの見し童に物い

ふなりけり。「故源中納言の女になむ。實にを

かしげにぞ侍るなる。かの御伯父の大將なむ、

迎へて内裏に奉らむと申すなる。」と申せば、

78–79 *izure, . . . yado. Izure = izuko*, modern *doko*. Note that there are here two separate questions: Where? Is it that house . . . ?

79 *wara wa = omae wa*. Not to be confused with the word *warawa* which occurs elsewhere, meaning a young servant-girl. This *wara* is derived from *ware* 我, which can also mean 'you'.

80 *nao* here, and in col. 86, seems to have something of what was presumably its original meaning (*cf. naosu*), straight, direct; and thence, simply, just.

80–81 *tayori arite:* while on some errand. It seems to imply 'having some business in the district (or: at that house)', and may imply further 'having a connection (i.e. mistress) in that household'.

81–82 *saru tokoro wa misi zo:* I have seen the place you speak of. Note, however, that it is also possible to interpret this sentence as a question: How is it that you know this place?

82 *kano misi warawa* refers to the girl whom the *syoosyoo* had seen in the garden. The subject of *monoyuu narikeri* is Mitusue.

83 *narikeri* = modern *no de atta:* It happened that . . .

83 *ko-Gen-tyuunagon no musume ni namu*. Although the *syoosyoo*'s questions have all related to the house, Mitusue now proceeds to enlighten him about the real object of his interest, the lady of the house (n.b. not the *warawa*, who was Mitusue's mistress). *Tyuunagon:* Middle Counsellor (of the Supreme Council of State).

83–84 *okasige:* charming, lovely (*cf.* col. 26).

85 *mukaete:* has become her guardian. (The word 'guardian' is here used in a very general sense, of course, and not in its Western legal sense. The situation is that, since the lady has no father, her uncle the *taisyoo* is going to act as her sponsor for the appointment at Court.)

85 *uti ni tatematuramu:* . . . is going to procure her an appointment at Court (introduce her into the Imperial harem).

「さらざらむ先に、猶たばかれ。」との給ふ。「さ

思ひ侍れど、いかでか。」とて立ちぬ。夕さり、か

の童は、ものいとよくいふものにて、ことよく

かたらふ。「大將殿の常に煩はしく聞え給へ

ば、人の御文傳ふることだに、伯母うへいみじ

くの給ふものを。」と、同じ處にてめでたから

む事などのたまふころ、殊に責むれば、若き人

の思ひ遣りすくなきにや、「よき折あらば今。」

といふ。御文は殊更に、けしき見せじとて傳へ

ず。みつすゑまゐりて、「言ひ趣けて侍る。今宵

ぞよく侍るべき。」と申せば、喜び給ひて、少し

夜更けておはす。みつすゑが車にておはしぬ。

わらはけしき見ありきて入れ奉りつ。火は物

の後へ取りやりたればほのかなるに、母屋に

いとちひさやかにてうち臥し給へるを、かき

抱きて乗せ奉り給ひて、車を急ぎて遣るに、

---

86 *sarazaramu saki ni* = *soo naranai mae ni. Sarazaramu* < *sa arazaramu.*

86 *nao* (*cf.* 80 *nao*)—you must just arrange something.

86 *tabakare:* plot, scheme. Some such phrase as 'to make her mine' should be understood here.

86–87 *sa omoi-haberedo, ikade ka:* I agree, sir, but how? For *haberu* see 44–46 *imizyuu hukoo . . . ika bakari.*

87 *yuusari:* one evening.

88 *kotoyoku* = *tyoosi yoku* i.e. freely and with the conversation going well.

89 *kataroo* = *katari-oo* (語り合ふ). The force of the ending *oo* can be brought out in translation by adding 'to Mitusue'.

89–90 *kikoe-tamaeba.* This verb seems to have *taisyoo-dono* as subject and is presumably made honorific by the suffixed *tamoo.*

90 *oba-ue.* This aunt, who is living with the lady and as we later discover is a nun, is almost certainly the (retired) wife of the *taisyoo.*

90–91 *imiziku notamoo:* make a fuss, scold.

91 *mono o*—adversative. Can be rendered by 'Oh, but . . .' at the beginning of the girl's speech.

91 *onazi tokoro.* Two interpretations are possible (1) the *taisyoo's* house, and (2) the lady's house. Note that time has passed between the girl's speech and this.

91–92 *medetakaramu koto:* the 'auspicious event' of the lady's entry into the Imperial service.

92 *koto ni semureba:* specially urged, urged more strongly than ever. The subject is Mitusue, who is pressing his mistress to assist in the *syoosyoo's* scheme.

93 *omoiyari sukunaki:* lacking in power of careful thinking.

93 *ni ya*—a half question. The implication is that it is perhaps on this account that she yielded to persuasion.

93 *yoki ori araba ima:* as soon as there is a good opportunity.

94 *on-humi*—a letter from the *syoosyoo* to the lady.

94 *kotosara ni = waza to.*

94 *kesiki:* what was going on.

95 *mairite,* i.e. to the *syoosyoo.*

95 *iimukete haberu:* I have persuaded (prevailed on) her. These words are spoken to the *syoosyoo* by Mitusue, the *syoosyoo* being the subject of the following clause. For *haberu,* see 44–46 *imizyuu hukoo . . . ika bakari.*

96 *yoku haberubeki = yokarubeki.*

97 *owasu:* an honorific word covering a variety of meanings; here equivalent to *iku* or *tatu.*

97 *Mitusue ga kuruma. Ga* here is possessive. The subject of the sentence is the *syoosyoo,* who went in Mitusue's carriage to avoid suspicion, Mitusue being well-known at the house.

98 *miarikite = miarukite.*

98 *ire-tatematuritu.* The depreciatory (negative honorific) suffix indicates that it was the *syoosyoo* whom she let into the house.

98 *hi:* lamp, light.

99–100 *moya ni . . . uti-husi-tamaeru o:* the tiny figure of someone who was lying asleep in the main room. This whole phrase is the object of the following verbs *kaki-idakite* and *nose-tatematuri-tamaite.*

101 *nose-tatematuri-tamaite,* The depreciatory *tatematuri* is used in deference to the lady's rank, while the honorific *tamaite* shows that the *syoosyoo* even in humbly doing the act is as worthy of respect as ever.

27

「こは何ぞ何ぞ。」とて、心得ずあさましう思さる。中將の乳母聞き給ひて、「伯母うへの後めたがり給ひて、臥し給へるになむ、もとよりちひきくおはしけるを、老い給ひて、法師にさへなり給へば、頭さむくて、御衣を引き被きて臥し給へるなむ、それと覺えけるも道理なり。」車よするほどに古びたる聲にて、「いなや、こは誰ぞ。」との給ふ。その後いかゞをこがましうこそ。御容貌はかぎりなかりけれど。

---

102 *ko wa na zo na zo.* These are the words of the kidnapped lady. *Na zo = nani zo (nan desu ka).*
102 *asamasyuu:* aghast, amazed—not the modern colloquial sense of *asamasii.*
103 *Tyuuzyoo-no-menoto:* the lady's nurse, (who was known as) Tyuuzyoo.
103 *kiki-tamaite:* hearing of the abduction (after it had occurred).
105 *hoosi ni sae.* The process of becoming a nun necessarily involved shaving the head; hence the point of the following phrase *kasira samukute.*
106 *on-zo:* clothing (of exalted person).
107 *kotowari nari:* it was only natural (that) . . .
108 *kuruma yosuru hodo ni:* when the carriage was brought up to the *kurumayose;* this was a platform for convenience in boarding and alighting from a carriage, which was part of the equipment of a high-class residence (here, of course, the *syoosyoo's*).
108 *ina ya*—purely an exclamation: Oh dear!
109–110 *sono noti . . . koso. Okogamasi:* farcical, ridiculous. One edition makes a stop after *ikaga* and would supply after it *narinikemu,* so that the sense would be *sono go doo natta ka wa bakabakasikute hanasi ni naranai.*
110 *on-katati.* The unanimous opinion of Japanese editors has been accepted that this refers to the old woman and not to the *syoosyoo.*

TAIHEIKI

—first part of section *Ootoo-no-miya Kumano-oti no koto*
(from near middle of 5th *maki* 卷)

THE *Taiheiki* 太平記, 'Chronicle of the Great Peace', despite its name, belongs, together with the earlier *Heike* (平家)-*monogatari* and a number of other works, to the class of War Chronicles (*gunki-mono* 軍記物) or Tales of Fighting (*senki-monogatari* 戰記物語). It deals primarily with stirring events over a period of nearly fifty years up to 1367, during the conflict between, on the one hand, supporters of the emperors Go-Daigo (Daigo II) 後醍醐天皇 and Go-Murakami (Murakami II) 後村上天皇 and, on the other, the military governors at Kamakura 鎌倉—first Takatoki 高時, the last of the Hoozyoo 北條 regents, and then Takauzi 尊 (or 高) 氏 and Yosiakira 義詮, the first two Asikaga 足利 *syoogun* 將軍; its sympathies are on the whole with the Imperial side. Some episodes from the earlier history and pseudo-history of Japan are also related in it. The reason for its inappropriate name is uncertain; the most plausible explanation seems to be that the name was given to the original form of the work, which was probably completed before 1352—see below—when for a brief space Go-Murakami was installed in the capital, and it was perhaps believed that lasting peace had been restored.

The authorship of the work is not entirely certain. A diary of 1374 says that a priest named Kozima 小島法師 had just died, and that he was the author of the *Taiheiki*. The latest event mentioned in the work itself belongs to 1367. There is a statement elsewhere, however, that the *Taiheiki* was seen, and that some of its facts were impugned, by someone who died in 1352. Although there seems to be no very strong reason for doubting the diary entry, it tells us in fact very little, since nothing else is known of Kozima. Most modern authorities think that the bulk of the work, at least so far as events up to about 1350 are concerned, may well have been written by a single author, but that many subsequent additions and revisions by different hands went to produce the text in its existing form. Already in the early Muromati 室町 period (fifteenth century) the *Taiheiki* was being recited for public entertainment, and by about 1600 professional reciters known as *Taiheiki-yomi* 太平記讀 were flourishing. If, as seems not unlikely, recitations had been given ever since the original form of the work was completed, say about 1350, the text as it now exists may well have been influenced by the reciters.

The general trend of the work may be said to be moralistic, in its praise of loyalty—especially loyalty to the Imperial House—and perhaps in its attribution to Buddhist and other supernatural beings of the power to influence events. But the chief aim of the author or authors was, it is clear, to produce a gripping story; certainly historical accuracy in any strict sense was neither achieved nor attempted.

The terminations of verb forms, etc. conform generally, at least in the earlier part of the work, to the accepted rules of Classical Literary style (*bungotai* 文語體). Note, however, in our extract (column 33) *midariitte*, presumably a spoken-language form, in place of *midariirite*.

Opinions about the literary value of the work have varied from extravagant praise to equally extravagant condemnation. There is a good deal of incoherence, particularly towards the end. Throughout, considerable use is made of literary devices, which it is possible to admire or deplore according to taste. The commonest of these is an elaborate parallelism between consecutive clauses or sentences; this device of *tuiku* 對句, as it is called, was almost certainly imitated originally from Chinese, but it was well established in Japanese by this time. Examples occur in our extract. The extract ends half-way through a passage of *mitiyuki-bun* 道行文, of which there are a number in the work; more will be said about this literary form in a moment. The reader will probably agree that, on the evidence of the present extract, the style of the work is vivid and forceful; the standard of the extract, however, may be rather above the average for the whole work.

Mitiyuki-bun is a kind of poetical prose or slightly irregular verse evoking rather than describing the experience of a journey. The names of places on the way are incorporated, together with the expression of thoughts and feelings regarded as appropriate to these places or to the circumstances of the traveller. There is much literary allusion and quotation, whole phrases being borrowed from *waka* 和歌 in the standard anthologies. This borrowing may be illustrated from the opening of the passage which is given in part in our extract, viz.:

Yura no minato o
miwataseba
oki kogu hune no
kazio tae /

When one (or he) looks across the harbour (? strait) of Yura, (it is seen that) the helm-thong (*kazio*) of the boat being rowed off shore is snapped.

ura no hamayuu
ikue to mo /
siranu namizi ni
naku tidori /

Crinum (a plant) of the strand [this is a *makurakotoba* 枕詞 introductory to *ikue*]—any number of folds (is descriptive of) the unknown wave-way, on which are crying dotterel—*or*, of number of folds unknown (is) the wave-way. . .

Ki-no-zi no tooyama
byoobyoo to /

Distant heights of the province of Ki (Kii), (seen) as dim and vast.

Huzisiro no
matu ni kakareru
iso no nami /

Waves of the coast, suspended on the Huzisiro pine-trees (i.e. seen through their branches—and suggesting clusters of purple wistaria [*huzi*] blooms).

(A more detailed explanation is given in the notes to the text. The Japanese has here been set out as verse for convenience, although in the text it is not distinguished typographically from prose. As will be seen, it is in *sitigotyoo* 七五調, alternate 'lines' of seven and five *onsetu* 音節, with occasional irregularities; this is the normal pattern of *mitiyuki-bun*.) Now, the opening 'lines' of the passage were almost certainly written with the following *waka* from the *Sinkokin-wakasyuu* 新古今和歌集 (No.1071 in the *Kokka-taikan*) in mind:

> *Yura no to o / wataru hunabito / kazio tae*
> *yukue mo siranu / koi no miti kana,*

and probably also with another in the same collection (No.1073) which is based on it (i.e. which takes it as its *honka* 本歌):

> *Kazio tae / Yura no minato ni / yoru hune no*
> *tayori mo siranu / oki tu siokaze.*

Not only are two of the phrases in our passage, *Yura no minato o* and *kazio tae*, identical (except for the final particle in the former) with phrases in one at least of these *waka*, but it seems very likely that *ikue to mo / siranu* in our passage is intended to recall *yukue no siranu*, 'does not even know the destination', of the *honka*, with a pun, that is to say, between *ikue*, 'how many folds', and *yukue*, 'destination'. Note too the phrases written wholly in capitals in the following *waka*; all these phrases are reproduced in our passage:

> *HUZISIRO NO / mi-saka o koete / MIWATASEBA*
> *kasumi mo yaranu / Hukiage no hama.*
>
>

Syokugosen- 續後撰 *wakasyuu*, No.1312

> *Yosa no umi / kasumiwatareru / akegata ni*
> *OKI KOGU HUNE NO / yukue sirazu mo.*
>
>

Huuga- 風雅 *wakasyuu*, No.1420

> *Sa si nagara / hito no kokoro no / mi-Kumano no*
> *URA NO HAMAYUU / ikue naruramu.*
>
>

Syuui- 拾遺 *wakasyuu*, No.890

> *HUZISIRO NO / mi-saka no matu no / konoma yori*
> *yuuhi ni miyuru / Awazi-simayama.*
>
>

Sinsenzai- 新千載 *wakasyuu*, No.1893

> *Yama takami / MATU NI KAKARERU / huzi no hana*
> *sora yori oturu / nami ka to zo miru.*
>
>

Sinsyuui- 新拾遺 *wakasyuu*, No.183

> *Kore mo mata / kami ya uekemu / Sumiyosi mo*
> *MATU NI KAKARERU / kisi no huzinami.*
>
>

Sinzoku-kokin- 新續古今 *wakasyuu*, No.206

In these *waka*, including the two from the *Sinkokin-wakasyuu*, there is already the association of *Yura no minato* with *kazio tae*, of *oki kogu hune* with *yukue sira . . .* (which, we have seen, probably suggested *ikue to mo / siranu*), and of *Huzisiro* with *matu*, as well as the idea of looking between pine-trees to the waves beyond. Further, the last two of these *waka* supply the idea of a resemblance between the waves and clusters of wistaria blooms on the pine-trees. It is not suggested that it was necessarily these particular *waka* (except those from the *Sinkokin-wakasyuu*) from which phrases were borrowed; most of the capital-letter phrases occur in other *waka*, some in a score or more. They were clichés in fact, all no doubt common currency among practitioners of *renga* 連 歌 ('linked verse').

The situation in which our extract opens is that the emperor Go-Daigo has taken refuge from Hoozyoo-Takatoki at Kasagi-yama, a mountain on the border between the provinces of Yamasiro 山 城 and Yamato 大 和, while his eldest son, Morinaga-sinnoo 護 良 親 王, referred to in the text as Ootoo-no-miya, waits for news. The warriors who come in search of the prince are on the Hoozyoo side.

The text followed is that of the NIHON-BUNGAKU-TAIKEI, vol.17, (pp. 118–20). Use has been made of the version in the YUUHOODOO-BUNKO (*Taiheiki, zyoo*, pp. 128–31) for many of the readings.

There are translations of some extracts from the *Taiheiki* in W. G. Aston's *A History of Japanese Literature* (London, 1899), together with a description of the work, which should be compared with that given in *Introduction to Classic Japanese Literature* (Tokyo, 1948), Kokusai Bunka Shinkokai.

F.J.D.

B.M.

---

5 *tora-no-o o humu:* tread on a tiger's tail. This metaphor or simile for incurring extreme danger comes from Chinese, where the phrase 履 虎 尾 is first recorded in the explanation of one of the sixty-four divinatory hexagrams (*sei*, 井) in the 'I-ching' (易 經, *Ekikyoo*, 'The Book of Changes'). The phrase in its Japanese translation had been used in the *Gen-Pei-seisuiki* 源 平 盛 衰 記, from which the author of the *Taiheiki* may well have taken it. It became known still more widely from its use in the *noo* 能 play *Ataka* 安 宅; a film with the title *Tora-no-o o humu otokotati* was shown in London in 1952 (this was based on the *kabuki* 歌 舞 伎 play *Kanzintyoo* 勧 進 帳). *Ataka* and *Kanzintyoo* are dramatizations of an incident during the flight of Minamoto-no-Yositune 源 義 經 from his brother, Yoritomo 賴 朝, about a century and a half before the Ootoo-no-miya incident, but the situations of the two heroes have much in common.

6 *on-minoue* seems to have here the sense of *on-mi*, 'his person', 'himself'.

6–8 *tenti hirosi . . . , zitugetu akiraka . . . kokoti site.* Note the parallel construction, which occurs again in the following pair of sentences. A literal translation on the lines of 'Though heaven and earth may be (said to be) wide, etc.' fails to do justice to the original on the ground of style, and it is suggested that 'How wide soever the heavens and the earth, etc.' is a better rendering.

9 *tuyu ni husu uzura no toko ni on-namida o arasoi. Uzura no toko*, 'quails' beds', is a recognized poetical circumlocution for *kusamura*, 'clumps of herbage'. Since the phrase is here elaborated with *tuyu ni husu*, one can hardly avoid bringing 'quails' into the translation. The construction is difficult to justify. It seems necessary to understand *arasoi* in a quasi-passive sense ('having his tears contending—rivalling—vying'); and also to take *tuyu ni* not only with *husu* ('couch *in the dew*') but also with *arasoi* ('contending—rivalling—vying —*with the dew*')—even though *tuyu to . . . arasoi* might seem more natural than *tuyu ni . . . arasoi*. The idea, at any rate, is that his tears would rival, or be as copious as, the dew. The translation suggested ('his tears outvying where the quails couch in their beds of dew') hardly strains English more than the original strains Japanese; though the Japanese may be easier to interpret in so far as *tuyu* is a stock poetical symbol for *namida*, whereas 'dew' and 'tears' in English are less closely connected.

大塔宮二品親王は、笠置の城の安否を聞召

されん爲に、暫く南都の般若寺に忍んで御座

ありけるが、笠置の城已に落ちて、主上囚はれ

させ給ひぬと聞えしかば、虎の尾を履むおそ

5 れ御身の上に迫りて、天地廣しと雖も御身を

藏さるべき所なし、日月明らかなりと雖も長

夜に迷へる心地して、晝は野原の草に隠れて、

露に臥す鶉の床に御涙を争ひ、夜は孤村の辻

10 にぞみて、人を尤むる里の犬に御心を悩まさ

れ、何處とても御心安かるべき所なかりけれ

Ootoo-no-miya Kumano-oti no koto

1 *Ootoo*—see 49 *Oo-too no Genzoo-Sanzoo*.

2 *nihon-sinnoo:* Imperial prince of the Second order. Under the Taihoo 大寶 code, Imperial princes held one of four 'orders' (*hon*), as distinct from the 'ranks' (*i* 位) awarded to subjects. [The use of 'order' and 'rank' respectively to render *hon* and *i* has been adopted from R. K. Reischauer, *Early Japanese History*.]

2 *Kasagi no siro*. Although *siro* in later times is usually to be translated as 'castle', nothing is known of any permanent military building at Kasagi-yama. At the time in question even permanent *siro* appear to have been little more than positions, often on high ground and sometimes with dwelling-houses built on them, surrounded by a wooden fence or series of fences, and perhaps by a ditch or ditches. 'Fortress' is here probably a fair translation.

2–3 *kikosimesaren:* honorific passive; and the *mesu* is itself honorific.

3 *nanto:* the Southern Capital, i.e. Nara 奈良.

3 *Hannya-zi:* temple of the Singon sect 眞言宗, founded in the seventh century. Late in the twelfth century the place had been razed by fire during the Gen-Pei 源平 war and then rebuilt, and further disastrous fires had occurred in the following century. There were still further fires after the time of the incident related in the *Taiheiki*. In recent times the temple has not been prosperous. A black lacquered chest, said to be the very one in which Ootoo-no-miya hid, was exhibited there till about 1936 and perhaps still is.

4–5 *torawaresase-tamainu*. The causative element as well as the *tamainu* (< *tamoo*) is honorific. (continued on p.32).

ば、かくても暫しはと思召されける處に、一乗
院の候人按察法眼好専、如何にして聞きたり
けん、五百餘騎を率して、未明に般若寺へぞ寄
せたりける。折節宮に附き奉りたる人一人も
なかりければ、一防ぎ防ぎて落ちさせ給ふべ
き様もなかりける上、透間もなく、兵既に寺内
に打入りたれば、紛れて御出あるべき方もな
し。さらばよし自害せんと思召して、既に推し
膚脱がせ給ひたりけるが、事叶はざらん期に
臨んで、腹を切らんことはいと安かるべし。若
しやと隠れて見ばやと思召し返して、佛殿の
方を御覧ずるに、人の讀みかけて置きたる大
般若の唐櫃三つあり。二つの櫃は未だ蓋を開
けず、一つの櫃は御經を半ば過ぎ取出して蓋
をもせざりけり。此の蓋を開けたる櫃の中へ、
御身を締めて伏させ給ひ、其の上に御經を引

12–13 *Itizyoo-in:* an institution (no longer in existence) inside the precincts of the *Koohuku-zi* 興 福 寺 in Nara, famous temple of the Hossoo 法 相 sect. 'Seminary' is suggested as a translation for *in* in cases like this; there does not seem to be any consistent line of division between a *zi*, temple, and an *in*.

13 *koonin:* a priest who was permitted to marry and whose duties were administrative rather than religious; the title was normally borne only by persons employed at a Buddhist institution whose head was or had been an Imperial prince. 'Lay-priest Administrator' is suggested as a translation.

13 *Azeti* was by this time a family name; earlier it had been the title of officials who made tours of inspection to the provinces.

13 *hoogen:* a priestly court rank (the Second rank) automatically bestowed on priests holding the office of *soozu.* The scheme of offices (*sookan* 僧官) and ranks (*sooi* 僧位) was as follows:

office	rank
soozyoo 僧 正 (High Priest of Buddhism)	*hooin* 法 印
soozu 僧 都 (Assistant High Priest of Buddhism)	*hoogen* 法 眼
rissi 律 師 (Master of Buddhist Asceticism)	*hokkyoo* 法 橋

[The suggested translations of the offices are R. K. Reischauer's in his *Early Japanese History.*] The collective name for these senior officials of the Buddhist heirarchy was *soogoo* 僧 綱. Though the scheme ceased to be officially recognized at the Meizi Restoration 明 治 維 新 (1868), it is still in use in some sects, the ranks now, of course, not being bestowed by the court.

14 *sos-site = hikiite.*

16 *hitohusegi husegite:* (by) putting up a (short) defensive fight.

19–20 *osi-hadanugase-tamaitarikeru. Osi:* 'forceful' prefix; *hadanugu:* 'bare the upper part of the body'. The causative element is honorific, and the rest of the compound needs no comment.

20 *kotokanawazaran.* From *kotokanoo:* (have) things go as desired, (have) matters turn out well for one.

22 *obosimesikaesite:* honorific equivalent of *omoikaesite.*

22 *butuden:* building or room housing the principal image or images of a temple.

23–24 *dai-hannya no karoodo. Dai-hannya* is for *dai-hannya-(haramitta-)kyoo,* the Mahā-prajñā-parāmitā-sūtra. *Karoodo* (< *karaudu* < *karahitu* = *Kara,* China; *hitu,* chest): chest of Chinese type with six legs (illustration in Sanseidoo *Koozirin* dictionary under *karabitu,* another form of the same word.)

27 *husase-tamai.* The causative element is honorific.

27 *on-kyoo.* One must understand by this 'some of the volumes or scrolls, as the case may be, on which the sutra was written'. The sutra is a very long one (600 fascicules). It is a moot point whether the paper on which the portions were written would have been rolled (*maki*) or folded concertina-wise (*ori-hon* 折本). *Maki* were older, but *ori-hon* had been used from the later Heian 平安 period (794–1191). Considering the fires from which the temple had suffered, it seems not unreasonable to assume that this copy of the sutra was in *ori-hon* form.

までもなしとて、兵皆寺中を出で去りぬ。宮は
て見けれどもおはせず、蓋開きたる櫃は見る
たる櫃二つを開いて、御經を取出し、底を翻し
れ。あの大般若の櫃を開けて見よ。」とて、蓋し
が、餘りに求めかねて、「是體の物こそ怪しけ
壇の下天井の上までも殘る所なく捜しける
淺かるべし。さる程に兵佛殿に亂れ入つて、佛
言を待たせ給ひける御心の中、推し量るも尚
指し當てて、兵、「こゝにこそ。」と云はんずる一
と思召して、氷の如くなる刀を拔いて、御腹に
坐しける。若し捜し出されば、頓て突き立てん
きかづきて、隱形の呪を御心の中に唱へてぞ

27–28 *hikikazukite*: pulling over so as to cover himself.

28 *ongyoo no zyu*: a spell (*zyu*) credited with the power of rendering the reciter invisible. The words come from what is known as the *Marisi-ten-kyoo* (經), the 'sutra of Marīci', and describe the divinity or bodhisattva *Marīci* (Japanese *Marisi-ten*, in which the *ten* 天 is a title, 'heavenly being', 'divinity'), a personification of the rays which were supposed to precede the sun and to be themselves invisible. The spell, which for full effectiveness required a particular hand posture, is said to have been widely used among Japanese warriors when hiding from their enemies.

29 *owasikeru*. *Owasu* is an honorific equivalent of *iru* or *aru*. Examples are found of a *simo-nidan* conjugation (apparently the older) as well as a *yo-dan*.

29 *yagate*: immediately. (The sense 'soon', 'before long', is modern.)

29 *tukitaten*: from *tukitatu* (v.t., *simo-nidan*), 'thrust in'.

31 *sasiatete*: from *sasiatu*, 'place, or press, (against)'.

32 *matase-tamaikeru*. The causative element is honorific.

32–33 *osihakaru mo nao asakarubesi*: 'even conjecturing would still be shallow', i.e. one would still fail to plumb the depths (of the prince's feeling) even if one 'put oneself in his place'.

33 *midareitte*: from *midareiru*, 'enter in a disorderly manner'.

33–34 *butudan*: the structure on which the Buddha image or images are placed. Perhaps 'altar' is not too misleading as a translation.

35 *kore-tei no* = *kono yoo na*. Presumably this refers to the things in the *butuden* in general, not to the chests in particular, since the speaker goes on to mention *ano* (those) *hannya no hitu*, which were therefore away from where he and whoever he addressed were standing.

37–38 *hirugaesite* = *hikkurikaesite*.

不思議の御命を續がせ給ひ、夢に道行く心地
して、猶櫃の中に坐しけるが、若し又兵立ちか
へり、委しく捜す事もやあらんずらんと御思
案あつて、頓て前に兵の捜し見たりつる櫃に、
入り替らせ給ひてぞ坐しける。案の如く兵共
又佛殿に立ちかへり、「前に蓋の開きたるを見
ざりつるが覺束なし。」とて、御經を皆打移し
て見けるが、からゝと打笑うて、「大般若の櫃
の中を能くゝ捜したれば、大塔宮はいらせ

40 *husigi no on-inoti o tugase-tamai.* The causative element in the verb is honorific. The phrase has to be taken as an example of something very like 'transferred epithet': logically it is the *continuance* of the prince's life, not the life itself, which is the *husigi.* 'The prince's life, of a marvel, had been preserved' is suggested as a translation, though it is not pretended that it really reproduces the figure.

40 *mitiyuku.* It seems that the *miti* and *yuku* should be regarded as forming a compound verb, rather than as separate words; if they were taken separately, the sense would be 'go along a road', which is hardly apposite, whereas *mitiyuku* would presumably mean 'make a journey', 'travel'. The noun *mitiyuki* is, of course, common, but dictionaries do not seem to record *mitiyuku.*

44 *irikawarase-tamaite zo owasikeru.* The causative element in the first verbal compound is honorific. It is not easy in English to bring out the force of the construction; perhaps 'transfers himself, he does (*zo*), and now that is where he was (*owasikeru*)' may give a clue. English idiom hardly admits of differentiating in normal translation between this construction and *irikawarase-tamaiki* or . . . *tamainu.* (The whole passage—even the whole of the *Taiheiki*—could perhaps be translated in the present tense, 'historical present', with the advantage of preserving more of the vividness of the Japanese, though probably at the cost of other elements of style.)

46–47 *uti-utusite;* and 47 *uti-waroote. Uti* in both cases is a 'forceful' prefix.

郎、彼此以上九人なり。宮を始め奉りて、御供

藏房、村上彦四郎、片岡八郎、矢田彦七、平賀三

玄豪、赤松律師則祐、木寺相模、岡本三河房、武

へぞ落ちさせ給ひける。御供の衆には、光林房

難ければ、則ち般若寺を御出ありて、熊野の方

袖を潤せり。斯くては南都邊の御隱家も叶ひ

の擁護に依る命なりと、信心肝に銘じ感涙御

ける。これ偏に摩利支天の冥應、又は十六善神

れければ、兵皆一同に笑うて門外へぞ出でに

給はで、大唐の玄弉三藏こそ坐しけれ。」と戯

48–49 *irase-tamawade*. The causative element is honorific. The verb is *iru*, 'enter', 'be in'.
49 *Oo-too no Genzoo-sanzoo*: Hsüan-tsang, Tripitaka, of the Great T'ang. Hsüan-tsang (Genzyoo—the traditional reading in the text is Genzoo, but Genzyoo is usual elsewhere) was a Chinese monk who set out for India in A.D. 629, and in 645 brought back a large number of Buddhist texts in Sanskrit, some of which he, with a number of helpers, spent the rest of his life translating; hence his nickname of Tripitaka (Sanzoo). The Mahā-prajñā-pāramitā-sūtra, on which he was engaged from 660 and which was completed just before his death in 664, was the greatest of his translations. (For particulars of Hsüan-tsang see *The real Tripitaka* by Dr. Arthur Waley.)

　　The reading of 大唐 as *Oo-too* is irregular, *Daitoo* being normal. Some commentators keep the reading *Daitoo* and bring the prince's appellation into line as 'Daitoo-no-miya'. But it seems almost certain that the place where the prince had had his official residence and from which he received his appellation was 'Ootoo', and it may perhaps be imagined that *Oo-too* was a nonce formation on the part of the warrior who made the joke.

49–50 *tawaburekereba*. *Tawaburu* is an earlier form of *tawamuru* (> colloquial *tawamureru*).
51 *Marisi-ten*: Marīci, see 28 *ongyoo no zyu*.
51 *myoo-oo*: the hidden (unostentatious, silent) bestowal of benefit by a divine being.
51 *zyuuroku-zenzin*: the Sixteen Beneficent Deities, (Buddhist) guardians of the good and enemies of evil. They were looked on as especially guardians of the Mahā-prajñā-pāra-mitā-sūtra, hence presumably the idea that they might have extended their protection to someone who had taken refuge in a receptacle used for this sutra. Note that the last two characters can also be read *zensin*.
52 *oogo* is the traditional reading here of the word represented by the two characters whose normal reading is *yoogo*. *Oogo* with the characters 應護 is '(divine) protection granted in answer to prayer', whereas *yoogo* with characters as in the text is 'protection' without

qualification. Presumably one of two things happened: either 擁 was written in error for 應 , and oral tradition preserved the true sounds; or *yoogo* was the word originally intended, but the pronunciation *oogo*, being substituted by reciters,—perhaps because they felt that *oogo* was a more 'religious' word—finally came to be regarded as correct. Since there is no mention of the prince's having prayed to the Sixteen Beneficent Deities, it might be argued that *yoogo*, with no implication of an answer to prayer, is the more logical word—which would point to the second alternative—but the argument is hardly conclusive. Some dictionaries (*Dai-genkai*, the Heibonsya *Dai-ziten*) recognize 擁護 as an alternative way of writing *oogo* with the answer-to-prayer sense, but it seems doubtful whether this can be justified; the example they quote in support of their account of the matter comes from another passage in the *Taiheiki*, where again the protection is vouchsafed by a divine being, but not clearly in answer to prayer. It may be best to regard the *oogo*, in these *Taiheiki* examples, as a different word from the *oogo* with the answer-to-prayer sense, and as meaning 'protection vouchsafed by a divine being (not necessarily in answer to prayer)'.

52 *sinzin kimo ni mei-zi:* (approximately) 'his feeling of faith was deeply impressed on his mind' (literally 'liver'). The exact interpretation seems to depend on how 'faith' is taken— more intellectually, as faith in the truths of Buddhism, or more emotively (and with a strong tinge of gratitude), as faith in (the power of) the divine being or beings responsible for his escape. Perhaps both are implied, since Japanese thought is little inclined to make a sharp distinction between the intellect and the emotions. 'The prince's faith was re-doubled' is proposed as a translation; *kimo ni mei-zu* was probably already a cliché.

55 *otisase-tamaikeru.* The causative element is honorific.

55–58 The traditional readings of the nine names (according to the Yuuhoodoo Bunko edition) are: *Koorin-boo-Genson, Akamatu-rissi-Sokuyuu, Kidera-Sagami, Okamoto-no-Mikawa-boo, Musasi-boo, Murakami-Hikoziroo; Kataoka-Hatiroo, Yata-Hikositi,* and *Hiraga-no-Saburoo.—Boo* 房, originally 'a room', came to be used for the building in which monks lived ('cloister' is suggested as a translation) and, in accordance with the common Japanese practice of referring to a person by the name of his dwelling, *Musasi-boo,* for instance, from meaning the Musasi Cloister, came also to be used for a monk of the Musasi Cloister. It is worth noting that *boo* 坊, from meaning a district, came to be used in the same Buddhistic senses as the other *boo,* as well as in a further extended sense in which *Musasi-boo* meant the monk Musasi rather than a monk of the Musasi Cloister. It does not seem that this last step was taken with 房.—*Genson* would have been a Buddhist *goo* 號.—For *rissi,* see 13 *hoogen,* above.—*Sokuyuu,* in *Akamatu-rissi-Sokuyuu,* is the *on* 音 reading of the characters for *Norisuke. Akamatu-Norisuke* is known from other records to have had a Buddhist *goo* unconnected with *Norisuke,* but perhaps it became traditional to read the characters in the *Taiheiki* as *Sokuyuu* instead of *Norisuke* to make the name sound as if it was his Buddhist *goo.*—There is doubt about the meaning of *Okamoto-no-Mikawa-boo,* whether *Okamoto* is the man's family name, the name of his birthplace, or the name of the place in which a Mikawa Cloister, to which he must then have belonged, was situated. The last seems most probable; there was a temple, the *Hooki-zi* 法起寺, at Okamoto near Nara.—*Kidera-Sagami* also presents difficulty. *Kidera* seems possible as a family name (though the characters with which *Kidera* are here written are normally, when they represent a family name, read as *Kodera*), but *Sagami* can hardly have been a personal name. There was a temple named Kidera at Nara (with 紀, not 木, for the first syllable, it is true, but this discrepancy need not be fatal to the identifi-cation) and this suggests the interpretation 'Sagami of the Kidera', whether Sagami is family name, or name of birthplace, or even used for *Sagami-boo,* '(monk of) the Sagami Cloister'. On the other hand, a family named Kodera (with 小, not 木, in the first syllable) served the Akamatu family generation after generation (see the Heibonsya *Dai-zinmei-ziten* under 'Kodera-Motoharu'), which makes one wonder whether it was not in fact a member of this family who accompanied Akamatu-Norisuke in this party, the character and the traditional reading in the *Taiheiki* having somehow become corrupt; 'Sagami' would still, however, be unexplained on this supposition.

58 *karekore izyoo:* (taking) this one and that one above; i.e., all together.

58 *o hazime-tematurite:* depreciatory (negative honorific) equivalent of *o hazimete* (equiva-lent to *o hazime,* the usual form in this idiom at the present time). The subject of the verb in this idiom (though it is never expressed) is the author or speaker.

の者までも皆柿の衣に笈を掛け、頭巾眉半に

責め、其の中に年長ぜるを先達に作り立て、田

舎山伏の熊野参詣する體にぞ見せたりける。

此の君元より龍樓鳳闕の内に長らせ給ひて、

華軒香車の外を出でさせ給はぬ御事なれば、

御歩行の長途は定めて叶はせ給はじと、御供

の人々かねては心苦しく思ひけるに、案に相

違して、いつ習はせ給ひたる御事ならねども

怪しげなる踏皮脚巾草鞋を召して、少しも草

臥たる御氣色もなく、社々の奉幣、宿々の御勤

め懈らせ給はざりければ、路次に行き逢ひけ

る道者も、勤修を積める先達も見尤むる事な

かりけり。由良の湊を見渡せば澳漕ぐ船の梶

緒たえ、浦の濱ゆふ幾重とも、知らぬ浪路に鳴

く千鳥、紀伊路の遠山渺々と、藤代の松に懸れ

---

59 *kaki no koromo*: persimmon robes; plain red robes worn by itinerant priests.
59 *oi*: travel boxes; cupboard-like containers with short legs, carried on the back and used by itinerant priests to hold clothing and various religious objects. (Illustrations in the Sinkoosya *Rekidai-huuzoku-syasin-taikan* by Ema-Tutomu 江馬務, pp.161–3; in the Ryuukoku-daigaku (Kyooto) *Bukkyoo-dai-zii;* and in the *Bukkyoo-dai-ziten* by Motizuki-Sinkoo 望月信亨).
59 *tokin*: name for a head-covering worn by itinerant priests, etc., and including a wide range of specific types, from heavy hooded caps covering head, neck, and the sides of the face, to diminutive birettas perched half above and half on the forehead. (Illustrations in the Sanseidoo *Zukai-gendai-hyakka-ziten*.)
62 *ryuuroo-hooketu*: Dragon Galleries and Phoenix Towers, an extravagant circumlocution for an imperial residence. The terms are Chinese and designate respectively the upper parts of a type of two-storey gateway, and watch-towers of a certain type on the walls, both being features of Chinese palace architecture.
62 *hitotonarase-tamaite*. The causative element is honorific. *Hitotonaru*: become adult, grow up.
63 *kaken-koosya*: Flowery Chariot and/or Scented Carriage; i.e., luxurious conveyance.
63 *no hoka o idesase-tamawanu*: had not gone outside the limits of, had been confined to; but it seems probable that the *idesase-tamawanu* should be taken also as signifying 'had not gone outside (the imperial palace)'. The causative element in the verb is honorific.
64 *kanawase-tamawazi;* and 66 *narawase-tamaitaru*. The causative element in both cases is honorific.
68 *hoohei*: '(making) an offering (to a god)'.
69 *okotarase-tamawazarikereba*. The causative element is honorific.
69 *rozi ni*: 'on the way'.
70 *gonzyu* = *syugyoo* 修行.

71 ff. *Yura no minato* . . . It is not clear from this *mitiyuki* 道 行 passage whether the prince's party is supposed to have gone overland the whole way, or whether some part of the journey was by sea. *Yura no minato* normally means Yura harbour, in the island of Awazi 淡 路. However, the *Sinkokin-syuu* poem which was almost certainly the author's first 'source' (see Introduction) has *Yura no to*, the Yura straits (the present *Yura-kaikyoo* 由 瓦 海 峽), which may moreover have indicated any part of the sea east of Awazi. It is likely therefore that *Yura no minato* (seven syllables) was substituted for *Yura no to* (five syllables) without any intention of changing the sense, especially in view of *miwataseba*, which suggests looking across a wide tract of water. But who looks? Is it the prince and his followers, or is it an outsider (in effect the reader)? If the prince's party, the boat they see has presumably no relevance to them except to turn their thoughts to the *Sinkokin-syuu* poem. Since the whole of the first four lines deal with the boat and its voyage, this seems to be making a lot of a rather marginal incident, whatever the value of this incident in evoking a mood (in the reader). If, on the other hand, it is an outsider (say, the reader) who is (in imagination) looking across Yura harbour or Yura straits, the boat is presumably occupied by the prince and his followers. The reference to the voyage (*namizi*) then becomes more apt, and the mood seems to be strengthened, since it is the prince himself who is 'adrift' on the 'unknown' sea. But why should he be in a boat? Had the party crossed over to Awazi and set sail from Yura harbour? This would be very round-about. Or did they go by sea for part of the way after reaching the coast of Izumi 和 泉 province? The normal route would have kept to the land, but they were in flight and might have had some special reason for avoiding a certain part of the normal route. However, this is pure conjecture. After all, the fact that so much is said about the boat may be due entirely to there being plenty of quotable material about it of a sort to evoke the right mood.—The order in which the other place-names are introduced does not seem to conform with the order in which they would have been reached or noticed. Huzisiro is further south than the Waka and Hukiage strands (*hama*), which were immediately south of the Kinokawa 紀 伊 川 river-mouth. Tamatusima was probably a little way inland from the Hukiage strand.

71–72 *kazio tae*. It is not quite certain what the *kazio*, literally 'rudder cord', 'helm-thong', was, but the best opinion seems to be that it loosely fastened the top of the rudder (at the base of the tiller) to an upright pin on the stern, enabling it to pivot on this pin; the snapping of this cord or thong would have made the rudder ineffective. (It may be noted that most older commentators—including apparently all those relied on by translators into English of the *Hyakunin-issyu* 百 人 一 首, which reproduces No.1071 of the *Sinkokin-syuu*—took the *o* to be a particle, reading *kazi o tae* and interpreting the phrase to mean that the rudder itself was broken or lost, but this seems unsatisfactory, both from the sense of *tayu* and from the fact that this verb is normally intransitive.) Irrespective of who was in the boat (see previous note), this hackneyed phrase is no doubt included only to add pathos, and not with any idea of recording a fact.

72 *hamayuu:* a plant, *Crinum Asiaticum Lycoris* var. *Japonicum BAK*, also called in Japanese *hamaomote:* 'crinum' is hardly a popular English name, and it seems to be legitimate to translate as 'amaryllis' with some indication of its seashore habitat, an amaryllis being very similar to a crinum. The stem of this plant consists of a great many overlapping leaves, for which reason 'hamayuu' was used as a *makurakotoba* for '*ikue*' (how many folds).

72 *siranu*. Probably to be taken both with and without *ikue to mo* (and, as stated in the Introduction, *ikue to mo siranu* is reminiscent of *yukue mo siranu*).

73 *Ki-no-zi: Ki-no-kuni* or *Kii-no-kuni*, the province of Kii, modern Wakayama-ken 和 歌 山 縣.

73 *byoobyoo* = *byooboo* 渺 茫.

る磯の浪、和歌吹上を外に見て、月に瑩ける玉
津島、光も今はさらでだに、長汀曲浦の旅の
路、心を砕く習ひなるに、雨を含める孤村の
樹、夕をおくる遠寺の鐘、哀れを催す時しもあ
れ、切目の王子に著き給ふ。

---

74 *tuki ni migakeru*. The central meaning is 'polished like the moon', but the phrase was no
doubt intended to suggest also 'bright in the moonlight'. *Migakeru* is used for its appro-
priateness with *tama*, polishing being something which is done to jewels.

74–75 *Tamatusima*. There is a Tamatusima-zinzya (神社) not far inland from what was
known as Hukiage-no-hama, the southern part of what is now Waka-no-hama, and it is
thought—though this is not certain—that the older shrine was on a hill behind this.

75 *hikari mo ima wa sarade dani*: even if the brightness was not as it is now. This can be taken
with *kokoro o kudaku narai naru*, two 'lines' ahead, though it can also be felt as independent
and elliptical, with some word or phrase understood expressing either the prince's emo-
tional state (How moved he would be!) or our reaction to his predicament (In what danger
he would be!) Presumably two ideas coalesce: that moonlight arouses a feeling of *aware*, or
poignant sadness, at all times, but at this time of exceptional brightness the feeling would
be exceptionally acute; and that the danger of discovery would be great enough even
without this exceptionally bright moonlight, and now must be greater than ever.

75 *tyootei*: long strand.

75 *kyokuho*: winding shore.

76 *kokoro o kudaku* approximates in sense to *sinpai suru*. (Translations such as 'tax one's
ingenuity'; 'rack one's brains' which will be found in Japanese-English dictionaries for the
modern sense are obviously not to the point here.)

76 *narai naru ni*: 'it is the normal thing (viz. for one to *kokoro o kudaku*), and yet', the *ni*
being adversative.

77 *enzi*: distant temple.

77 *si*: an emphatic particle (fossilized in *kanarazu si mo*) having much the same function as
zo or *koso*. The use of the *IZENKEI*, here *are*, is optional after *si*—not compulsory, as it is,
except in the very earliest texts, after *koso*.

FROM

OTOGI-ZOOSI

—one story: *Sazareisi*

As a common noun, *otogi-zoosi* is used of a class of reading matter which came into being chiefly during the Muromati 室町 period (1397–1573) but continued to be produced well on into the Tokugawa 德川 period (seventeenth century and later). The word *togi* means entertaining or a person who entertains; the prefixing of the honorific *o* should imply that the one entertained is a superior, though *o-togi* seems often to have been used when this implication did not strictly apply, so that the *o* practically ceased to be felt as a prefix. An *otogi-zoosi*, then, was an 'entertainment book', consisting of a story or stories such as a nurse might tell to her charge, a maid to her mistress, a concubine to her master—or indeed almost anybody might tell to almost anybody else—in order to beguile the time. The stories are very varied in type: traditional nursery and folk tales, miracle stories with a Buddhist background, and tales of war and love, sometimes with a more or less contemporary setting. They vary a good deal also in length, though none is as long as a novel. Their language is probably fairly near to that of the speech of the time, and there is little literary embellishment. They were clearly intended to have a popular appeal; in the later part of the period during which they flourished there was no doubt a large and growing reading public in the big towns among which they would have found a market, but it is uncertain who bought and read them in the earlier part.

As a specific title, *Otogi-zoosi* 御伽草紙 refers to a book of stories of the class described which was published in Oosaka during the Kyoohoo 享保 era (1716–35). It is from this book that the present story, the shortest one in the book, has been taken.

The text used is that given in the YUUHOODOO-BUNKO edition, *Otogi-zoosi*, pp. 167–70.

F.J.D.

さゞれいし

神武天皇より十二代成務天皇と申し奉る
は、限なくめでたき御世なり。此帝に男みこ、
姫宮三十八人の皇子おはしける。卅八人めは
姫宮にて渡らせ給ふ。数も知らぬほどの皇子
たちの御末なればとて、その御名をさゞれ石
の宮とぞ申しける。御容貌世に勝れてめでた
くおはしければ、数多の御中にもこえて、御寵
愛斜ならずいつきかしづき給ひける。さるほ
どに御年十四にて、摂政殿の北の政所に移し
まゐらせ給ふ。めでたき御おぼえ、一天四海の
うちに上こす人こそなかりけり。
さゞれ石の宮、世間の有爲轉變のことわり
を、つくづく思召しよりて、それ佛道を願ふに、
浄土は十方にありと聞けども、中にもめでた
き浄土は、東方浄瑠璃世界に若くはなしと思

Sazareisi

2 *Zinmu-tennoo yori zyuu-nidai Seimu-tennoo.* Seimu is now counted as the thirteenth, not the twelfth, of the *tennoo*. The reason for the discrepancy is not known. It is conceivable that *yori* is being used in an anomalous way, so that the sense is 'the twelfth of those who came after Zinmu-*tennoo*', but this seems very unlikely.

4 *owasikeru*, and 5 *watarase-tamoo*: honorific substitutes for *ari*, the second showing the higher degree of respect (to the person designated by the subject of the sentence).

6–7 *Sazareisi-no-miya. Sazareisi:* little stone, pebble. It is uncertain whether the reason for the name was the Princess's smallness, she being the 'baby' among the Imperial offspring, or whether it was that with her arrival the number of the offspring reached 'innumerableness', typified by pebbles because they are commonly found together in multitudes. But the second reason seems the more probable: a poem in the *Mosiogusa* 藻鹽草, a work of the Muromati 室町 period, associates 'unlimited in number' with *sazareisi: Kimi ga yo ni / iwao to naran / yuku sae mo / kazu mo kagiranu / Sazareisi-yama* (Mountain of pebbles, which may well become the rock of [i.e. associated with] the Emperor's span of years [*yo*], whose number, even though one should go there [and attempt to count them], is boundless.) Sazareisi is said to have been the name then borne by a mountain in Tango 丹後, modern Kyooto-hu 京都府. And see 36–37 *Kimi ga yo . . . .*

7–8 *On-katati yo ni . . . owasikereba* might be rendered more or less literally as 'Since there was no-one in all the world (or 'all the land') as lovely as she was', but this probably makes too much of *yo ni*. 'Since she was of extraordinary beauty' or 'Her beauty was so extraordinary that', seems adequate.

9 *itukikasizuki-tamaikeru*. Both *ituku* and *kasizuku* mean approximately the same thing, 'bestow care or attention on'. The final *ru* (*RENTAIKEI*) instead of *ri* (*SYUUSIKEI*) may be accounted for by regarding the (compound) verb as nominal (equivalent to modern verb plus *no* or *koto*), with exclamatory force. However, the rule of *kakari-musubi* was not always observed at the time of our text (is not, in fact, always observed in the text itself, see 12 *nakarikeri*), so that the shade of sense here intended is in some doubt.

10 *sessyoo-dono*. During the Huziwara ascendency the Kanpaku 關白, Civil Dictator, regularly added to himself the title of *sessyoo*, Regent, which had previously been conferred only when the *tennoo* was either a minor or a female. Seimu-*tennoo*, however, assigned by the old official chronology to the years A.D.131–192, is nowhere said to have ruled through a regent. The writer has credited this 'pre-historical' reign with a late-Heian (平安) institution.

10 *kita no mandokoro:* literally, the Office in the North. In the Kanpaku's palace in late-Heian times this was used as the women's quarters, and the word, in accordance with the wide-spread Japanese practice of referring to persons by the name of their place of residence, came to mean 'wife (of the Kanpaku)'. Although here, with *utusimairase-tamoo*, it is the place which is primarily intended, the implication is that the Princess was made the wife of the 'Regent'.

11 *on-oboe:* the Imperial favour.

12 *nakarikeri*. Note non-compliance with the rule of *kakari-musubi*, which would require *-kere* (*IZENKEI*) after *koso*.

14 *o, tukuzuku obosimesiyorite*. The verb is an honorific substitute for *omoiyorite*. Japanese dictionaries differ as to whether *omoiyoru* is transitive or intransitive: the more recent ones opt for intransitive, but none of them seems to allow that it may be sometimes one and sometimes the other. They are agreed, however, in attributing to it a meaning more or less the same as that of *omoituku* (transitive), i.e. something like 'have [an idea, etc.] come to one', which, if *omoiyoru* were intransitive, would have to be re-interpreted as '[an idea, etc.] comes to one'. This sort of meaning does not fit the present example. It may be that dictionaries are deficient in not including another meaning of *omoiyoru;* on the other hand, the present example may be quite anomalous. One possibility seems to be that the writer intended to end the clause with *obosimesi* (gave deep thought to . . .) and to append *obosimesiyorite* (and a thought occurred to her) as a separate clause but that one of the two *obosimesi* came to be omitted either by mere inadvertence or from a desire to avoid the rather awkward repetition, it being overlooked that *obosimesiyorite* alone was then inconsistent with the . . . *o tukuzuku*. However, there is no real evidence to warrant 'restoring' the text on these lines. Taking it as it stands we seem forced to assume that *obosimesiyorite* here hardly differs in sense from *obosimesi(te)*.

14 *sore* at the head of a clause or sentence (see also 52) suggests that some new information is about to be given; 'now' is perhaps the nearest equivalent.

15 *zippoo:* the ten directions (eight compass points, up, and down).

16 *zyooruri-sekai:* the Pure Beryl Realm, supposed to be situated in the east and to be the abode of Yakusi.

じとりて、つねに怠らず、藥師の御名號、南無

藥師瑠璃光如來と唱へ給ふ。ある夕暮の事な

るに、月の出づる山の端打ちながめ給ひ、わが

生れん淨土はそなたぞと思しめし、獨りた〲

ずみ給ふに、御前に虚空より黄金の天冠を額

にあてたるくわんにん一人まゐり、さゞれ石

の宮に瑠璃の壺を捧げ申しければ、藥師如來

の御つかはしめ、金毘羅大將なりとぞ申しけ

る。

此壺に妙藥あり、これすなはち不老不死の

藥なり。これをきこしめされば、御年もよりた

まはず、わづらはしき御心ちもなく、いつも變

らぬ御姿にて、御命の終もなく、いつまでも〲

でたく榮え給はんとて、かき消すやうに失せ

にけり。さゞれ石の宮、此壺をうけ取らせ給

ひ、あらありがたや、年月願ひ奉るしるしかな

16–17 *obositorite:* honorific substitute for *omoitorite.*

17 *Yakusi:* in Sanskrit, Bhaiṣajyaguru; the Medicine Master.

17 *(go-)myoogoo* is normally used only of the invocation to Amida (*namu Amida-butu*), but here designates the invocation to Yakusi which is represented by the following nine characters.

17–18 *Namu Yakusi-rurikoo-nyorai:* Hail! Bhaiṣajyaguru, the tathāgata (*nyorai*) of beryl light (*rurikoo*). *Namu* represents Sanskrit namaḥ, which, derived from a root meaning bend, signifies humility or worship; *namu* used as an exclamation before the name of a buddha may perhaps best be rendered 'hail!' The Sanskrit word tathāgata is an honourable title of buddhas. Its etymology is disputed. According to that which was apparently accepted by those who translated it into Chinese by 如來, it is compounded of two words equivalent respectively to 'thus' and 'come' and originally meant '(he) who has thus (i.e. like former buddhas) come (and manifested himself in this world)'. See also 23 *ruri.*

18–19 *naru ni* = *de aru ga.*

19 *uti-nagame-tamai.* The *uti-* is a 'forceful' prefix, adding nothing to the sense except perhaps a suggestion of 'intently' (gazing intently).

21 *tenkan:* sort of ornamental head-dress.

22 *kannin:* an official.

23 *ruri* is from Sanskrit vaiḍūrya (the dot under the *d* is important, 'vaidūrya' being a different word), which it now seems certain meant beryl (not lapis lazuli or cat's-eye), though, since the less precious rock crystal closely resembles beryl and has sometimes been passed off for it, the line between the two may perhaps not always have been strictly observed (see A. Master, 'Indo-Aryan and Dravidian', II. Pāli *veluriya* 'beryl', in *BSOAS* XI: 1943–46,

pp.304–6). The commonest type of beryl is the aquamarine, and another particular type is the emerald, both these names implying a colour, but there are also yellow, pink, or even colourless beryls (see J. C. Brown and A. K. Dey, *India's Mineral Wealth* [3rd ed., 1955], Oxford University Press, pp.597–602). Whether *rurikoo* (vaiḍūrya-prabhāsa, 'beryl light') as part of Bhaiṣajyaguru's descriptive title implied colour or mere brilliance is uncertain; *a priori* it seems likely that the idea of brilliance was at least well to the fore. Perhaps it may be assumed that the colour originally associated with *ruri* in Japan was aquamarine, though the matter is complicated by the fact that the 'beryl' word in many of the languages concerned was also used for glass, which might be of many different colours. Modern Japanese dictionaries (sometimes no doubt influenced by the false identification of vaiḍūrya with lapis lazuli and/or cat's-eye) assign to *ruri-iro* meanings ranging all the way from pale yellowish green to indigo with a purple tinge; the word does not seem to be in popular use. It is impossible to be certain what precise shade the writer had in mind when he calls a *ruri* jar *aoki*, i.e. any sort of green or blue (col. 34)—if indeed he had any precise shade in mind at all—or, come to that, whether the *ruri* jar was supposed to be made of beryl or of glass.

24 *tukawasime:* messenger (of a divine being).

24 *Konpira-taisyoo:* the General Kumbhīra, one of the twelve Generals 十 二 大 將, retainers of Bhaiṣajyaguru.

31–32 *uketorase-tamai.* The causative element (as well as the *tamai*) is honorific.

32 *sirusi:* a response (to a prayer), the ensuing reward (of a meritorious act), the effect (of a spell, of medicine).

とて、三度禮し、良藥嘗め給ふに、あまた味ひ

言ふばかりなし。青き壺に白き文字あり、よみ

て御覽ずれば、歌なり。

君が代は千代に八千代にさゞれ石の

いはほとなりて苔のむすまで

とあり。これすなはち藥師如來の御詠歌なる

べし。それより御名を引きかへて、いはほの宮

とぞ申しける。

其後年月を送り給ふに、聊か物の悲しき事

もなく、いつも常磐の御姿にて、榮花にほこり

給ふ。御命長く渡らせ給ふことは、すべて八百

餘歲なり。成務天皇、仲哀天皇、神功皇后、應神

天皇、仁德天皇、履仲天皇、反正天皇、允恭天皇、

安康天皇、雄略天皇、清寧天皇、十一代の間、い

つもかはらぬ御姿にて、榮えさせ給ふなり。さ

ゞれ石の宮、あるよもすがら燈火を揭げ、藥師

---

34 *yuu bakari nasi:* be indescribable.

36–37 *Kimi ga yo wa / ti-yo ni yati-yo ni / sazareisi no / iwao to narite / koke no musu made:*
As for your life, / a thousand, eight thousand, ages, / till pebble is changed to rock, / and moss has grown. One could also translate 'till pebbles have become a rock' (or 'rocks'); and *kimi* is 'Lord', i.e. the Emperor, as well as 'you'.

In the earliest recorded form of the poem, in the *Kokin-syuu* 古今集 (A.D.905), the first 'line' reads *Waga kimi wa.* The poem is also found in the *Wakan-rooei-syuu* 和漢朗詠集 (early eleventh century), where, although MSS. vary, the second 'line' is often *ti-yo ni masimase.* In the *Kokin-syuu*, where both the *dai* 題 (heading, explaining the circumstances of the composition) and the author are stated to be 'unknown', it is the first poem in the section of 賀歌 *ga no uta*, which seem to have been the same as *iwai no uta* (*iwai* from verb *iwoo*), perhaps meaning no more than congratulatory poems (or songs), although *iwai* was originally a *Sintoo* 神道 rite of worship for which the worshipper prepared himself by purification.

Kubota-Utubo 窪田空穂 in his commentary on the *Kokin-syuu* (*Kokin-waka-syuu-hyoosyaku* [Tookyoo, 1935], Tookyoodoo, vol.I, pp.562–3) says that there was a widespread belief in Japan 'at the time' その當時 that stones grew slowly in size. [A similaɪ superstition has existed in rural England up to recent times—see C. Hole, *English Folklore* (London, 1940), Batsford, p.108.] Although Japanese commentators do not seem to have suggested this, may not a pun have been intended between *iwao*, rock, and the verb *iwoo?*

The poem, with a meaningless refrain, is said to have been used as a song in the course of the *Ennen-no-e* 延年ノ會, Life-prolonging meeting, at the *Koohuku-zi* 興福寺 in Nara 奈良, but when this was is not clear. These entertainments were given at many important temples and were at their height from the ninth to the fourteenth centuries. Originally, the *kimi* does not seem to have referred particularly to the Emperor, but it may be that the change to *Kimi ga yo* (from *Waga kimi wa*) marks a recognition of such special reference, although in our story it clearly does not have this. It was of course taken to refer to the Emperor when the poem was adopted (in 1870 or 1871) as the Japanese national anthem.

It seems curious that the *sazareisi* and *iwao* of the poem should have been seized on as names for the heroine of a story. One suspects some traditional connection between one or other of the words and a long-lived woman. The only clue that comes to mind is the story of Iwanaga-hime in the *Koziki* 古事記 (Chamberlain's *Translation of 'Ko-ji-ki'*, 2nd ed., pp.138–40). If Ninigi-no-mikoto had accepted her as a bride as well as her better-looking sister, his descendants would have lived 'eternally immovable like unto the enduring rocks'. It is true that he rejected her because she was 'alarmingly hideous', whereas Iwao-no-miya was of extraordinary beauty, but at least they share both an *iwa* in their names and the quality of long-lastingness. Iwanaga-hime became in popular belief a goddess who protected long life (see Heibonsya *Sintoo-dai-ziten* 神道大辭典 under *Iwanaga-hime*) and her hideousness may well have been forgotten. However, this suggestion of a possible connection between Iwao-no-miya and Iwanaga-hime is purely conjectural.

48 *aru yomosugara*. Dictionaries treat *yomosugara* only as an adverb, but it seems necessary to regard it here as a noun, so used, presumably, to avoid the repetition in *aru yo yomosugara*. It is, of course, possible that the author intended this, but that one *yo* dropped out inadvertently.

48 *tomosibi o kakage*: keeping a light (i.e. lamp) burning.

眞言を念じおはしけるに、かたじけなくも藥
師如來、いとも貴き御姿にて、いはほの宮に對
ひのたまふは、汝はいつまで此世界にあらん、
人間の樂はわづかの事なり、それ淨瑠璃世界
の地は、すなはち瑠璃なり、汝を移さん淨土
は、七寶の蓮花の上に玉の寶殿を立てて、黄金
の扉をならべ、玉のすだれをかけ、床には錦の
しとねを敷き、綾羅莊嚴を以て身を飾りたる、
數千人の女官、時々刻々に守護を加へ、百味の
飲食をさゝぐる事ひまもなし、此世界にて契
深き人は、目の前に竝み居つゝ、何事も心のま
ゝの極樂なれば、さのみはいかで八苦の世界
にあらんとて、いはほの宮を東方淨瑠璃世界
に導き給ふ。其身をもかへずして成佛し給ふ
こと、稀代不思議のためしとかや。上代も末代
もかゝるめでたきためしなし。今は末世のこ

58-59 *tigirihukaki hito:* persons to whom one is deeply attached.
59 *namii-tutu = narande i-tutu.*
60 *sa nomi wa:* that being so.
60 *hakku:* the eight afflictions (of human life), as detailed in the Nirvāna sūtra (*Nehan-gyoo*), viz. birth, growing old, illness, death, parting from dear ones, encountering hatred, seeking but not obtaining and—grouped together as one 'affliction'—the five skandhas, or components of life (having form, or 'the flesh'; sensation, or the response to things and events; perception, i.e. of good and bad; predisposition, or action; and consciousness).
62 *mi o mo kaezu site:* without undergoing (death and) rebirth (in another form).

65

と、か程にこそはおはせずとも、神や佛を念ず
る人は、やはか其しるしの無かるべき。南無藥
師瑠璃光如來〳〵、おんころ〳〵せんだりまと
うきそはか〳〵。

67-68 *on korokoro sendari matooki sowaka*. This is the mantra of Bhaiṣajyaguru, or rather the Sino-Japanese reading of the characters with which the (Sanskrit) mantra was rendered, more or less phonetically, into Chinese. The corresponding Sanskrit appears to be: oṃ huluhulu caṇḍālī mātaṃgī svāhā. 'Oṃ' and 'svāhā' are the words normally used at the beginning and end respectively of a mantra, 'oṃ' signifying solemn affirmation (it has been compared to 'amen', only that it occurs before instead of after the statement to which it refers) and 'svāhā' being an exclamation originally used in making an oblation to a Hindu god. The body of the mantra now makes no relevant sense although the words are Sanskrit. It is possible that their being words at all is due to corruption: a mantra was often a series of meaningless syllables; meaningless, that is to say, except that their repetition (with the appropriate finger gestures) was supposed to effect the conjuration of a particular being or spirit.

FROM

HUUZOKU-MONZEN

—two pieces: *Huzi no hu*; and *Minomusi no setu*

THE *Huuzoku-monzen* 風俗文選 was compiled in 1706 by Morikawa-Kyoroku 森川許六 (1656–1715). It is a collection of small essays etc., by Basyoo 芭蕉 and other *haiku* 俳句 poets, on all kinds of subjects. The form of the pieces is often based on a Chinese model; the sentiment that fills them is typical of *haibun* 俳文 in its lighter mood. Many of them are concerned with objects in nature, and the two here deal with Mt. Huzi and an insect. The first is a *hu* 賦, or 'prose poem', the second a *setu* 説, 'essay', 'monograph' (see E. D. Edwards, 'A classified guide to the thirteen classes of Chinese prose', *BSOAS* XII, p.770). The writer of *Huzi no hu* was Matukura-Ranran 松倉嵐蘭 (1647–1693), and that of *Minomusi no setu*, Yamaguti-Sodoo 山口素堂 (1642–1716), both of whom were friends and pupils of Basyoo.

Both pieces are so full of allusions that, even with a translation before him, the reader is likely to feel somewhat baffled if he does not have recourse to the detailed notes.

The texts used are those of the ITYOOBON edition, (Tookyoo, 1936). *Kootyuu Huuzoku-monzen-tuusyaku* by Huzii-Sikei 藤井紫影, otherwise Huzii-Otoo (乙男), (Tookyoo, 1944), was of great assistance in interpreting them.

$$(Huzi\ no\ hu) \begin{cases} \text{F.J.D.} \\ \text{C.J.D.} \end{cases}$$

(*Minomusi no setu*)   C.J.D.

---

5 *Kaguya-hime:* the heroine of the *Taketori-monogatari* 竹取物語, exiled from the moon to spend a period on earth, and taken back (via Mount Huzi) after maintaining her chastity. In Tokugawa times she seems to have virtually supplanted, in popular belief, the *sintoo* 神道 deity of the mountain, Konohanasakuya-hime 木花開耶姫.

5 *rei o todomu:* lets her spirit remain, still has her spirit (here). This is equivalent to saying that her spirit inhabits the mountain.

6 *hatiyoo:* eight leaves. This numerative is applied to the rim of the crater of Huzi with the implication that it resembles the (Buddhist) eight-petalled lotus, each high point being regarded as a petal. Apparently the eight points are not particularly obvious, other counts giving five or eleven; the number of course depends on what degree of prominence is regarded as giving a bump the requisite status. The points were given Buddhistic names (chiefly those of Buddhas and Bodhisattvas), but these names are no longer in normal use.

6 *sisyuu:* viz. Kai 甲斐, Suruga 駿河, Sagami 相摸, and Izu 伊豆.

6 *mikuti. Kuti* is the beginning of a road and, more particularly, the point from which one starts to climb a mountain, an 'approach'. Japanese commentators are in agreement that two of these points are Yosida 吉田, north-east of Huzi, and Oomiya 大宮, south-west, but they differ about the third.

7 *susono:* skirt moor, skirting plain. Huzi-no-susono is the name of the comparatively level tract of country south of Huzi but north and north-east of Asitaka 愛鷹. The extent of this tract from east to west is in sober fact about eight *ri*, or somewhat over thirty km.

富士ノ賦

嵐 蘭

不二は日本の蓬萊山なり。昔、孝靈五年、山はじめて現ず。徐福も此山に登りて仙藥を求め、赫夜姫も神と化してこゝに靈を留む。峰は八葉にわれて根は四州に跨がる。道路は三口よりのぼりて、千筋に別れ、裾野は東西に長うして、百里に列る。形削りたるが如く、高き事北斗に近し。夜陰に旭をかゞやかし、夏天に雪

Huzi no hu

3 *Huzi.* 不二 is one of many imposing combinations of characters used to write the name as if it were Sino-Japanese. The name is almost certainly Ainu in origin, *fuji* or *huchi* in that language meaning fire, more particularly sacred fire, and *fuji-so* meaning the crater of a volcano.

3 *Hoorai-san*, Chinese P'êng-lai Shan: one of three 'island-mountains' which Chinese legend placed in the sea to the east of China; it was a happy land where the herb of immortality grew and was sometimes identified with Japan. In Japan, Hoorai or Hoorai-san has been used as an ornamental or commendatory name for Mount Huzi, Mount Kooya 高野山, and other 'sacred' mountains. A Hoorai-dai (臺), a tray landscape having on it sprays or representations of pine, bamboo, and plum-blossom (*syoo-tiku-bai* 松竹梅), with models of a crane and a tortoise (*turu-kame* 鶴龜) and of an old man with a bamboo rake and an old woman with a besom (*zyoo to uba* 尉と姥)—all being emblems of longevity—is a traditional object at weddings.

3 *Koorei gonen.* Koorei, the seventh in the official list of *tennoo* 天皇 starting with Zinmu 神武, reigned, according to the old official chronology, from 290 to 215 B.C. There is a legend that an earthquake in the fifth year of this reign (thus, 286 B.C.) resulted in the simultaneous formation of Lake Biwa 琵琶湖 and Mount Huzi.

4 *Zyohuku:* Hsü Fu, a Chinese, who according to Chinese accounts set out with a band of emigrants in search of Pê'ng-lai Shan or some other island where the herb of immortality grew, and did not return. A Japanese tradition says that he reached Japan, and his grave is said to be in Singuu-si 新宮市 in Wakayama-ken 和歌山縣. (continued on p.52).

を頂く。山間に海をた〻へ、山上は眞砂を攀

づ。和國異朝類するものなく、三國名山と稱し

て、義楚六帖に甚だ譽めたり。日本武尊は、東

夷をたひらげて、草薙の名を改め、右大將賴朝

は、武士を集めて、牧狩をかる。鳴澤の池は、俊

成の仇名をとり、人穴の奧は仁田が無分別さ

うなり。十郎の宮、五郎の社、西行は五文字を

するゑかね、探幽は墨色にあぐむ。烟は古今の序

---

10 *sankan ni umi o tatae. Umi* = lakes (*mizuumi*), viz. the five Huzi lakes (*Huzi-goko* 富士五湖) to the north of the mountain. *Sankan* is best taken here as meaning something like 'fold (in the mountain)', since to take *sankan ni* as = 'between the mountains' would lead one to think too much of the other mountains beyond Huzi, true though it is that the lakes do in fact lie between Huzi and them; the absence of distinction in Japanese between singular and plural enables the difference between these two interpretations to go more or less unnoted. Dictionaries are inadequate in their explanation of *tatoo* (colloquial *tataeru*). When used of water in topographical or scenic descriptions, the verb normally has no explicit subject. The sense of *umi o tatoo* seems to be the same as that of *umi ga aru* plus the idea that the *umi* are held—supported—sustained—by what or whom it is no more necessary or profitable to enquire than into the identity of 'it' when we say 'it rains' in English. 'Held in its folds are lakes' is suggested as a translation.

10 *sanzyoo*. It seems that the interpretation here must be '(somewhere) on the mountain (i.e. as distinct from the situation of the "folds" at its base)', since the *masago* is found on the slopes which one clambers up, not on the top (see illustration in Huzanboo encyclopaedia, *Kokumin-hyakka-dai-ziten*, under *Huzi-san*).

11 *sangoku*: the three lands—Japan, China, and India.

12 *Giso-rokuzyoo*. I-ch'u (Giso) was a Chinese priest of the Sung period, *Soo-dai* 宋代 (960–1279). His 'six books' deal largely with Buddhism and Confucianism.

12–13 *Yamatodake-no-mikoto . . . no na o aratame*. There are various versions of the legend of how Yamatodake (or Yamatotakeru), when in Suruga 駿河, escaped from a heath-fire started by treacherous enemies. According to the second version in the *Nihongi* 日本紀, or *Nihon-syoki* 日本書紀, the sword he had with him (the one extracted by Susanoo from the tail of the serpent, or *oroti*, which he vanquished) spontaneously cleared a space round him by mowing down the herbage, and so acquired the name *Kusanagi*, Herbage-mower. (See Aston's translation of the *Nihongi*, I, p.205; also pp.53, 56, 57, and 58. *Cf.* Chamberlain's translation of the *Koziki* 古事記 [*Ko-ji-ki*], 2nd ed. p.256; also pp.75–6.) *Kusanagi no na o aratame*, 'renames Herbage-mower', must surely be accounted a somewhat perverse way of saying that the new name of Herbage-mower is given to a sword previously bearing another name.

13 *u-daisyoo*: abbreviation of *ukon-e no taisyoo* 右近衞大將, General of the Right (of the Imperial Guards).

14 *makigari* is a battue, a hunt at which the game is driven in to a central clearing. *Huzi no susono* was a favourite place for such large-scale massacres; of all those held here, Mina-moto- (源) Yoritomo's hunt in the fifth month of 1193 is the most famous, because it was the occasion on which the Soga 曾我 brothers avenged their father's death (16 *Zyuuroo . . . Goroo*, below).

14 *Narusawa*. (Huziwara- 藤原 no-) Syunzei (1114–1204) composed a poem in which the name 'Narusawa' occurred, but the final syllable had to be read as the particle *wa*. Hence he was nicknamed *Narusa no nyuudoo* (入道) 'the priest of Narusa'. The *Narusawa*, or *Narusawa-no-ike*, referred to in this and many other early poems seems to have been at the summit of Huzi, and not at the site of the present village of Narusawa. It owed its fame, and probably its name, to the noise it made. The prevailing opinion is that it was a place where small stones were continually falling, and that there was no water there, though the noise made by the stones resembled that of rushing water. The reason for calling it an *ike* is not clear.

15 *Hitoana* is the name of a cave formed in the solidifying lava at the base of Huzi on the west. A Bodhisattva was reputed to dwell here. *Hitoana* may be a corruption of Hutoana (big cave), as some Japanese writers have suggested, but no evidence in support of the supposi-tion has been adduced so far as is known

15–16 *Nitta ga muhunbetu soo nari*. The Nitta in question is Nitta-Tadatune (忠常), also known as Nitta-no-Siroo (四郎), who, according to the *Azuma-kagami* 吾妻 (or 東) 鑑, was ordered by Minamoto-Yoriie 源賴家 during a hunting expedition in 1203 to explore the Hitoana cave. Nitta is supposed to have had the various Buddhist heavens and hells revealed to him while in the cave. The story of this revelation is elaborated in *Huzi no Hitoana-zoosi*, an *Otogi-zoosi* 御伽草子, and later became the subject of a *kabuki* 歌舞伎 play. *Muhunbetu* is a technical Buddhist term for freedom from memory, reason, and self-consciousness—these being regarded as obstacles to knowledge of absolute truth, or reality—the term therefore implying the acquisition of such knowledge. The word is presumably used with this implication to the fore. The *soo nari* is not altogether clear; the probability seems to be that it is equivalent to modern colloquial *da soo da*, 'it seems (from report) that', 'they say that'. Some such translation for this clause as 'Nitta, it seems, confronts reality' is perhaps as good as any.

16 *Zyuuroo . . . Goroo*. Our text now becomes little more than a list. Zyuuroo and Goroo are the Soga brothers (see 14 *makigari*). Kudoo-Suketune 工藤祐經 had murdered their father. Notwithstanding that Suketune enjoyed Yoritomo's favour, the two brothers took advantage of his presence at Yoritomo's battue to carry out the vengeance which the warrior code required of a murdered man's son. Zyuuroo was killed on the spot (actually by the same Nitta-Tadatune who later explored Hitoana) immediately after he and his brother had despatched Suketune, and Goroo was executed later. The brothers' exploit, performed at the cost of their lives, procured them lasting fame and reverence.

16–17 *Saigyoo . . . suekane*. The reference is to a poem by Saigyoo-hoosi (法師), poet-priest who lived 1118–90: *Suruga naru / Huzi no keburi / itu tote ka / yukue mo siranu / waga omoi kana*. Syunzei (see 14 *Narusawa*) objected to the first line and substituted *Kaze ni nabiku;* Huziwara-no-Teika (定家), 1162–1241, reversed this decision. *Suekane*: unable to establish.

17 *Tan-yuu*: (1602?–74) one of the Kanoo 狩野 school of painters. The meaning is that he despaired of ever being able to draw Huzi.

17–18 *Kokin no zyo ni, niryuu ni yomare*: is mentioned in two ways in the preface to the *Kokin-syuu*. The 'two ways' are, first, in a quotation from a poem in which the poet's burning love is likened to smoking Huzi and, second, in an allusion to a lost poem in which the poet seeks consolation for the fact that there is no longer any smoke on Huzi. (It may be noted that the last eruption of Huzi was in the winter of 1707–8, after the composition of our text.)

に、二流に讀まれ、雲は廻船に怖れて、一尺八寸の號をとゞむ。禪定の人は、實冠に頭をつゝみ、下向道は、小袖の砂をふるふ。絶頂の鰷半腹の雀、巣鷹は大心にして、伊與の松山におとし、水鳥の羽音には、臆病になつて、都の方に

---

18 *kaisen*. The word was used for a cargo-boat and, in the Tokugawa period, specifically for those sailing at regular times on a fixed route. Here it would refer to those plying between Edo 江戸 and Oosaka 大阪.

18–19 *issyaku-hassun:* a name for a cloud of a particular form (*kasagumo* 笠雲 or *o-kasa*) sometimes seen on or round Huzi and feared by shipping because it is a harbinger of rough weather. For superstitious reasons, sailors avoided using the more specific names and substituted *issyaku-hassun*. The most plausible of several explanations which have been given is that there was a type of very wide-brimmed hat, one *syaku* and eight *sun* across, which the cloud resembles in shape.

19 *zenzyoo:* a religious procedure which consists of climbing Huzi, or certain other mountains, and there performing various rites, mostly Buddhist but with admixture of other elements.

19 *hookan:* literally, jewel crown, but here used apparently to mean a sort of hood (*zukin* 頭巾). The *hookan* worn by *Dainiti-nyorai* 大日如來, who is associated with Huzi, is a pentagonal one known as *goti* (五智) *no hookan*, and the hood of *yama-busi* 山武士, itinerant priests, is said to have been modelled after it. (The *noo* 能 play *Ataka* 安宅 has the line, referring to a *yama-busi: zukin to ippa, goti no hookan nari*.) Presumably the devotees of the mountain cult wore a hood either the same as that of *yama-busi* or some further development of this. In recent times pilgrims making a circuit of the cone of Huzi (see 20–21 *hanpuku no suzume*) still wore (perhaps still wear) what was called a *hookan*, but was in fact a very distinctive kind of hood made from a 6-foot length of white cloth.

20 *gekoodoo:* the way down—usually after visiting a temple, but presumably the word is not inappropriate when more or less Buddhist rites have been performed on a mountain, even if there is no actual temple there.

20 *Zettyoo no konosiro: konosiro* at the summit. (The *konosiro* is a sea fish, *Chatoessus punctatus*, with a long spine pointing up and back behind its more normal dorsal fin.) Japanese commentators on the text are not very helpful about this phrase; they cite the *Wakan-sansai-zue* 和漢三才圖會 (preface dated 1713) to the effect that *konosiro* abound in the rivers or streams 江河 at the base of Huzi and are 'loved' by the god of the mountain; hence those who climb Huzi for religious purposes refrain from eating them. There seems to be no other evidence, however, that the name *konosiro* was ever used of a freshwater fish; nor does this bit of folklore as reported connect *konosiro* with the summit. More to the point is a statement by Dr. Takeda-Hisakiti 武田久吉 on p.46 of the *Huzi-san* volume of the Kaizoosya NIPPON-TIRI-TAIKEI (1931), viz. that on the north-west of the crater rim there used to be a small, flattish depression which held water after the snow had melted and that, 'according to legend', this was called Konosiro-no-ike, 'Konosiro pond'. Unfortunately, he says no more about the legend; possibly the *Wakan-sansai-zue* passage relates to some variant of this. One wonders whether the name may have been given in the first place because some natural formation suggested a *konosiro*—there is near the site of this 'pond' a rock known as Tiger Rock to some people and as Lion Rock to others because of a fancied resemblance in shape. There used, too, to be numerous 'volcanic bombs' 火山彈 *kazandan* lying about, especially round the rim—lumps of lava which had solidified, while spinning in the air, into balls, or egg- or spindle-shaped forms—though now all but the largest have been picked up and taken away. Might not some of these lying in the depression have appeared fish-like and so have given rise to the name? In any case, whatever the reason for the name may have been, if there was a 'Konosiro pond' at the summit, that seems to be enough to account for our phrase.

20–21 *hanpuku no suzume:* sparrows of the middle slopes. Again commentators are unhelpful. One of them remarks that sparrows are not normally found on mountain slopes and suggests that the author intends to praise sparrows on Huzi for being there at all! The suggestion now put forward is admittedly conjectural. There is a practice of circuiting the cone of Huzi well below the summit (*go-tyuudoo* 御中道 or *tyuudoo-mawari* 中道廻り); it is done chiefly by members of the *Huzi-koo* (講, subscription-club) and it brings great merit to those who take part. The tradition is that this practice was initiated by a man who was head of the *koo* (the sixth in succession) probably during the Kyoohoo 享保 period (1716–1735), i.e. after the date of our text; but may his part not rather have been to popularize in the *koo* an already existing practice? Guides are employed by those who take this route, which is rather strenuous even now and used to be dangerous in places. Since the word *suzume* was used of a guide (e.g. *miya-suzume*, guide at a shrine; *sato-suzume*, brothel-quarter guide), may not *hanpuku no suzume* refer to guides who led parties on this route? After *konosiro* which can certainly not be real fish, it would be in keeping to have *suzume* which, or who, are not real sparrows.

21 *sudaka:* hawks caught in the nest (to be trained for use in sport).

21–22 *otosi* presumably means to bring down their prey, to strike. Young hawks captured on Huzi were reputed to be particularly spirited, and capable of flying as far as Matuyama in Iyo (Sikoku 四國).

22 *mizudori no haoto.* This refers to an incident on the Huzi-gawa 富士川 in 1180 when a strong Heike 平家 force fled at night before an inferior Genzi 源氏 one without offering fight. The legend recorded in the *Heike-monogatari* (物語) is that the Heike soldiery mistook for camp fires of the Genzi the scattered fires of peasants who had fled to avoid the armies, thus greatly overestimating the enemy's strength, and that a sudden flight of water-fowl suggested an imminent attack and caused panic (see p.248 of A. L. Sadler's translation of *The Heike Monogatari* in *TASJ*, XVLI, pt.II [December, 1918]). The phrase has become proverbial in the sense of a trivial or inadequate cause for alarm.

逃る。富士海苔、不盡灰、富士甘草、富士黄茋、栗、柿、松、檜の木のたぐひ、往還は竹の下越、根原越。關は足柄の關、横ばしりの關、あら井の渡口、佐夜の山越、海を隔て、峯を重ぬ。三保清見寺の見越、箱根、鎌倉の姿、日本、兩國の橋上には、馬上の人の首をめぐらし、赤坂駿河臺には、乗物の窓に眸をさく。遠くは朝熊山をかぎり、近くは、原よし原のあたりなるべし。諏訪の湖には、倒の影を浸し、甲州の府には三つ峯に見えて、扇の繪はこゝなるべし。昔より、詩

23 *Huzi-nori:* a variety of freshwater algae which was, and perhaps still is, used as food in the form of wafer-thin sheets prepared as *Asakusa-nori* is from marine algae. Other names for it are *kawamozuku* 川水屑 and *sibakawanori* 芝川苔; it owes its name of *huzinori* to being found in streams on or near Huzi (pictures of its collection and preparation, with description, in *Huuzoku-gahoo* 69, 10 March, 1894). Perhaps 'Huzi waterweed' may serve as a translation.

23 *huzi-bai:* 'Huzi censer ash', a powder, consisting of seed-pods of the water-caltrop burnt to ashes, used as the base on which powdered incense is burnt in an incense-burner. The word is corrupted from *hisibai, hisi* 菱 being the water-caltrop; it is normally written 藤灰, as though it were 'wistaria ash'. Our author may well have been perfectly aware that *huzibai* had nothing to do with the mountain and have had his tongue in his cheek when he included it in his list of Huzi products. If so, he may have deliberately chosen the characters 不盡 for writing the name in allusion to the 'inexhaustible' volcanic ash on Huzi, the *masago* already mentioned. (This way of writing 'Huzi' is found early, in the preface to a poem in the *Man-yoo-syuu* 萬葉集.) On the other hand, it is possible that *huzibai* was sometimes written with these characters—perhaps as the name of some commercial brand of the article, since to suggest that it was 'inexhaustible ash' might assist in selling it. Even then our author may well have intended the allusion to volcanic ash when he decided to use these characters.

23 *huzi-kanzoo:* a leguminous shrub which apparently owes its name to being found on Huzi. One of a number of other Japanese names for this plant is *kanzoo-damasi*, false liquorice. It seems legitimate to translate here as 'Huzi liquorice'.

23 *huzi-ooki. Ooki* (with the second character 茋 ; the bottom stroke of the character in our text must be a mistake) is a root, probably the sneezewort, used in Chinese medicine, and

huzi-ooki appears to have been the name of a Japanese substitute. Although there is some evidence to suggest that this may have been the bulbous root of the *hamasuge* 濱菅 or *koobusi* 香附子, if this was so, its nature and use must have differed considerably from those of the Chinese *ooki*. 'Huzi sneezewort' is suggested as the translation. In view of what follows in the text, it seems likely that a pun is intended with *oo-ki*, large trees.

24 *kuri, kaki, matu, hinoki*. It is uncertain whether all four trees were supposed to be found on Huzi, or, irrespective of being found there or not, are mentioned because there existed kinds of trees whose names were a combination of '*huzi*' with one of these tree names. The only such combination that can be traced is '*huzimatu*'; the tree so named, and otherwise known as '*karamatu*' 唐松, is the larch, which is in fact common on the mountain. *Kuri*, chestnuts, are fairly common on the lower slopes, but it cannot be traced that *kaki* or *hinoki* are to be found there. *A priori* it would seem more likely that '*huzikaki*' was the name of some variety of persimmon than that *kaki* flourished on Huzi. In translating '*matu*' it is perhaps legitimate to say 'pine' rather than 'larch' (actually the two trees are of different genera).

24 *Takenosita-goe*. This and *Nebara-goe* seem to indicate roads running north and south on each side of Huzi. These places are on such roads at the present day.

25 *Asigara-no-seki, Yokobasiri-no-seki*. These were on the Tookaidoo 東海道 when it ran between Huzi and Asitaka in pre-Tokugawa times. Asigara was either near to or identical with Takenosita; Yokobasiri was further west. The places are marked on the historical map of the Tookaidoo (in the article under this name) in the Huzanboo *Kokumin-hyakka-dai-ziten*.

25–26 *Arai no tokoo*: more usually called *Arai no watari*, a place where in Tokugawa times travellers on one loop of the Tookaidoo crossed by boat over a narrow part of Hamana-ko 濱名湖, since 1498 an inlet of the sea, though earlier a land-locked lake (the ancient Tootuaumi 遠淡海 > Tootoomi 遠江). The connection with Huzi is merely that a distant view of the mountain is possible from here. From this point in the text as far as the middle of col. 29, the reader is being taken in imagination along the Tookaidoo, going east towards and finally into Edo 江戸, and is asked to consider various famous places on the route, at the time of the text or earlier, from which Huzi is visible.

26 *Sayo no yamagoe*: the mountain pass of Sayo. This is the Saya-no-nakayama celebrated in many early poems. In Tokugawa usage the form seems to have varied between Saya . . . and Sayo . . . , with the latter prevailing. The main Tookaidoo route by Tokugawa times ran somewhat to the south of the old pass, but the place was too famous not to be mentioned.

26–27 *Miho Seikenzi*. Seikenzi is a little to the north of Miho-no-Matubara (松原). (Incidentally, the pronunciation of Miho varies, and probably has done so for a long time, between that represented by this spelling, and Mio.)

27 *mikosi*: looking across; the view (from).

27 *sugata*. Thus must refer to the shape or appearance of Huzi as seen from the places mentioned.

27 *Nihon, Ryoogoku no kyoozyoo*, i.e. on the Nihon and Ryoogoku bridges (Nihon-basi and Ryoogoku-basi) across the Sumida-gawa 隅田川 in Edo.

28 *Akasaka Surugadai*: two places in Edo, on opposite sides of the castle, which, being on high ground, offer views of Huzi. The palanquins are to be imagined as taking important personages to or from the castle.

29 *manaziri o saku*: literally, tear the eye-corners, i.e. strain the eyes (to see something).

29 *Asama-yama*. In spite of the characters with which the name is written, this pronunciation seems to be the preferred one, though Asakuma-yama is also used. This mountain is in Ise 伊勢 (present Mie-ken 三重縣). The more famous Asama-yama 淺間山 is in Sinano 信濃 (present Nagano-ken 長野縣); it is both greater in altitude and nearer Huzi than the Asama-yama of our text.

30 *tikaku wa, . . . narubesi*: literally, 'as for near places, it must be around Hara and Yosiwara (places south of Huzi on or near the coast)', i.e. for the best near view one must be thereabouts.

31 *sakasima no kage o hitasi*: (it) immerses its inverted image.

31 *Koosyuu no hu*: the capital of Kai, i.e. the city of Koohu.

32 *oogi no e*: the pictures on fans.

59

歌連俳の句數、合せてこれをつまゝば、大かた
此山の高さには比せむ。されど古今の間、たゞ
一首秀でたる者は、赤人の自妙なるべし。其餘
は此山に對して、萬が一にも及ばず。吾翁、富
士吉野の句、一生なしとかや。東路に趣く人
は、かくなりがたき富士の詠に、心力を費し、
又あづま路に趣かぬ人は、かく有難き富士を
見ずして、一生を終るも、共に殘多き事なるべ
し。

---

33 *renpai* = *renga to haikai* 連歌 と 俳諧, both being linked-verses, but *haikai* differing from *renga* in that they included words and themes not hallowed by their previous use in the classical *uta*. 'Linked-verses, of both serious and lighter sort' may serve as a translation.

33 *tumamaba*. This must be for *tumaba* (< *tumu*, pile up). No explanation can be given of the 'error'; it is not known for instance whether parallel forms occur in other contemporary texts such as to suggest that there was any tendency in speech towards a 'stutter' of this sort.

35 *Akahito no sirotae*. Yamabe (山部)-no-Akahito was an early Nara (奈良)-period poet whose work is included in the *Man-yoo-syuu*. The reference, however, must be to one of his poems, not as he presumably wrote it, but in the altered form in which it appears in the *Hyakunin-issyu* 百人一首; in its *Man-yoo-syuu* form (where it is a *hanka* 反歌 to a *tyooka* 長歌) the word *sirotae* does not appear. The poem is: *Tago-no-ura ni / uti-idete mireba / masiro ni zo [sirotae no] / Huzi no takane ni / yuki wa huri-tutu*. Clay MacCauley (*Hyakunin-isshu*, 1917) translates it as: When to Tago's coast / I my way have gone and see / Perfect whiteness laid / On Mount Fuji's lofty peak / By the drift of falling snow.

36 *waga okina* = Basyoo. He did in fact write a number of *ku* on Huzi!

38 *kaku narigataki Huzi no ei*: the composing of verses to this so intractable Huzi. *narigataki* = *dekinikui*.

40 *nokori ooki*: almost the same in sense as *nokoriosiki*.

みのむし〳〵、聲のおぼつかなきをあはれぶ。ちゝよく〳〵と鳴くは、孝に專なるものか。いかに傳へて鬼の子なるらん。清女が筆のさがなしや。よし鬼なりとも瞽叟を父として舜あり。汝は蟲の舜ならんか。

みの蟲〳〵、聲のおぼつかなくて、かつ無能なるをあはれぶ。松蟲は聲の美なるが爲に、籠中に花野をなき、桑子は絲を吐くにより、からうじて賤の手に死す。

みのむし〳〵、無能にして靜なるをあはれぶ。胡蝶は花にいそがしく、蜂は蜜をいとなむにより、往來おだやかならず。誰が爲にこれを甘くするや。

みのむし〳〵、かたちの少しきなるを憐ぶ。

Minomusi no setu

2 *Sodoo.* See Introduction.

3–4 *awarebu.* It is probably best not to take too narrow a meaning of this verb; 'exclaim at'.

5 *Sei-zyo:* Sei-Syoonagon 清少納言. The *minomusi* is mentioned in the section on insects in her *Makura no soosi* 枕草子; for a translation see Beaujard, *Le livre de chevet de Séi Shōnagon*, pp.57–8.

6 *Kosoo . . . Syun.* Shun (Syun) was a legendary Chinese emperor renowned for his sagacity; his father was Ku Sou (Kosoo), whose name can be interpreted as 'blind old man'. He is said to have been called this because he was unable to distinguish good from evil. The names Shun and Ku Sou have come to exemplify sagacity and lack of discrimination respectively. The reference is the antithesis of 'Like father, like son'.

10–11 *karoozite* is here equivalent to *yooyoo* or *yooyaku*.

14–15 *kore o amaku suru. Kore* presumably refers to honey, which bees 'make sweet' only to have it eaten by hive-robbers.

にすがりて、定家の心を起し、秋は荻吹く風に

蓑蟲〳〵、春は柳につきそめしより、櫻が塵

猶忘れざるなり。

深く入る。遍照が蓑をしぼりしも、ふるづまを

惑ひなからん。鳥は見て高くあがり、魚は見て

蓑の島の名にかくれずや。いけるもの誰か此

みのむし〳〵、玉蟲ゆゑに袖濡らしけむ、田

げらる。

るの謗あり。子陵も漢王に一味の閑をさまた

ときて、酒にあてむとする。太公すら文王を釣

父は魚を忘れず、風波にたへず。幾度かこれを

蓑蟲〳〵、漁父が一絲を携へたるに同じ。漁

汝がすこしきなるには。

あるも、多くは人の爲に身をそこなふ。若かじ

を得れば、これがすみかとなれり。龍蚭の勢ひ

わづかに一滴を得れば、其身をうるほし、一葉

---

17 *uruosi*. *Uruosu* means (*a*) to moisten, and (*b*) to enrich. It seems that (*b*) is intended here with a side-glance at (*a*).

19 *hito no tame ni*. This use of *tame ni* to show the agent is an example of the influence of *kanbun* 漢文.

19–20 *sikazi . . . ni wa*. More *kanbun* influence; *sikazi* is to be thought of as coming after *ni wa*.

21–22 *gyohu:* 'fisherman'; who characteristically wears a *mino*.

22–23 *kore o . . . atemu to suru*. *Kore* is a *mino*, which the fisherman removes (*tokite*) and tries to 'put to' (i.e. pawn for) *sake*. Huzii says that this passage is derived from a Chinese poem and gives the author as Yeh T'ang-ch'ing 葉唐卿; no information has been discovered about him.

23 *Taikoo . . . Bunnoo*. Wên Wang (Bunnoo, B.C.1231–1135) is the canonical name of Hsi Po 西伯, 'Chief of the West', who was accounted the virtual founder of the Chou 周 dynasty (although the dynasty began officially with his son). One day, before going out hunting, Hsi Po dreamt (or was told by an oracle) that he would catch no ordinary game. He encountered an old man fishing, who seemed so wise that he chose him as his minister and, because he had been told by his grandfather that when a wise counsellor should be found the fortunes of Chou would flourish, he gave the minister the name of T'ai Kung Wang 太公望 (Taikooboo, 'grandfather's expectation'—the dropping of the last syllable in our text is unusual). The malicious report (*sosiri*) was that T'ai Kung Wang was not fishing for fish, but for Wên Wang. Until the time of this incident T'ai Kung Wang had had a career full of misfortune; on one occasion he sank so low as to have to sell salt for his living, and even that got maggots in it.

24 *Siryoo . . . Kannoo.* When Han Wang (Kannoo, 'the prince of Han'), the founder of the Han dynasty (B.C.202–220 A.D.), began his reign, Tzǔ Ling (Siryoo), who until then had been his tutor, went into retirement. But the emperor recalled him and made him his minister. The references in this section contrast the state of the *minomusi* with the less happy ones of a fisherman battered by the elements, and of another fisherman and a retired gentleman who were not left alone, but made into ministers.

26 *sode nurasikemu*—i.e. with tears of love; a very common figure.

26–27 *Tamino no sima:* a reference to a poem by Ki-no-Turayuki 紀貫之 in the *Kokin-syuu* 古今集: *Ame ni yori / Tamino no sima e / kyoo yukeba / na ni wa kakurenu / mono ni zo arikeru*, made when he went to Mantle Island one rainy day.

27–28 *kono madoi.* The distraction of love, which affects not only fish and birds, but even Henzyoo.

28 *mite . . . mite.* The object is *tuma*, to be supplied from *huruzuma*.

29 *huruzuma:* his wife he had left when he shaved his head. The incident is in the *Yamato-monogatari* 大和物語. This passage appears to be giving examples of overcoats in literature coupled with the theme of love.

31 *haru . . . yori* may refer to a poem by Huziwara-no-Teika 藤原定家 in *Syuui-gusoo* 拾遺愚草: *Harusame no / hurinisi sato o / kite mireba / sakura no tiri ni / sugaru mino-musi.*

32 *ogi huku kaze ni:* a reference to a poem by Zyakuren in *Hubokusyoo* 夫木抄: *Tigiriken/ ogi no kokoro mo / sirazu site / akikaze tanomu / minomusi no koe.*

63

音をそへて、寂蓮に感をすゝむ。木がらしの後
は、空蟬に身をならふや、骸も躬も共にするつ
るや。

又以男文字述古風

蓑蟲々々　落入慁中　一絲欲絶　寸心共空
似寄居狀　無蜘蛛工　白露甘口　靑苔粧躬
從容侵雨　飄然乘風　栖鴉莫啄　家童禁叢
天許作隱　我憐稱翁　脫蓑衣去　誰識其終

---

36 ff. *mata* . . . The Japanese reading of the introductory sentence and the poem is as follows:
　　　Mata otoko-mozi o motte kohuu o nobu
Minomusi, minomusi / Otite sootyuu ni iru
Issi taen to hossu / Sun sin tomo ni munasi
Goona no katati ni nite / Tityu no takumi nasi
Hakuro kuti ni amaku / Seitai mi o yosoou
Syooyoo to site ame o okasi / Hyoozen to site kaze ni zyoo-zu
Seia tuibamu koto nakare / Kadoo muragaru o kin-zu
Ten wa yurusu in o nasu koto o / Ware wa awaremu oo to syoo-suru koto o
Sai o das-si saraba / Tare-ka sono owari o siranu

36 *otoko-mozi*. As opposed to *kana*, which is women's writing.

37 *minomusi*. The eighth, sixteenth, etc. characters rhyme in this poem.

37 *sun sin*. It seems best to interpret *sun* and *sin* separately as body and mind, *sun* representing the insect's tiny body; then *tomo ni* has its proper value; 'mind and body both undisturbed'.

39 *seia*: homing crows.

39 *nakare, kin-zu*. The mood of these verbs is difficult to ascertain; *nakare* suggests the imperative.

40 *nasu koto o*. The inversion here and following shows an infiltration of Chinese construction into Japanese; *cf.* 19 *hito no tame ni*.

40 *oo*. The reader will now have a rather confused idea of what a *minomusi* is. Actually it is the name given to the larvae of certain moths, which construct cocoons out of fragments of wood and leaves. These cocoons protect the hinder parts of the body, and 'wearing' them, the insects crawl in search of food and dangle on silken threads from trees. In them the insects hibernate and pupate. The insect's name of 'mantle-grub' or 'overcoat-insect' derives from the way in which its head emerges from this cocoon, resembling an old man—whence this reference, which also carries an allusion to *Basyoo-oo* (翁), the sage Basyoo—in a *mino*. The tradition that the insect produces a sound is widespread but presumably unfounded.

TUUHUU-ISE-MONOGATARI

Out of the feudal wars of the late Muromati 室町 period a single family, the Tokugawa 徳川 finally emerged to hegemony. The period of Tokugawa rule is often divided into two parts, with the year 1720 as approximately the crucial date in the gradual shift of the cultural and commercial centre of Japan from the Kyooto(京都)-Oosaka(大阪) area to Edo 江戸. It was still in Kyooto and Oosaka that the great flourishing of the arts—writing, painting, drama, lacquer-work and the like—took place in the Genroku 元祿 era (1688–1704), nearly a century after the establishment of the Tokugawa government in Edo; it was in Oosaka that Saikaku 西鶴 lived and wrote and that Tikamatu 近松 had his plays performed, and it was in Kyooto that the Hatimonzi-ya 八文字屋 press produced its stream of popular reading. But the importance of Edo grew steadily for, being the seat of government, it was the town in which, under the *sankin-kootai* 參覲交代 system of attendance at the Syoogun's court, all the feudal lords and their wives and families were required to spend a large part of their time. The resultant concentration of wealth there attracted merchants and craftsmen, so that eventually it eclipsed the western cities, first in size and then in cultural importance. Various events dating from about the second quarter of the eighteenth century may be cited to illustrate the change, but it is to be seen clearly enough in the field of literature: Kamo-Mabuti 賀茂眞淵 decided that Edo, rather than Kyooto, was the most profitable place in 1738 in which to attempt to propagate the study of ancient Japanese literature; from about 1750 onwards book production was concentrated almost exclusively in Edo; it was to Edo that would-be authors came to offer their wares; and it was the tastes of the Edo merchants which largely determined the type of literature that was produced.

Although the popular literature of Edo during the Tokugawa period is generally divided under such headings as *aka-hon* 赤本, *kuro-hon* 黑本, *ao-hon* 青本, *ki-byoosi* 黄表紙 and *gookan* 合卷, it really forms one continuous stream. The different names, derived from the varying format of the books, do not signify distinct changes in content. The earlier books, in particular the *aka-hon*, were largely picture-books for children, either, somewhat like the *otogi-zoosi* 御伽草紙 of earlier times, versions of fairy stories —Momotaroo 桃太郎, the rats' wedding, and so on—or tales of warriors of fabulous strength. They consisted of little more than series of drawings connected by short explanatory sentences or made intelligible by pieces of dialogue attached to persons represented in the pictures. The *kuro-hon* and *ao-hon*, however, showed a gradual increase in the importance of the text and had a wider range of content in that they often summarized *kabuki* 歌舞伎 and *zyooruri* 淨瑠璃 pieces which dealt with stories of war, personal revenge, the subjugation of demons and the like, or, on occasions, depicted the contemporary scene. *Ki-byoosi* continued to give increasing importance to the text and came to be distinguished from the earlier types by dealing essentially with the contemporary life of the merchant class in Edo. The genre was firmly established by the immediate popularity, on its publication in 1775, of *Kinkin-sensei eiga no yume* 金々先生榮花夢, a work with both text and pictures by Koikawa-Harumati 戀川春町. *Ki-byoosi* often dealt with the activities of the *tyoonin* 町人 in the brothel quarters of Edo, as in the present story.

The *Tuuhuu-Ise-monogatari*, which was written in 1782, is not particularly noteworthy, but it is typical of *ki-byoosi* in style and subject-matter. The original *Ise-monogatari* dealt with the love affairs of the ninth-century court noble and poet Ariwara-no-Narihira 在原業平, and, as the *ki-byoosi* story concerns a latter-day would-be Narihira, it was given the same name preceded by *tuuhuu*, meaning something like 'current', 'brought up to date'. Little is known of the author, Iba-Kasyoo, except that he died in 1783 at an uncertain age and wrote over thirty *ki-byoosi*. The importance attached to the text by his time is clear from the fact that he and the famous artist Kiyonaga were given equal prominence at the head of the piece, but it was perhaps still the latter's drawings which were the main attraction. Oota-Nanpo 大田南畝 in his *Okame-hatimoku*[1] 岡目八目, a critical work on *ki-byoosi* published in 1782, mentions the *Tuuhuu-Ise-monogatari* and gives it an average-to-good rating in his scale of excellence, but the discussion of the piece contains little of interest.

The language of the story is a mixture of the old written language and the contemporary colloquial. *Da ga* rubs shoulders with *naredo mo*, and *-eba* is sometimes hypothetical and sometimes not, but on the whole the classical forms of verbs still predominate. The chief feature of the author's style is the looseness of his sentence structure, which comes very largely from his marked tendency, common among Tokugawa writers, to use a series of conjunctive forms and so to delay bringing his sentences to an end. While this helps to speed the pace of the narrative, it sometimes tends also to obscure the sense. The story has an undeniable liveliness, however, stemming largely from the frequent use of contemporary slang and from the comments interpolated here and there by the author. He also makes typical Tokugawa play with Chinese characters, writing certain words with characters which, while usually having more or less the required meaning, are not the ones normally used; *sinsyoo* 身上, for example, is written as 財産, and *hudan* 不斷, as 平常.

The story also has some interest as a social document of the period. Apart from passing references to points of current fashion, the piece illustrates the ideal type of master-servant relationship in its account of the career of Tokubee. There are mentions of such characteristic features of the Edo merchants' quarters as the long blocks of tenements known as *nagaya*, the barber's shop, the bath-house, and the *zisinban* (huts provided for the watchmen who were employed to guard against fire and burglary); and, in the exchange between Koosuke and his landlady, one can see how relatively free and easy were the relations between men and women in merchant society in

[1] Contained in *Tokugawa-bungei-ruizyu* (KOKUSYO-KANKOOKAI ed., 1913), vol.12.

contrast to the restraint and formality required among members of the samurai class.

The text used is that published in the KINDAI-BUNGAKU-TAIKEI, vol.12, *Ki-byoosi-syuu*. Another publication, in the ZOKU-TEIKOKU-BUNKO, vol.34, *Ki-byoosi-hyaku-syuu*, has also been consulted. No original text was available, and so it is not known whether the illustrations would help to clear up any of the uncertainties. Hollow quotation marks, '⌐', '∟', enclose passages of dialogue or 'thinking aloud' taken from the illustrations. (In the transcription these passages are indented.) It is the custom of the Japanese editors of reprints (unillustrated) of these illustrated books to insert such passages where they consider them most appropriate; it should be borne in mind that they are not part of the main body of the story.

R.P.D.

P.G.O'N.

昔男を寫して　通風伊勢物語

伊庭可笑作

鳥居淸長畫

爰に酒商賣をせし伊勢屋德右衞門と云ふ
ものあり。近き頃より段々しんしやう（財産）
しだし、國元より年期子供二人呼び寄せ、得意
を廻らせ、日々繁昌せしなり。

『これ德吉目を覺せ。われ（汝）も幸助といつ
しよに湯にでもい（浴）つて來い。アノ帶の仕
樣を見さつしやれ。』

『あれごらう（御覽）じませ。幸助も德吉も同
じ年恰好なれども、幸助めは每晚湯にでも行
き、髮も此方から云はぬ先に催足して結ひま
すに、德吉は襟も耳も眞黑にして、たゞ居眠り
が得手ものさ。』
扨も德右衞門方の二人の御用は、日々得意

Tuuhuu-Ise-monogatari

1 *Mukasi-otoko*. As most of the episodes in the original *Ise-monogatari* begin with these words, they have come to be a kind of composite noun meaning, like the name Narihira itself, a 'Don Juan'.

1 *utusite*: 'copying', 'in imitation of'.

4 *Koko ni*. It is unlikely that this is intended to draw the reader's attention to an accompanying picture, as might be supposed; it is probably used only as a vague introductory phrase, very similar uses being found in a number of places in the works of Saikaku, for example.

6 *nenki-kodomo*. Apprentices taken on for a fixed number of years; that is, boys on articles of apprenticeship.

6 *tokui*: customers.

8 *ware*: you. Though primarily a first-person pronoun, *ware* was also used for the second person. At this time it was normally used only to inferiors. These first remarks were apparently made by Tokuemon.

9 *ano*. An exclamation.

9–10 *sizama* means either 'way of doing', or 'the making-up' of a kimono, etc. Used here in connection with an *obi*, it presumably means 'way of tying' rather than the 'style' of the belt itself.

10 *mi-sassyare.* *-syaru* (as in *kawasyaru* from *kau*, or *kakasyaru* from *kaku*) and *-sasyaru* or *-sassyaru* (as in *mi-sassyaru* or *tabe-sasyaru*) are suffixes derived from the passive and passive of the causative forms *sareru* and *saserareru*. These started as elaborate honorifics, and the derivative *-syaru* still had an honorific (or at least polite) tone in the Tokugawa period. This would, however, have been weakened somewhat when the verb was used, as here, in the imperative. The verb in the text is perhaps equivalent to the modern *mi-nasai*, and the remark is therefore presumably addressed to Tokuemon's wife, rather than to the boy. This form of the verb was not as polite as the *goroo-zimase* which follows, in a passage that must be attributed to the wife.

12 *tosi-kakkoo:* approximate age, age-group.

12 *Koosuke-me.* *-me* is a derogatory suffix. (See also col. 67 of text.)

13–14 *saisoku site yuimasu ni.* *Yuimasu*, though literally 'do one's hair', here implies 'get one's hair done' (*cf. ie o tateru*, literally 'build a house' but often used to mean 'have a house built'.) Thus, 'he has his hair done, having suggested (it to us) . . .' The *ni* has here an adversative sense, like the modern *no ni*.

16 *go-yoo.* Usually this would mean 'the requirements (of a customer)', 'an order' (as in col. 17), but here it is equivalent to *go-yoo-kiki* 'roundsman', 'errand-boy'.

を歩き、昔と違ひ今時は、「御用はよう御座り
ますか。」とは云はず、誰が前へでも懐手をし
て、のそり〳〵と覗くばかり、それでも用は足
りるなり。幸助は近所の神様や澀むけた娘な
どに、「ええ子だから、いい酒を早く持って來
てくりや。」と云はれ、いい酒は忘れても、ええ
子と云はれたが何より嬉しく、忽ち持って來
るやうなきだて（氣質）なれば、ふだん（平常）か
らして尻をはしより、内を出ても近所を離れ
ると尻を卸して、たゞ彼所の髮結牀、此所の自
身番の緣端へ横倒しになって、彼所の女房は
いき（粹）だの、此所の娘は雜だのと、云ふやう
な話が面白く、忽ち此の頃は、鹽辛でも食つた
やうな聲になりぬ。
それに引きかへ、德吉は朝から晩まで、内へ
百度參して用を足し、髮もふだん（平常）煤掃

18 *hutokorode*. Pulling one's hands out of the sleeves of a kimono and folding them across the chest inside the garment. A disrespectful pose when talking to someone, equivalent to keeping one's hands in one's pockets.

19 *nosorinosori*. Gives an impression of something ponderous and slow. Applied to the verb *nozoku*, it could be translated by something like 'dully', 'stolidly', 'lumpishly'.

19 *nozoku*. In addition to the meanings usually given in dictionaries, *nozoku*, as used here, covers the sense of 'look up at', 'give a sidelong stare at'.

19–20 *yoo wa tariru nari*. Literally, 'requirements are fulfilled'; hence, 'they do what is required of them'. *Cf. yoo o tasu*, the transitive form of the expression, used in col. 32.

20 *kami-sama*. A jocular use of the character 神. The word itself, as (*o-*)*kami-san* (おかみさん) 上さん, is still used to mean wife, especially with reference to the tradesman class.

20 *sibumuketa*. More commonly found as *sibukawa no muketa*. This is a metaphor used to describe a quite attractive young woman, especially one who, having come up from the country, has come to lose her rusticity and acquire a little sophistication. *Sibukawa* is the inner and usually astringent skin of, for example, a chestnut; *mukeru* 'peel off'.

21 *ee*. This use of *ee* for *ii* clearly gave the word a peculiar flavour; perhaps this may be indicated by translating it as 'nice' rather than 'good'.

22 *kur'ya*. *-yaru* is a polite ending added to the *REN-YOOKEI*. The imperative *-yare* can be abbreviated to *-ya;* hence, *kureyare > kureya > kur'ya = kudasai*.

24–25 *hudan kara site*. An emphatic form of *hudan;* '(even) in the ordinary way', '(normally) as a matter of habit . . . and now' (i.e. it suggests that some new departure is about to be mentioned).

25, 26 *siri o hasyori; siri o orosite. Siri* here means the lower back part of the kimono, and *hasyoru* is from *hasioru* 'to bend the edge'. For walking about or working, men of the lower classes would tuck their skirts up into the belt. *Siri o orosu* refers to the opposite process of letting them down again—a more fitting form of dress for a smart young man-about-town. The *tyon* after *hasyori* seems to be misplaced: the sense must be, not 'he tucked up his skirts and even if he went out . . .', but 'even if he went out of the shop with his skirts tucked up (for work, he smartened up his appearance as soon as he was out of sight)'.

26–27 *zisinban*. Huts for fire-watchers and street-police.

29 *siokara*. Very strongly salted fish or fish offal. Such fare was supposed to make the voice husky (*cf. siokara-goe* 'a husky voice'). The implication here is that the boy's voice has broken and he has now reached puberty.

31 *Sore ni hikikae:* In contrast.

32 *hyakudo-mairi*. In its literal sense, a religious rite, performed usually to obtain some special favour, consisting of walking or running on a fixed beat in the precincts of a shrine or temple and making obeisance each time at an appropriate spot. Here, it refers to an assiduous to-ing and fro-ing.

32 *susuhaki*. The removal of accumulated soot on the ceiling, etc., regularly performed at the end of the year or, as here, the besom with which this is done.

45　　　　　40　　　　　35

のやうにして、耳も襟も眞黒になつて歩き、近

所の子供が五六人むくろんじを持ち、ふきむ

くをしたり、或はけてあつたを取りて遊ぶを

つく〲見て、面白くなり、何うでもおれ（吾）

もして見たいと思へども、むくろんじもなく、

二三日も心がけ、通りの店下にてむくろんけ

しやうろんけを始め、仕合とひとつ（一個）の

むくが六ツ七ツになり、夜は大切に布腰上げ

の中へ押し込み、寐るにも抑へて寐る程に大

事にして、又二ツ殖え三ツ殖え、後には二三十

にもなりけり。是れより悪く賭事に身の入る

ものなり。徳吉は只元手ひとつ（一個）でも、精

出してひとつ（一個）を大切にして稼げば利倍

することに心がけ、あけくれ親方の帳面算用

する傍にて、幾何も利ありと云ふこと面白く、

後には徳右衛門が白鼠は此の徳吉なるべし。

---

34 *mukuronzi* (also *mukurozi*): the soap-berry tree, and, by extension, its hard black berries. These were used in the game of *hukimuku* mentioned in the next phrase. (They are still used, with feathers inserted, as shuttlecocks.) *Hukimuku* seems to have been the same as *mukuronge* (col. 38), a game more commonly called *mukuuti*. It was played by digging a small hole, or drawing a circle, about four inches across and trying to throw the berries into it from a set distance. Each player first contributed a fixed number of berries to a pool. The first player then threw all the berries, retaining as many as went into the hole. The next player then threw the remainder, keeping as many as he could get in, and so on. (*Anaiti* 穴 一, a variant of this game played with coins instead of berries, had been a popular form of gambling during the Genroku era.)

35 *keteatta*. Clearly another game, but it has not been possible to discover anything about it.

38–39 *mukuronge syooronge o hazime*. Although no *nigori* signs are used in either of the first two words, the voicing of their final consonants can be assumed from the existence of the word *mukuronge*. Nothing can be discovered about *syooronge*, but the clause presumably explains how Koosuke acquired the one berry which, the author goes on to say, he turns into six or seven.

The following conjecture is put forward for what it is worth: that *mukuronge syooronge* was the cry used by children when a berry, instead of going into the hole, hit the edge or another berry and bounced away, or when they found such a berry, in order to establish possession of it (*cf.* 'Finding's keepings' or, as a cry, 'Finders!'); and that here the expression signifies a berry which has done this. The very slender warrant for this conjecture rests on the existence of the word *syorosyoro* (also found as *tyorotyoro*, *tyorori*, etc.) which expresses a quick movement of a small object (or the trickling of water). The form *syooronge*, it is suggested, is merely *syoro* (which presumably would have the same suggestion of quick movement as the reduplicated form) with the first vowel lengthened and the same ending as *mukuronge* added so as to make a balanced jingle with that word. (*Mukuronge* itself is of uncertain derivation. A combination of *mukurozi* and *nage* seems possible, but there was apparently a vogue for endings in *ge*, especially when the words were used as a refrain, e.g. *tyotyoge matyoge*.) If this very tentative suggestion is accepted *mukuronge syooronge* could perhaps be translated as a 'spurter' or 'shooter'.

40 *muku*. Abbreviation of *mukuronzi*.

40 *nunokosiage. Nuno*, usually just 'cloth', here means the kimono. *Kosiage* is a large waist-pleat put in a child's kimono to be let out as he grows. This pleat makes a convenient hiding-place, as is clear from the text.

41 *osaete:* putting (keeping) a hand over.

43 *Kore yori = konna koto yori.*

43 *waruku:* 'to (deplorable) excess' or, as in English 'badly (addicted to gambling)'.

44 *mono nari*. Although this is not *mono* 者 meaning 'person', it may be convenient to make the English less impersonal than the Japanese. Thus, the sentence could be translated by something like 'It is from such a beginning as this that people become badly addicted to gambling'.

44 *motode hitotu*. A common phrase used to describe the meagre resources of someone starting a business career, *motode* meaning 'capital' and *hitotu* 'a little', 'a small amount'.

46 *tyoomen-san-yoo:* adding up the items in the register, doing the books.

48 *sironezumi*. The faithful servitor of a family, or an old and trusted clerk in business. The expression gets this meaning from the fact that Daikoku-ten 大黑天, the god of wealth, is always shown with pet white rats.

73

其ののち光陰矢の如しと云っては、何うか
敵討めいて堅くろしいから平ったく、子供の
伸びるは竹の子のごとく、幸助徳吉は早十五
六歳になり、鬼若衆では昔めいて悪いと、徳右
衞門夫婦は世話を燒き、二人とも元服させ、幸
助は願ひにて、「矢張幸助がよろしい。」と云ふ
ゆゑ其のまゝ置き、さて徳吉は徳兵衞と名を
改め、幸助とは年一ッ劣りしが、店の事も能く
呑込み萬事見所ありとて、まづ番頭下地にし
て、徳右衞門が口眞似もさせける。
徳兵衞は若い者になりしゆゑ、もう子供で
はなく、すこしの仕落も今までとは違って重
くなる道理と、いよ／＼心を付けて勤めしに、
幸助はのらくら者の癖に、年下な徳兵衞に帳
面をされ、少しくや（口惜）しくは思へども徳
兵衞が身持の眞似はならぬと諦め、いよ／＼

49 *kooin ya no gotosi*. *Kooin* stands for 'sun' (*koo*) and 'moon' (*in*), its meaning of 'time' being derived from the movements of these bodies. The expression, which therefore means 'Time is like an arrow' or 'Time flies', was a stock phrase of the *katakiuti-mono*, the stories of personal revenge (see introduction). These stories of blood-feuds were mostly variations on the same theme: someone is killed, leaving a young son who is deprived of his birthright; time then has to fly to cover the prosaic intervening years before the son is old enough to avenge his father's death.

50 *katakurosii kara hirattaku*. *Katakurosii* (now *katakurusii*) 'painfully stiff', when applied to speech, generally refers to an excess of Chinese words like *kooin*. *Hirattaku* (*yuu*) is the opposite, meaning '(say something) in easy language'.

52 *oni-waka-syu*. Although this does not seem to have been a recognized term, it makes sense to regard it as *waka-syu* (a common word in the Edo period for boys who had not yet gone through *genbuku* 元服 and still wore the characteristic forelock of their kind) and *oni* used as a prefix to make a word descriptive of young imps with long hair who were still free of the restraints that came with manhood. *Oni-waka*, however, was the child-name of Musasi-boo-Benkei 武藏坊辨慶 and from this it came to appear in the titles of several puppet plays and to be used of a certain puppet head with the distinctive hair-style of a boy which represented such a robust, active lad as the young Benkei. Thus, *oni-waka-syu* may well have been just a plural form of *oni-waka* meaning youths who had not yet assumed the status of adults.

54 *negai nite:* by request, i.e. at his own request; an adverbial phrase which links up with *oki*. It was usual for new names to be taken at the *genbuku* ceremony.

57 *banzi midokoro ari tote:* on the grounds that he shows promise in every respect.
57 *bantoo-sita-zi. Bantoo* means the manager (as distinct from the proprietor) of a shop or the chief clerk of a business. *Sita-zi* means primarily 'groundwork', 'basis', and although its use in a context such as this seems unusual, *bantoo-sita-zi* presumably means one who is being 'grounded' in the duties of a *bantoo*. The point thus is that he was no longer made to run errands but was brought into the shop to be trained as Tokuemon's assistant.
58 *kutimane:* mimicry of speech. The meaning is that, in his dealings with customers Tokkiti was now allowed to make undertakings and to employ turns of phrase which would normally only be appropriate to the proprietor himself.
60 *sioti:* a slip, indiscretion.
61 *doori = wake:* the situation was such that . . .
62–63 *tyoomen o sare.* A good example of the indirect passive of the verb (i.e. being caused trouble or displeasure by the action in question), the feeling behind which is here made explicit in the *kuyasiku omoedo mo.*
64 *naranu = dekinai.* The idea is that he resigns himself to being passed over, telling himself that he could not possibly imitate Tokubee's 'goody-goody' behaviour.

男振りをみがきければ、一體生まれつき横ぶ
とり（肥滿）にて姿が平ッたく、德兵衞とは男
振りもおとりしが、手前の氣にては、彼の德奴
は飛んだ野暮ななり（體）だと、矢張うぬ（奴）が
方から男がええと心得、頭も百介が枸杞と云
ふ所で、鬢は蟋蟀籠のやうにして、惜しい眉毛
を云譯のために少し殘して剃りつけ、諸事き
んゝめかし大きにかぶる。
德右『幸助こゝへ出ろ。われ（汝）が髮の風は何
だ。さうして此の頃見れば途方もない、三升の
手拭を持つて湯に行き二時程の長湯だ。ソレ
其の煙管は何だ。鴈首も吸口の穴も同じやう
だ。』
幸『ハイゝゝ、此の煙管の名は大粒張と申し
て、近頃大ぶん流行ります。』
德『向後、髮の風も直させますから御免なさ

66-67 *otokoburi mo.* That is, in manly looks as well (as in competence and assiduity).

67 *temae no ki nite wa. Temae* is here a humble first-person pronoun, the part from here to *otoko ga ee (to kokoroe)* (col. 69) being what Koosuke thinks to himself. The phrase is thus an apologetic way of introducing one's own view—'In my own humble opinion . . .'

68-69 *unu ga hoo kara.* Besides being a rather rude second-person pronoun, *unu*, as here, was used as equivalent to *zibun-zisin* 自分自身. The phrase is thus very similar in meaning to *temae no ki nite wa;* its implied apology for saying what follows could be brought out in translation by 'Though I say it myself, . . .' or, perhaps, 'I make bold to say that . . .'.

69 *otoko.* Here = *otokoburi.* Something like *ware wa* or *zibun no hoo ga* should be understood. before it.

69-70 *atama mo . . . to yuu tokoro de.* The *mo* implies much the same as 'for instance', and the last phrase is equivalent to *to yuu gurai de* 'he goes so far as . . .' Together they give the idea that this is just one example of the extent to which his self-decoration went.— *Hyakusuke ga kuko.* Nakazimaya 中島屋-Hyakusuke was a cosmetics merchant of Asakusa famous for his brilliantine. *Kuko-abura* (油) 'box-thorn oil' was his most famous creation.

70 *bin wa kirigirisukago no yoo ni site.* The meaning is that his side whiskers were so neatly combed out that they looked like the regular strands of thin wicker from which crickets' cages were made.

70 *osii:* which anyone *ought to* (or normally *would*) grudge losing, precious.

71 *iiwake no tame ni:* as a (mere) apology (for eyebrows), as a token.
71–72 *syozi kinkin-mekasi. Kinkin,* which may be written 金金, was an Edo cant-word of
the period meaning 'splendid', 'stylish', etc. (See the Introduction as to the famous
ki-byoosi, Kinkin-sensei eiga no yume.) *Mekasu* (from *meku*) = 'make (oneself) seem'.
Thus, for the whole phrase, 'everything (about him) has the "flash" touch'. (See also
col. 85 in text.)
72 *kaburu:* show off, put on airs; a slang use of the word with a meaning similar to that of the
modern colloquial *syotte'ru* (< *syou*).
74 *tohoo mo nai* does not really modify *tenugui,* but is more in the nature of a mid-sentence
interjection.
74 *sansyoo.* The acting-name of several members of the line of famous actors known as
Itikawa-Danzyuuroo 市川團十郎. The name was derived from their *mon* 紋 or crest,
which consisted of three concentric squares and, like the *mon* of other popular players,
was a fashionable decoration on towels among the smart set.
76 *Gan-kubi:* the bowl-piece.
76 *suikuti:* the mouth-piece.
78 *oo-tububari. -bari* = 'style'. Both ends of the *oo-tubu*-style pipe were round and stubby,
so that the bowl-neck did not protrude as much as usual.
80 *Kyookoo:* henceforth.

れて遣はされませ。』

幸助は何でも一つとして我が氣に入らね

ば、ならうなら親方も徳兵衛も叩き出してし

まひたけれども、その株はなし。所詮驅落して

腹一杯にきん〳〵と色男にこしらへ、世間の

女に氣を揉ませて樂しみませうと、金子百兩

ぬすみ出し首に懸け、隨德寺と出掛ける。

『今までは人のあたま(髪)や著物の身幅ま

で、どうだの斯うだのと大きにお世話。どいつ

も〳〵一生へんてこで朽ち果てるのであら

う、氣の毒な事だ。エ、犬まで野暮だ、氣の利

かねえ。静かに吠えろシッシッ』

德右衞門內にては、何時もの通り朝起きた

る處、金箱の抽斗へ置いたる百兩の金見えず。

鍵は箱の傍に捨ててあり。然れども幸助が驅

落にて外へ疑ひもかゝらず、家內膽を潰す。

---

81 *tukawasaremase*. An honorific form of *tukawasu* which is itself an honorific verb used in a similar way to *kudasaru* in modern Japanese. Tokubee's politeness here is contrasted with Koosuke's nonchalance.

82 *hitotu to site*. The basic meaning is 'in (their) entirety'; hence, following *nan de mo*, it amounts to 'absolutely everything'.

83 *naroo nara*: 'if he could manage it', *naru* being used in the sense of 'succeed', 'be able to', = *dekiru*.

84 *kabu*. This, the present word for a share in a firm, was used in the Tokugawa period for the (negotiable) title to membership of a trade guild holding monopolistic rights in a certain trade in a certain district. From this came a wider meaning of 'standing', 'competence'. Thus, here, ' . . . but he is in no position to do that'.

84 *syosen*. Although now normally used only with a negative verb in the same way as, and with the same meaning as, *tootei* 到底, the word here means simply 'finally', 'in the end'.

84 *kakeoti*. Here merely 'running away' and not 'elopement', its usual meaning at the present day.

85 *hara-ippai ni*: to one's heart's content.

85 *ni kosirae*: get myself up as, deck myself out as.

87 *zuitokuzi to*. *Zui to nigeru* ずいと逃げる means 'be off in a flash and leave no trace'. This expansion of *zui to* into the name of the temple is a piece of Tokugawa slang. (It was carried even further to *zuitokuzi suru* 'do a bunk'.)

89 *doo dano koo dano to ooki ni o-sewa*: 'It's none of their business (*ooki ni o-sewa*), all this fuss they're making'. In the phrase *ooki ni o-sewa*, the attention (*o-sewa*) is always unwelcome.

90 *henteko*. An extension of *hen* 變 'queer,' here meaning unfashionable uncouthness.

93 *Tokuemon-uti = Tokuemon no uti.*

95–96 *Koosuke ga kakeoti . . . kakarazu.* Literally, 'there being a flight by Koosuke, not even suspicion falls elsewhere'; that is, ' . . . no one else is even suspected'.

96 *yanuti = ya no uti*, the household.

幸助は主人の金を盗み取り、少しのしるべ
（知己）にて谷中邊へゐさふらふ（食客）となり、
吾がおもひ入れに衣類をこしらへ、何がさて
横廣い男で、引きずるやうな黒七子の裕羽織
に小紋縮緬、かはり八丈と云ふ所をふり重ね、
鮫鞘一本落差し、帶は黑繻子に赤絲で菊壽を
織り込み、裏付はふんぐり返す様なのを履き、
ふだん（平常）淺草、山下、兩國、其の他、向島は
勿論江戸中を歩くに、何うも不恰好に平ッた
いなり（體）の男と、人の目に付き、彼所の娘此
所の女房、茶屋女までなり。。ひら〳〵と、綽名を
云ひけるをええと聞き付け、「昔の業平はお公
卿であつたさうだが、多くの女の心をかけら
れた色男さうな。おれ（吾）も男がええからそ
れで業平と云ふと見えて、是は斯く綽名を付
けたか。併し江戸中の女に惚れられるには翁

97–98 *sukosi no sirube nite:* on (the strength of) a slight acquaintance.

99 *kosirae.* Here means 'have (clothes) made', 'order'.

99–100 *nani ga sate yokobiroi otoko de. Yokobiroi,* like *yokobutori* (col. 65–6), means squat and tubby. *Nani ga sate = motiron.* The whole phrase should be taken closely with the following *hikizuru yoo na,* thus: ' . . . which, since he is so undeniably squat, seems to drag the ground'.

99–106 The author manages to go from col. 97 to col. 113 before using a final verb in the main structure of the passage, but natural breaks can be made in translation. One can be made at *kosirae* (col. 99), for example, as there then follows a digression into the details of Koosuke's sartorial splendour. The suspensive forms of the verb which follow one after the other in these lines all depend grammatically on *aruku ni* (col. 105); and the verbal structure is therefore *hurikasane . . . otozasi . . . orikomi* (sic—see 102–103 *obi wa . . . kikuzyu o orikomi*) . . . *haki . . . aruku ni . . . hito no me ni tuki* 'When he walks . . . wearing . . . beswarded with . . . with woven . . . shod in . . ., he appears . . .'

100–101 *kuro-nanako . . . o hurikasane. Kuro-nanako:* a black silk twill material; *awase-baori:* a lined *haori; ko-mon-tirimen:* a crêpe-de-chine material with a small pattern.— *Kawari-hatizyoo. Hatizyoo,* an abbreviation of *hatizyoo-ginu* (絹), is a check-patterned silk material. *Kawari* is an abbreviation of *kawarizome* 變染め which means a special method of dyeing or the goods so dyed.—*To yuu tokoro.* See 69–70 *atama mo . . . to yuu tokoro de.*—*Hurikasane. Huri* is a prefix of little or no meaning. As *Haori ni A, B o kasane* would normally be taken to mean 'wearing A and B *over* his *haori*', the *ni* after *awasebaori* in the text is probably unrelated to *kasane.* The clause should perhaps be read to mean 'wearing *kawari-hatizyoo* over *komon-tirimen* with his lined *haori*'.

102 *samezaya:* shark-skin scabbard.

102 *otosizasi.* Means wearing a sword, etc., stuck upright in the belt instead of at the proper angle.

102–103 *obi wa . . . kikuzyu o orikomi:* (having) a waist-band with chrysanthemums and the character for 'long life' woven into it . . . This clause would fit into the sentence better if it ended with a verb meaning 'to wear' (see note to col. 99–106) and was in some such form as . . . *kikuzyu o orikonda obi o sime.*

103 *uratuki.* Short for *uratuki-zoori* (草履), sandals with more than one layer of sole. The more expensive ones might have as many as five or six.

103 *hungurikaesu.* Presumably a corruption of *humikurikaesu* 踏みくり返す which is perhaps a combination of *hunzorikaeru* 踏ん反り返る 'to send flat on one's back' and *hikkurikaesu* 引つくり返す 'to overturn'. Presumably the sense is that the high-soled sandals, though very expensive and elegant, tended to make him lose his balance.

107 *NARIHIRA.* Koosuke was given this name because his *nari* 'form' was *hira(ttai).*

107–108 *adana o iikeru o ee to kikituke:* he hears their calling him by this nickname as (something) good; i.e. the nickname they give him sounds to him as if they are being nice.

108 *Mukasi no Narihira.* See Introduction.

110 *soo na.* A regular ending of the period for what would now be either *soo da* or *da soo da.*

110–112 *Ore mo . . . adana o tuketa ka.* The middle clause *sore de Narihira to yuu to miete* is a general observation prompted by the preceding *otoko ga ee* (*koto*) 'manly good looks', which is what *sore* refers to. Thus, the whole thing could be translated as 'I'm another chap with nice looks—and it's apparently on their account that anyone gets called Narihira—so they've given me this nickname, eh?'

つたす。」と、自惚はますく〳増長する。其のの

ち幸助は、何處へ出ても通りのもの、まして女

と名の付いた程の者は目引き袖引き笑ふを、

皆おれ（吾）に惚れたと心得、此の廣い江戸中

の女に惚れられて、ひよつと一人の女にええ

返事をして想ひをかなへたらば、四方八方か

ら恨み居らうし、どれもく〳少しづゝ叶へて

やつては、まア身體が續かぬから、さりとは罪

だが、此處を耐へてまづ養生食ひを専一とし

て、大丈夫となつて、世間の女の百分一もかな

へてやらうと思ひ、成るたけ精のつく物を好

む。

それから幸助は、とんだ氣のながいのか鼻

の下の長いのか、五六年になれども、日々鰻や

籠膃肭臍、その外寒に入ればあらゆる練藥を

用ゐ、それでも内に居る事はならず、をり節出

112–113 *yowatta su.* *Yowatta* is very much the same in meaning as *komatta.* *Su* is an unusual exclamatory particle.

115 *mehiki sodehiki:* catching (each other's) eyes and pulling (each other's) sleeves.

115–116 *warau o . . . to kokoroe:* he interprets their smiles as (meaning) . . . (*cf.* 154 *idesi o*).

118 *omoi o kanaetaraba:* if I were to comply with her wishes.

118–119 *sihoo happoo kara urami oroo.* This refers to the jealous resentment of the women he does not favour. Although the construction is not felt as elliptical in Japanese, it can be taken as equivalent to *sihoo happoo kara no onna ga urami oroo.*

120 *sari to wa.* Is equivalent to *soo sitara* or *soo nattara* and refers forward to the idea of temporarily withholding his favours. 'It may be wrong to do so, but . . . '

121 *koko o koraete:* containing myself *for* the present.

122 *dai-zyoobu.* Here means 'very strong'.

123 *sei no tuku mono:* energy-building foods.

123–124 *konomu.* The context requires a slight extension of the usual meaning of 'like', 'have an inclination for', etc. to something like 'turn to', 'go in for'.

125 *tonda.* Although adjectival in form and sentence position, this word really operates adverbially; thus, 'extraordinarily patient'.

125–126 *hananosita no nagai:* foolishly susceptible where women are concerned, amorous.

126 *gorokunen ni naredo mo, nitiniti.* This would normally be taken to mean 'although it goes on for five or six years, day after day', and it was apparently so taken in the brief discussion of the piece in Oota's *Okame Hatimoku* (see Introduction). But a little further on (col. 140–2) the author clearly states that Koosuke decides to start his love-making after three years have passed. As such a flat contradiction in so short a space seems unlikely, the author may have intended it to be taken hypothetically with the meaning 'although it should go on for five or six years', i.e. 'even though it should take him five or six years (to reach the state he requires), day after day'.

て見れば、此の頃業平が見えなんだが、アレ向
うを通るの、今浅草の方へ行つたの、昨日は孔
雀茶屋へ入つたのといふ評判なれば、いよ〳〵
身を大事にして、「もう十年も養生をして、そ
れから腹一ぱい樂しまん。」と云ふを、梁の上
を通る鼠が笑ふももつとも（道理）なり。さう
〳〵人の世話になつても居られず、押入店を
借りて、一人暮しとは成つたれども、いつ（何
月）何時でも女房を持ちたければ、五百人持た
うが千人持たうが、好きなことととをさめて居
る。

今業平と綽名されて、おれ（吾）もよほどの
色男と思ふ聞にはや三年になり、もう少しづ
ゝ色事を始めようとは思へども、始めたと言
つたならば、世間で女どもが朝湯のくゞりが
明いたやうに、どろ〳〵と押しかけて來るで

---

127 *neri-yaku*. Any sort of medicine which is kneaded, generally with a base of honey or molasses; an electuary.

128 *sore de mo*. It is not clear what exactly is meant by *sore*, but it probably refers to Koosuke's decision to keep himself aloof mentioned at the end of the previous paragraph.

128 *narazu*. See 83 *naroo nara*.

129–131 *konogoro . . . tooru, ima . . . itta* and *kinoo . . . haitta*. These are three examples of the things people say about Koosuke, such as the extent of his *hyooban*. The *no . . . no . . . no* act here like *dano . . . dano . . . dano*.

129 *mienanda = mienakatta*; this is a form of the verb now usually found only in West Japan.

133–134 *hari no ue o tooru nezumi ga warau*. This recalls the proverb *Rainen no koto o yuu to oni ga warau* 'The devil laughs at next year's plans', that is 'Don't count your chickens before they are hatched'.

134 *mottomo:* not to be wondered at, only natural (for).

134–135 *Soosoo = itu made mo, sonna ni*.

135 *osiiredana*. As *osiire* means a built-in cupboard, the expression is presumably used here humorously to mean a rented house no bigger than a cupboard or, since it appears later that he is in lodgings, a minute rented room in a house. It probably originated in a pun on two meanings of *tana*: 'shelf' and 'rented house'.

137–138 *motoo ga . . . motoo ga*. The *ga* give a concessive sense to the verbs in this construction which is usually most conveniently translated 'whether . . . or . . . ' Cf. *yukoo ga yukumai ga* 'whether (he) goes or not . . .'

138 *suki na koto = zibun no katte*.

138–139 *to osamete iru*: contents himself, disposes of any anxiety, with the thought that.

143 *kuguri*. Short for *kugurido*; a small door, usually set into a bigger gate.

144 *dorodoro to* indicates a rumble, boom, or clatter. Here it presumably refers to the clackety-clack of *geta* as the women rush along.

あらう。何うぞチラホラ女の惚れるやうにし
たいものと思ひ、淺草の因果地藏へ願をかけ
る。

『私は女に多く惚れられて困ります。どう
ぞ五人か十人ぐらゐで止まりますやうに、お
守り下さりませ、南無地藏菩薩。』

幸助は願はかける、もう（最う）よしと思ひ、
馬道邊を通りしに、ある格子造りの内より、下

女と見えて小綺麗なる女、澁團扇に唐茄子の
へたやら種がらを載せて、捨てに出でしを、是
れもおれ（吾）に惚れて態と捨てに出たと心
得、矢庭に後より抱き付きしを、女は膽を潰し
振り切つて遁げる。

光源氏ならば、岡扇へ載せた唐茄子で腰折
と云ふ所だが、此の業平は歌を詠む風でなけ
れば、鼻歌で此の場を歸る。

145 *tirahora* = *mabara ni*, 'sparsely', 'here and there'.
146 *Inga-Zizoo*. The name of a figure of Zizoo which stands near one of the gates of the Asakusa-dera. Zizoo is a *bosatu* (bodhisattva), treated in Japan as a god of mercy and the patron of travellers and children.
152 *Umamiti*. The name of a road in the Asakusa district of Edo, so called because it was much used by people who rode along it on horseback on their way to the Yosiwara.
152 *koosi-zukuri*. The latticed front door of a house.
153 *sibu-utiwa*. A round fan made from paper treated with persimmon juice to stiffen it. Being stiff, it is often used about the house for such things as fanning fires and carrying odds and ends, as in the text.
154 *idesi o*. The *o* can be explained as the accusative particle, taking the construction to be *idesi (koto) o . . . to kokoroe* (cf. 115–6 *warau o . . . to kokoroe*); but the word order in Japanese is such that, on coming to the *o*, a reader would be more likely to take it as a conjunction equivalent to the modern *ga*.
156 *tukisi o*. In this case the *o* can only be a conjunction with adversative force.
158 *toonasu de*. Here equivalent to *toonasu ni tuite*.
158 *kosiore*: a poor *tanka* 短歌. The expression is said to come from poems in which the first part, ending with the *kosi no ku* 腰 の 句, the middle line of five syllables, is out of harmony with the second. Hence, a 'broken-backed' poem.

幸『ハテナ斯ういふ筈ではないが、きのふ地藏樣へお願ひ申したので惚れぬと見える。』それより幸助は、彼所此所の女にかまつて見ても、所々にててらされ、吾が長家の大家の神樣はどうか來て居る様子、是れは大丈夫出來ると、いやみをいひかけしに、常の通り神樣も半分なぶる氣にて少し綾なした處が、ほん（實）のことになりきうな鹽梅ゆゑ、外して近所へ出る。

女『幸助さんえゑ所へ來なすつた。チツトの内留守を頼みますよ。』幸『いつもいけぬわゑ。地藏樣が餘り利き過ぎて一人も出來ぬ。』

幸助つく〲考へて見るに、免角おれ（吾）が男がよすぎるゆゑ、女ども力味があつて、一ツも相談が出來ぬと見えた。いつそ地色は思ひ

---

164 *tokorodokoro nite*. Here means 'everywhere' rather than 'here and there'.

164 *terasare*. *Terasu* was used in brothel areas in the Tokugawa period to mean 'make (a client) feel ill at ease', 'treat badly'. The passive form is equivalent in this context to something like 'be given the cold shoulder'.

165 *kite iru*: feel amorous towards (a man), be forthcoming. *Kuru* can have this meaning only when the subject is a woman.

165–166 *dekiru to*. *Omotte* may be understood after this.

166 *iyami*: doubtful remarks, *double-entendres*.

167 *ayanasita*: 'dealt skilfully with' or, in the context, 'led (him) on'.

167 *hon = hontoo, honkakuteki*.

170 *titto = tyotto*.

171 *rusu*. Here used in its original meaning of 'stay and look after'.

175 *rikimi ga atte*. An obscure phrase, but since the meaning of *rikimi* is 'forcefulness', 'intensity (of emotion)', or the appearance thereof, the meaning is probably that the woman were 'violently affected'.

176 *zi-iro*. Literally 'local love', as opposed to liaisons with professional women in the brothel areas. Hence, it can be translated here as 'amateur love affairs'.

切ッて、女郎買ひと出やうと思ひ付き、吉原に

て名ある女郎を彼所此所にて買へども、兎角

思ふやうに先から惚れた様子は見えず、数年

耐へた程の面白味はなく、いろいろ氣を揉む。

幸助は其の後も諸所にて遊びしが、何處で

も面白可笑しくされる許りで、根ッから返え

ぬ故、ちと場所を變へて遊ばんと品川と出か

け、或内にてお菊と云ふ廻り女郎を揚げしに、

能く／＼のぶいきもの（不粋者）と見えて、飛ん

だよくせし故、始めて女は斯うしたものと云

ふことを知り、さア行く程に、滅多無性に通ひ

しゆゑ、親方德右衞門方にて盗みし金も、養生

喰ひその外店賃にな（失）くした上、少しの残

りを北國にて遣ひちらし、肝心面白く遊ぶ段

に成つた所で貧乏に成り、少しはあつた衣類

もぶちころし、此の頃は人のものを借著して

177 *to deyoo*. Here means something like 'set out to', 'start (. . . -ing)', being an emphatic expression roughly equivalent in meaning to *o yatte miyoo*. This use of *deru* is probably connected with its meaning of 'assume (an attitude)', 'make (a move)', in such expressions as *Doo deru ka wakaranai* 'I do not know what attitude (he) will take', ' . . . what move (he) will make'.

179 *saki* = *saki-kata*, (one's) companion.

182 *nekkara* (or *nekara*) = *sappari*, *mattaku*.

182–183 *saenu*. From the idea of 'being skilful', *saeru* acquired in brothels the meaning, as here, of 'get pleasure', 'have fun'.

183–184 *asoban to Sinagawa to dekake*. The meaning of the first *to* can be made clear by supplying some, such word as *omotte* after it, but the way in which the second *to* is used seems slightly different and less common. It too could be explained as giving the last phrase the meaning of 'he sets off with Sinagawa in mind', taking it as an abbreviated form of *Sinagawa e (ikoo) to omotte*. But such a use here seems unusual and it is at least possible that the part *tito . . . Sinagawa* is a quotation, perhaps a line from a popular song, which would make the meaning 'He sets off, saying to himself the words: "With the idea of just changing our haunt, Sinagawa!"'

184 *mawari-zyoroo*. A term used in the Edo period for low-class prostitutes who did not have a room of their own, but went to the rooms hired by their clients.

184 *agesi*. *Ageru* is the verb used of summoning *geisya* 藝者 and the like.

185–186 *tonda*. See 125 *tonda*.

187–188 *saa yuku hodo ni . . . kayoisi. Yuku* here is a *double-entendre*. Taking it in its ordinary sense of 'go', the interpretation would seem to be 'The more he goes, the more recklessly he makes his visits'. One is then inclined to regard the whole thing as a circumlocution for 'He makes his visits with more and more abandon'. But the context makes it possible to take *yuku* here in its sense of 'ejaculate'. *Saa*, with the decent sense of *yuku*, must be attributed to the author; with the other, it is most likely to go closely with *yuku* to add vividness.

188 *Tokuemon-kata nite:* at Tokuemon's place.

190 *Hokkoku*. Another name for the new Yosiwara brothel district, so called because it was situated to the north of Edo castle from 1657 onwards after the old site had been abandoned.

190 *kanzin omosiroku asobu dan*. That is, *omosiroku asobu kanzin na dan*, (when it comes to) the all-important stage where he gets pleasure from his dissipations.

192 *butikorosi*. Here means 'pawning', 'selling'; *cf.* the slang expression 'flogging (something)' in English.

192–193 *hito no mono o karigi site no zyoroo-kai to narisi wa*. The *karigi site no* phrase describes *zyoroo-kai* and *narisi wa* = *natta koto wa*. Thus, the whole thing means 'to have come to whoring in borrowed clothes'.

の女郎買ひとなりしは、はかなし。

人の身の成行きはあぢなものにて、主人の

目をくらまし、おもいれ女色の道を修行する

心にて養生喰ひをし、さらばと思つた時は先

の思はくが違ひ、やう〳〵品川の果てにて女

に思ひ付かれ、面白いと思ふと落ちぶれるが

一時にて、今は身の置所さへなく、菰一枚を八

丈とも縞縮緬とも思ひ、身にまとひながらも

矢張己惚はやまず、昔の藤屋伊左衛門は、夕霧

と云ふ女に金銀を遣ひ捨て、紙衣一枚と成つ

て其の名を残したとやら、我は其の上を行つ

て、菰を冠るといふも、伊左衛門よりは色男な

りと、是ればかりを本望とあきらめて、往來の

人に一錢二錢を貰ひ世を送りける。又德右衞

門が方にては、德兵衞を養子として家を讓り、

夫婦は隱居して、今は德兵衞の身代となり、或

---

193 *hakanasi:* 'how sad!', 'what a wretched/sorry plight!' etc.

194 *azi na mono.* Originally 'something tasty/spicy'. Here the meaning is that the course of human life is *azi na* in being so unpredictable.

195 *omoire.* An abbreviation of *omoi-ire*, 'to one's heart's content'.

195 *syuugyoo.* More commonly written 修業, the characters in the text usually being read *syugyoo.* Since the seventeenth century at least, *syuugyoo* or *syugyoo* has been used in such phrases as *iro-syugyoo* meaning, as here, serious concentration on love affairs.

196 *saraba to omotta toki. Saraba* can be regarded as an abbreviation of some such prase as *saraba yukoo* 'Right, now for it!', and the whole rendered as 'when he thought the time had come . . .'

197 *Sinagawa no hate nite. Hate* has the idea of distance, remoteness, with the slight derogatory implication which can be read into the English '(way) out at Sinagawa'. The reason for its use here is that Sinagawa was considered rather outlandish, compared with the more central Yosiwara.

198 *omoitukare.* A passive form from *omoituku*, used here with the meaning 'to feel attracted towards', 'to be taken by (someone)'.

198–199 *omosiroi to omou to otibureru ga it-toki nite*: he no sooner begins to enjoy himself than ruin comes in a moment. *It-toki* was, strictly, a period of approximately two hours under the old Japanese system of measuring time.

199 *komo itimai o.* Should be taken with both *omoi* and *matoi-nagara*.

201 *Huziya-Izaemon.* The lover of a woman called Yuugiri. The story of their love, which took place in the 1670's, became well-known and was made the subject of numerous songs and plays.

かの間に利買ひして、だん〳〵と繁昌しける。

（君が）身のたはけ（白癡）を悔み稼ぎしかば、僅

させ、鹽屋をさせしに、幸助も今になってわが

せよ。」と許せしゆゑ、金を與へ同町へ店を出

居夫婦も德兵衞が仁心に免じ、「どうなりとも

本）を遣はし、世話致したき。」と願ひければ、隱

見して、隱居へも詫言云ひて、「少しもとで（資

德右衞門は幸助を連れ歸り、いろ〳〵と意

れ歸りけり。

助に巡りあひ、先づ世話をしてやらんとて連

時淺草觀世音へ參りし歸りに、以前の朋輩幸

---

203 *to yara.* The same in meaning as *to zo* 'it is said', 'I hear'.
204 *komo o kaburu.* Has two meanings here; the context makes the literal one of wearing a straw mat over his head the stronger of the two, but the phrase also signifies the condition of a beggar, a state of dire poverty.
204 *to yuu mo:* even the fact that, the very fact that.
204–205 *nari to. Omotte* may be understood after this.
209 *Asakusa-Kanzeon.* Strictly speaking, the tiny gold figure of Kannon, just over two inches high, which is the principal image in the Asakusa-dera; but it is commonly used, as in the text, to mean the temple itself.
209 *mairisi kaeri ni. Mairisi* qualifies *kaeri;* 'on his way back from the temple'.
210 *mazu.* Used here in its basic sense of priority; 'to begin with . . .', 'the first thing is to . . .'
212 *Tokuemon.* A misprint; for this read 'Tokubee'.
214 *tukawasi.* Here used in the sense of *yaru, ataeru;* that is, 'give Koosuke some capital'.
214 *itasitaki.* Something like *mono de gozaimasu* may be understood after this *RENTAIKEI.*
215 *Doo nari to mo* = modern *doo de mo.*
215–216 *Tokubee ga zinsin ni men-zi . . . to yurusesi:* yielding to Tokubee's kindness of heart, they pardoned (Koosuke), saying . . .
217–218 *waga mi no* = *zibun* (自分) *no.* It is difficult to see any reason for the use of the character 君.
218 *kuyami kasegisikaba.* These words do not make a compound verb but mean 'repented and worked hard'. Note too that *kasegisikaba* is *not* a conditional.
219 *ri-gai* has not been found as a recognized word but, on the analogy of *ri-uri* 'selling at a profit', it should mean 'buying profitably'. Here it may be used loosely to mean no more than 'trading at a profit'. Alternatively, it may have been used with some such specific meaning as buying or replenishing stock out of the profits while keeping the capital intact.

誠に二ながら連立ちて、鼻ッ垂しの時分伊勢

より江戸へ來ても、人の心はきつ（甚）い違ひ

なものにて、悪事をなし主人の恩を捨て驅落

したると、主人の子となり家を續ぐとは、下駄

と燒味噌ほどの違ひなれども、末に繁昌せし

が不思議。是れも慾心でせず唯好色のみゆゑ、

神の惠みと見えたり。

其の後徳兵衞も親類内より女房を呼び、其

の序に又隠居へ願ひ、幸助にも世話してお菊

を添はせ、兩家ともに繁昌日に増し、徳兵衞夫

婦は隠居徳右衞門夫婦へ孝行を盡し、目出た

き春を迎へ家業榮える。此の目出たい序に、

つまらぬ二人の伊勢物語の御評判も、唯よい

〳〵と御贔屓を願ひまゐらせ候かしく。

220 *hutari-nagara:* both of them, the two of them.
220 *hanattarasi no zibun:* when they had runny noses; i.e. when they were still young boys.
221 *kitui.* As the character indicates, it here means simply 'very great'.
223–224 *geta to yaki-miso.* The equivalent here of 'chalk and cheese'. When spread on platters and baked, pieces of *miso* are somewhat like *geta* in appearance, hence the comparison.
231 *haru.* Here means the New Year.
231 *Kono medetai tuide ni:* 'At this happy juncture we should like to take the opportunity of . . . ' This last sentence is couched in fulsome terms typical of a letter from a tradesman to a customer, and is intended to be humorous in its overwhelming politeness to the reader.
233 *kasiku = kasiko;* a humble word used at the end of a letter almost exclusively by women.

UGETU-MONOGATARI

—one story: *Muoo no Rigyo*

THE late eighteenth century saw the rise of the *yomi-hon* 讀 本, that is, novels in which the text was intended to stand on its own, and not, as in *ki-byoosi* 黃 表 紙 and some earlier types of Tokugawa 德 川 fiction, to serve as explanations of pictures which were as important as the text itself. One of the most famous of these *yomi-hon* is the *Ugetu-monogatari* 雨 月 物 語 by Ueda-Akinari 上 田 秋 成, published in 1776. This is a collection of nine stories, all derived from older collections, some Japanese and some Chinese, and all containing the elements of the legendary, the fantastic, or the supernatural which are typical of *yomi-hon* as a whole. It is work in the tradition of the collections of tales of the supernatural which had been made from the very earliest days of Japanese literature.

Ueda-Akinari (1734–1809) was a man of humble and obscure origins and very poor health, who, nevertheless, gained a great reputation as a novelist, poet, aesthete, and scholar, and exerted a great influence on later writers of *yomi-hon*. His first works were *haikai* 俳 諧, produced in the *demi-monde* of Oosaka 大 阪, but from the age of about thirty-three his interests turned more to the Japanese and Chinese classics, and led him, on the one hand, to enter the field of scholarship, where he derived much from the great Kamo-Mabuti 賀 茂 眞 淵 and had a series of disputes with Motoori-Norinaga 本 居 宜 長, and, on the other hand, to compile the *Ugetu-monogatari*.

Our story, *Muoo no Rigyo*, though given a Japanese setting on the shores of Lake Biwa 琵 琶 湖 in the early part of the Heian 平 安 period (794–1191), is based on one called *Yü-fu-chi* 魚 服 記, 'The Story of the Fish's Apparel', included in a fourteenth-century Chinese collection of stories by Lu Chi 陸 楫, called *Ku-chin shuo-hai* 古 今 說 海, 'Sea of Tales Old and New'. The influence of the Chinese language on the style of the Japanese version may be seen, for instance, in the quotation constructions, e.g. *hito-goto ni tawaburete yuu* '. . . *ataezu' to nan* (cols. 16–19).

The influence of Chinese may also be seen in the author's use of *kanzi*, though not all his idiosyncrasies in this matter can be ascribed to this cause. There are a number of places in this story where the author has assigned unusual readings, indicated in the original by *hurigana*, to *kanzi* (both single characters and compounds); or perhaps it would be more accurate to say, since the *hurigana* readings are really as much part of the original text as the characters to which they were attached, that he has written a number of Japanese words with very unusual *kanzi*, characters which often elaborate or define more accurately for the reader the meaning of those words. Thus 貼 is used for the word *osu* (col. 12), though this is not an accepted *kun* reading of the character. Again, *kuwasiki* is written with the Chinese compound 細 妙

91

(col. 9), while *asobu* (cols. 7–8) is written 遊 躍, without any *kana* after it to show the ending of the verb. Other examples of Chinese influence may be seen in the use of 去 for *yuku* and of the characters 許 多 for the Japanese word *amata*. Occasionally, too, the author appears to have used certain characters in direct imitation of the original Chinese version of the story, as, for instance, 心 頭 read *mune* (col. 23). In our text, all readings of characters which the student will be unable to find given as such in dictionaries are included, in *kana*, in the body of the text, followed by the characters in brackets with which they were written by Ueda-Akinari.

The text followed is that in *Yomi-hon-kessaku-syuu* (Tookyoo, 1935), by Wada-Mankiti 和 田 萬 吉. Translations by Wilfrid Whitehouse of five other tales from the *Ugetu-monogatari* appeared in *Monumenta Nipponica* I (1938), pp.242–258 and 549–567, and IV (1941), pp.166–191.

C.B.
W.E.S.

むかし延長の頃、三井寺に興義といふ僧あ
りけり、繪に巧なるをもて名を世にゆるされ
けり、常に畫く所、佛像山水花鳥を事とせず、
寺務のいとま（間）ある日はうみ（湖）に小船を
うかべて、綱引釣するあま（泉郎）に錢をあた
へ、獲たる魚をもとの江に放ちて、其の魚のあ
そぶ（遊躍）を見ては畫きけるほどに、年を經
てくはしき（細妙）に至りけり、或時は繪に心
を凝して、眠をきそへば、ゆめの裏に江に入り
て、さばかり（大小）の魚と倶に遊ぶ、覺むれば
卽て見つるまゝを畫きて壁にお（貼）し、みづ
から呼びて夢應の鯉魚と名付けけり、その繪
の妙なるをめで（感）て、乞要むるものついで
（前後）を爭へば、たゞ花鳥山水は乞ふにまか
せてあたへ、鯉魚の繪はあながちに惜みて、人

Ugetu-monogatari

1 *muoo:* in response to a dream, inspired by a dream. The title of this story is taken from the title of the picture of a carp painted by the main character, Koogi, as a result of a dream (cols. 9–20). It also refers to his later dream experiences as a carp, which form the larger part of this story (col. 20 ff.).

2 *Entyoo no koro:* A.D.923–30.

2 *Mii-dera:* a temple of a branch of the Tendai 天臺 sect, near Ootu 大津 at the southern end of Lake Biwa (the 'lake' of this story).

3–4 *. . . o mote na o yo ni yurusarekeri.* A literal translation would be: He was widely allowed a reputation for . . .

4 *sezu.* It is possible to interpret this either as a conclusive form (*SYUUSIKEI*), or as a conjunctive or suspensive form (*REN-YOOKEI*).

6 *abiki:* fishing with a net, as opposed to *turi*, fishing with a hook and line.

6 *ama:* fisherman. Generally written 海人.

7 *e*—here 'lake', rather than the usual meaning of inlet, bay.

11 *sabakari = sorehodo,* but the meaning here is presumably that indicated by the characters, i.e. large and small, of all sizes.

12 *osi*—here means 'stick on', hence the use of the character 貼. This meaning of *osu* is a rare but recognized one.

毎に戯れていふ、「生を殺しあざらけき（鮮）を

喰ふ凡俗の人に、法師の養ふ魚必しも與へず」

となん、其の繪とわざごと（俳諧）とともに天

下にきこえけり、

一とせ病にかゝりて、七日を經て忽に眼を

閉ぢ息絶えてむなしくなりぬ、徒弟友どちあ

つまりて歎き惜みけるが、只むね（心頭）のあ

たりのすこ（微）し暖なるにぞ、若しやと居め

ぐりて守りつも三日を經にけるに、手足少し

動き出づるやうなりしが、忽ちためいき（長

嘘）を吐きて、眼をひらき、醒めたるが如くに

起き上りて、人々にむかひ「我人事を忘れて既

に久し、幾日をか過しけん」、衆弟等いふ、「師三

日前に息たえ給ひぬ、寺中の人々をはじめ、日

頃睦まじくかたり給ふ殿原も詣で給ひて葬

の事をもはかりたまひぬれど只師が心頭の

17–19 . . . *yuu* . . . *to nan*. The word order in which the verb of saying precedes the reported speech is found in Japanese styles influenced by Chinese. The use of *to nan* after this construction is a characteristic of Akinari's style.

17 *azarakeki:* raw, fresh. Though this word is cognate with the modern *azayaka na*, the meaning here is pejorative (equivalent to *namagusai*), conveying the Buddhist distaste for eating flesh.

19 *wazagoto:* joke, witticism.

21 *hitotose:* one year.

22 *totei:* disciples.

22 *tomodoti*—an older form of *tomodati*.

24–25 *imegurite* = *mawari ni ite*.

25 *mamoritu mo*. The *SYUUSIKEI* followed by *mo* was in earlier times exclamatory, but here the sense seems to be that of *mamorituru tokoro*.

29 *syuutei:* disciples.

31 *tonobara* = *tonogata* 殿 方, gentlemen.

暖なるを見て、柩にも藏めでかく守り侍りし
に、今や蘇生りたまふにつきて、かしこくも物
せざりしよと怡びあへり」與義點頭ていふ、
「誰にもあれ一人檀家の平の助の殿のみたち
(館)に詣てまう(告)さんは、法師こそ不思議に
生き侍れ、君今酒を酌み鮮き鱠をつくらしめ
給ふ、暫く宴を罷めて寺に詣でさせ給へ、稀有
の物語聞え參らせんとて、彼の人々のあるさ
ま(形)を見よ、我が詞に露違はじ」といふ、使異
しみながら彼の館に往きて其の由をいひ入
れて窺ひ見るに、主の助を始め、おとうと(令
弟)の十郎、家の子かもり(掃守)など居めぐり
て酒を酌みゐたる、師が詞のたがはぬを奇と
す、助の館の人々此の事を聞きて大に異しみ、
先づ箸を止めて、十郎・掃守をも召し具して
寺に到る、

---

33 *mamori-haberisi*. *Haberu* here is a deferential suffix, and is not to be taken as a separate word meaning attend on.

34 *kasikoku mo* is exclamatory, showing the feeling of the speakers in the face of this miracle (*cf.* modern *yoku mo*).

36 *tare ni mo are:* literally, let it be anyone (any of you).

36 *mi-tati:* mansion. The *mi* is honorific.

37–40 *moosan wa* . . . *tote:* what he will say is ' . . . ' and . . . *Moosan wa* thus has here an imperative force.

38 *namasu*—presumably used here in its older meaning of finely chopped fish and not in its present-day meaning.

40 *kikoe-mairasen = o hanasi site agemasyoo.*

41 *tuyu:* in the very least.

42–43 *ii-irete:* sending in a message.

44 *ie no ko:* retainer.

44 *kamori:* servant, sweeper. Though used here in a general sense, this word more strictly denotes an official of the Bureau of Housekeeping at the Heian Court, the *Kamonryoo* (*kamon* being an alternative form of *kamori*). It is said to have had its origin in the *Kanimori* of a legendary incident. The legend, as it appears in the *Kogo-syuui* 古語拾遺, relates that when Toyotama-hime, the daughter of Watatumi, the Sea God, was about to give birth to *Hikonagisa-take-ugayahukiaᵉzu-no-mikoto*, a special hut was built for her on the seashore. There Amenoosibito-no-mikoto made a broom, and swept out the crabs which had invaded the hut. Those who claimed descent from Amenoosibito were charged with the duties of supervising the sweeping and cleaning of the Palace, with the title of *Kanimori-no-tukasa* 蟹守寮, crab-watcher officials.

47 *mazu:* at once, immediately.

47 *mesi-gu-site:* taking with him.

興義枕をあげて路次のわづらひ（勞）をかた
じけなうすれば、助も蘇生のことぶき（賀）を
述ぶ、興義先づ問ひていふ、「君試に我がいふ
事を聞かせ給へ、かの漁父文四に魚を誂へた
まふことありや」、助驚きて、「まことにさるこ
とありいかにして知らせ給ふや」、興義、「かの
漁父みたけ（三尺）あまりの魚を籠に入れて君
が門に入る、君は賢弟と南面の所に碁を圍み
ておはす、掃守傍に侍りて桃の實の大なるを
啗ひつゝ弈の手段を見る、漁父がまな（大魚）
を携へ來るを喜びて、高坏に盛りたる桃を與
へ、又盃をたまうて三獻飮ましめ給ふ、かしは
びと（膾手）したり顔に魚をとり出でて膾にせ
しまで、法師がいふ所たがはでぞあるらめ」と
いふに、助の人々此の事を聞きて、或は異し
み、或は心地惑ひて、かくつばら（詳）なる言の

49 *makura o agete:* raising his head from the pillow.
49 *rozi no wazurai:* the bother of travelling.
51 *kokoromi ni*—literally, for trial, to see what you think, but means little more here than English 'just'.
53 *saru = sa aru:* be so, be such.
55 *mitake. Take* is not strictly any specific unit of measurement, but is presumably used here in the sense of *syaku*, since it is written with the character 尺.
56 *kentei*—an honorific term for someone else's younger brother.
56 *minamiomote no tokoro:* a room facing south. In Japanese houses, which traditionally face south, this would be the front, and also the best, room.
57 *owasu*—honorific equivalent of *ari, ori*, etc.
58 *eki:* playing go.
58 *mana.* In older Japanese, *na* was a general term for food. The prefix *ma*, normally written 眞, may be translated as 'fine', but really does little more than give a poetical flavour to the word to which it is prefixed. Here, however, as with e.g. *sabakari* (see 11), it is the sense of the characters, big fish, that has to be taken as the meaning rather than that of the Japanese reading.
59 *takatuki:* a tall, lacquered dish or tray on a stand, used for holding cakes, fruit, etc.
60 *sankon. Kon* is a 'unit' for counting cups of *sake*.
60–61 *kasiwabito.* In ancient Japan the leaf of the *kasiwa*, oak, was used as a plate. Thus *kasiwabito* or *kasiwade* means literally the one who is in charge of the plates, i.e. the cook. Note that Ueda-Akinari has here used characters meaning literally the one in charge of the *namasu*.

由を頻に尋ぬるに、興義かたりていふ、

「我此の頃病に苦しみて堪へ難きあまり、其
の死したるをも知らず、熱き心地少しさま
んものをと、杖に扶けられて門を出づれば、病
もやゝ忘れたるやうにて籠の鳥の雲井にか
へるこゝちす、山となく里となく行きゝて、
又江のほとり（畔）に出づ、湖水の碧なるを見
るより、現なき心に浴びて遊びなんとて、そこ
に衣を脱ぎすて（去）て身を跳らして深きに飛
入りつも、をちこち（彼此）に游ぎめぐるに、わ
か（幼）きより水に狎れたるにもあらぬが、お
も（懲）ふに任せて戯れけり、今思へば愚なる
夢ごころなりし、されども人の水に浮ぶは魚
のこゝろよきにはしかず、こゝにて又魚の遊
びをうらやむ心おこりぬ傍にひとつの大魚
ありていふ、『師のねがふ事いと易し、待たせ

61　*toriidete = toridasite*.

61–62　*namasu ni sesi made.* Everything would be just as Koogi said, 'even to the fact that the cook made (the fish) into a dish of chopped fish'.

62　*tagawade zo arurame.* Zo is normally followed by the *RENTAIKEI*, not the *IZENKEI*. One would expect here either *tagawade zo aruramu* or *tagawade koso arurame*.

64　*tubara:* detailed.

66　*amari:* through excess of (unbearableness).

66–67　*sono si-sitaru.* Koogi is looking at himself from outside, as it were—'the death of that person (who was I)'.

68　*mono o.* Usually used in the middle of a sentence, with adversative meaning. Following the *mu* form at the end of a sentence, it adds an overtone of wistfulness to a statement of desire or intention. A modern colloquial equivalent for the phrase *samasan mono o* here would be *samasitain' da ga na*.

69　*ko* is the reading here for 籠.

69　*kumoi.* 井 is an *atezi* for 居.

70　*yama to naku sato to naku:* over mountains and through villages. The sense is arrived at by taking it to mean 'literally': 'not particularly over mountains nor particularly through villages', i.e. traversing mountains and villages alike.

71–72　*miru yori = miru to sassoku*.

72　*asobinan = asobinamu.* The verb-ending *namu*, the *MU* form of the suffix *nu*, expresses intention.

73　*mi o odorasite:* literally, making my body leap. A translation of the 跳身 of the Chinese original of this story.

74　*iritu mo*—see 25 *mamoritu mo*.

80　*matase*—an honorific use of the causative form.

給へ』とて、杳の底にゆく（去）と見しに、しばし
、、冠装束したる人の、前の大魚に跨りて、
あまた（許多）のうろくづ（鱗魚）を牽ゐて浮ひ
きたり我にむかひていふ、『わたづみ（海若）の
詔あり、老僧かねて放生の功徳多し、今江に入
りて魚の遊躍を願ふ、権に金鯉が服を授けて
水府のたのしみをせさせ給ふ、只餌の香ばし
きに昧まされて、釣の絲にかゝり身を亡ふこ
となかれ』といひて去りて見えずなりぬ、不思
議のあまりにおのが身をかへり見れば、いつ
のまに鱗金光を備へてひとつの鯉魚と化し
ぬ、

81–84 *yuku to misi ni . . . ukabikitari*. The equivalent in modern colloquial would be *itta to omottara . . . ukande kaette kita*.

82 *kamuri = kanmuri*. This, and the following *soozoku* together form the Court dress. *Soozoku* has in modern Japanese become *syoozoku;* its first syllable illustrates a common feature of classical, particularly Heian, Japanese, namely the avoidance in many words of Chinese origin of *yoo-on* 拗音, 'twisted sounds', i.e. syllables such as *sya, syu, syo, zya, zyu, zyo,* etc.—*cf.* 140 *zusa*.

83 *urokuzu*—also *irokuzu*—scales of a fish, or fish and other creatures that live in the sea; here the latter.

84 *watazumi*—the God of the Sea. The form *watazumi*, as in this text, may be a mistake, the usual form being *watatumi*. In fact there were in legend four sea-gods, Oo-watatumi, and three lesser deities, Soko-tu-watatumi, Naka-tu-watatumi and Uwa-tu-watatumi, who presided over the lower, middle and upper depths respectively. The word *watatumi* occurs from the earliest times, and though it is often said to be a compound, its elements cannot be identified with entire certainty.

85 *roosoo*—here used as a respectful mode of address—you, venerable priest.

85 *hoozyoo:* releasing living things, i.e. buying things like fishes and birds, which have been caught by men to be killed, and releasing them as an act of Buddhist piety.

86 *kinri:* golden carp.

87 *suihu*—strictly the Palace of the Sea-God, but can also mean the regions under the water.

91 *kinkoo:* the glitter of gold.

91–92 *ke-sinu*. 化 is often read *ke* when it means a magical transformation.

あやしとも思はで、尾を振り鰭を動かして

心のまゝに逍遙す、まづ長等の山おろし、立ち

95

居る浪に身をのせて、志賀のおほわだ（大灣）

の汀に遊べば、徒歩人の裳のすそぬらすゆき

かひにおど（驚）されて、比良の高山影映る、深

き水底に潜くとすれど、かくれ堅田の漁火に

よるぞうつゝなき、ぬば玉の夜中の潟にやど

100

る月は、鏡の山の峯に清みて、八十の湊の八十

---

94 *Nagara no yamaorosi:* the wind blowing down from Mount Nagara. This mountain lies to the west of the city of Ootu.

96 *katibito:* pedestrians. *Kati* is usually written with 徒 alone.

96 *mo:* a kind of skirt.

97 *Hira no takayama:* presumably the modern Hira-san (Mount Hira), the highest peak in the range of mountains on the western side of Lake Biwa.

98 *kakure-Katada*—a *kakekotoba* on *kakuregatai*, hard to hide in, and Katada 堅田, the name of a village. The sense of the passage is: Though I tried to dive down . . . I found myself drawn unawares towards the fishing-fires at the village of Katada, where it was hard to hide (because there was no shelter).

99 *nubatama*—literally the seed of the *hioogi* grass, but used as a *makurakotoba* for *yo*, night. This use appears in the *Man-yoo-syuu*, though in such early works it occurs mostly in association with compound nouns having *kuro*, black, as their first element, e.g. *kuro-gami*, black hair, *kurogoma*, black pony. In later works it is found as a *makurakotoba* for *kami*, *koma*, etc., without the *kuro*. Alternative forms of the word are *mubatama* and *ubatama*, and it is written with a variety of characters.

100 *Kagami-no-yama:* a mountain on the border between Yasu-gun 野洲郡 and Gamoo (蒲生)-gun, east of the Lake. *Kagami*, mirror, is closely connected in Japanese thought with *sumu*, be clear.

100 *yaso*—literally eighty, but here means countless.

100 *minato:* inlet, creek.

隈もなくておもしろ、沖津島山、竹生島、波に
うつろふ朱の垣こそおどろかるれ、さしも伊
吹の山風に、朝妻船も漕ぎ出づれば、葦間の夢
を覺され、矢橋の渡りする人の水なれ棹をの
がれては、瀬田の橋守にいくそたびか追はれ
ぬ、日あたたかなれば浮び、風あらきときは千
尋の底に遊ぶ、
にはか(急)にも飢ゑてもの(食)ほしけなる
に、彼此にあさ(饗)り得ずして狂ひゆくほど

100–101 *yasokuma mo nakute*. The epithet *kumanaki* is frequently applied to moonlight, meaning with no dark corner, i.e. brilliant. *Tuki wa . . . yaso no minato no yasokuma mo nakute* means 'with the moon there were none of the many dark corners of the many inlets'.

101 *omosiro*. This use of the stem of the adjective is exclamatory.

101 *Okitusimayama*—now called Oki-no-sima, the largest island in Lake Biwa.

101 *Tikubusima*—an island near the northern end of the Lake, having on it a shrine to Benten. It is the red fences of this shrine which are referred to here.

102 *kaki koso odorokarure*. The use of the passive here is similar to its use in the modern colloquial in a case like *to kanzirareru*, 'one cannot help feeling that'. The difference between X *ni odorokareru* and X *ga odorokareru* (the *koso* in our text approximates to *ga*) is something like the difference between 'one marvels at X' and 'X is enough to make one marvel'.

102–103 *sasimo Ibuki*. *Sasimo* here, meaning 'that famous', is also a reference to the central play on words in the poem by Huziwara-Sanekata 實 方 (included in the *Go-syuui-syuu* 後拾遺集) which made a certain Mount Ibuki famous: *Kaku to dani / e ya wa Ibuki no / sasimogusa / sasimo sirazu na / moyuru omoi o*. Note however that the Mount Ibuki of this poem is in fact not that of this story, being in the province of Koozuke 上 野.

103 *Asazuma-bune:* the ferry-boats which used to ply across the inlet of Asazuma, on Lake Biwa, north of Hikone 彦 根.

104 *Yabase no watari suru hito:* the man who worked the ferry between Ootu and Yabase, which is opposite Ootu.

104 *minarezao:* a boat-pole, literally a pole accustomed to the water. Other compounds in this story where *mi* occurs with the same meaning as *mizu*, are *minasoko, migiwa* and *minato*.

に、忽文四が釣を垂るゝにあふ、その餌甚だ香
し、心又かはがみ（河伯）の戒を守りて思ふ、我
は佛の御弟子なり、しばし食を求め得ずとも、
なぞもあさましく魚の餌を飲むべきとてそ
こを去る、暫時ありて飢ますく甚しければ、
かさねて思ふに、今は堪へ難し、たとへ此の餌
を飲むとも嗚呼に捕れんやは、素よりかれ
（他）は相識るものなれば、何のはゞかりかあ
らんとて遂に餌をのむ、文四はやく絲を收め

---

105 *Seta no hasimori:* the keeper of the bridge at Seta, which is at the extreme south end of Lake Biwa, guarding the approach to Kyooto from the Kantoo.

105 *ikuso-tabi ka:* literally any number of tens of times, i.e. scores of times.

108 *monohosige naru.* It is rare for *-ge naru* to be used, as here, applied to the first person; such a use indicates an objective attitude on the part of the speaker towards himself—not 'I felt in need of food' but 'I seemed to be in need of food'.

109 *asari-ezu site* does not mean being unable to hunt for food, but hunting for food and not getting any. The character here appears to have been invented for the occasion; the original Chinese version of the story, as also several editions of the *Ugetu-monogatari*, has here 求食.

111 *mata* in this context has to be translated into English as an adversative.

111 *kawagami:* the River-God. It is presumably Watatumi who is indicated here, since our story had this name earlier where the Chinese version of the story used the word 河伯. This latter is actually a rare name for the God of the Yellow River.

112 *hotoke no mi-desi.* The *mi* is honorific to the Buddha, not to the *desi*.

113 *nazo mo . . . tote:* literally, why should I meanly swallow a fish's bait? *Nazo* (= *nanzo*), like any other use of *zo*, is followed by an attributive form, here *nomubeki*.

116 *oko ni:* foolishly. This word is often written 烏滸, the name of a country of Later Han times, whose inhabitants had customs so strange to the Chinese that they were constant objects of ridicule. *Cf. okogamasii,* ridiculous.

117–118 *. . . aran tote.* The conclusion of Koogi's reflections starting at *ima wa taegatasi,* col. 115.

て我を捕ふ、こはいかにするぞと叫びぬれと

も、他かつて聞かず顔にもてなして、縄をもて

我が腮を貫き、葦間に船をつなぎ、我を籠にお

し入れて君が門に進み入る、君は賢弟とおも

て（南面）の間に弈して遊ばせたまふ掃守傍に

侍りてこのみ（菓）を啗ふ、文四がもて來し大

魚を見て人々大に感させ給ふ、我其のとき人

々にむかひ聲をはり上げて、『旁等は輿義をわ

すれたまふか、宵にかへさせた

まへ』と連に叫びぬれど、人々知らぬ形にもて

なして、只手を拍つて喜び給ふ、繪手なるもの

まづ我が両眼をひだり（左手）の指にてつよく

とらへ、みぎり（右手）に礪すませし刀を・とり

てまないた（俎盤）にのぼし、既に切るべかり

し時、我くるしきのあまりに大聲をあげて、佛

弟子を害する例やある、我を助けよ〳〵とな

118–119 *osamete:* gather in.
119 *ko wa = kore wa.*
120 *katute kikazu-gao ni motenasite. Katute = sukosi mo, mattaku,* and emphasizes the negative *kikazu. Kikazu-gao,* a not-hearing face, means a look as though one had not heard. *Motenasu:* behave.
125 *medesase*—also *yurusase* and *kaesase,* col. 127.—*Cf.* 80 *matase.*
131 *migiri.* Possibly formed by analogy with *hidari.*
131 *katana:* knife.

（哭）き叫びぬれど聞き入れず、終に切らるゝ
とおほえて夢醒めたり」と語る、人々大に感で、
異しみ、「師が物がたりにつきて思ふに、其の
度ごとに魚の口の動くを見れど、更に聲を出
すことなし、かゝることまのあたりに見しこ
そいと不思議なれ」とて、從者を家に走らしめ
て殘れる鱠を湖に棄てさせけり、興義是より
病癒えて杳の後よはひ（天年）をもてまか（死）
りける、其のをはり（終焉）に臨みて畫く所の
鯉魚數枚をとりて湖に散せば、畫ける魚紙繪
を離れて水に遊戲す、ここをもて興義か繪世
に傳はらず、其の弟子成光なるもの、興義が神
妙をつたへて時に名あり、閑院の殿の障子に
鶏を畫きしに、生けるとり（鶏）この繪を見て
蹴たるよしを、古き物がたりに載せたり、

---

140 *zusa*—modern pronunciation *zyuusya*. *Cf.* 82 *kamuri*.

142 *yowai o mote:* of (old) age. The characters indicate that *yowai* here means one's natural term of existence.

142–143 *makarikeru:* literally, departed; but here means died, as the character indicates.

145 *yuuge su:* sport, disport oneself—modern *yuugi suru*.

146–147 *sinmyoo:* something which is beyond human understanding, mysterious gifts, wonderful skill.

147 *tutaete*—here used probably in a double sense, both 'inherited' and 'passed on to the world' (the latter contrasting with *tutawarazu*).

147 *Kan-in no tono:* the residence of Huziwara-Huyutugu 冬嗣 (775–826) in Kyooto, afterwards, as a palace, called Kan-in Dairi.

149 *huruki monogatari*—recorded in *maki* XI of the *Kokon-tyomonzyuu* 古今著聞集, a miscellaneous collection of tales and anecdotes compiled by Tatibana-no-Narisue 橘成李 in 1254.

TAMAKATUMA

—two extracts: *Hitomuki ni katayoru koto no ageturai;*
and *Sakinoti to tokigoto no kawaru koto*

THE *Tamakatuma* 玉 勝 間, or *Tamagatuma* as it is also called, is a collection of notes by Motoori-Norinaga 本 居 宣 長 on early Japanese literature, language, history, religion, administrative and legal institutions, education, etc., as well as statements of his own views on a wide variety of topics, ranging from life in general, to methods of study, and the corrupting influence of Chinese ideas and institutions. They are a selection from jottings Motoori made while working at his commentary on the *Koziki*. The first three volumes (*maki* 卷) were published in 1794, and others, three at a time, appeared at intervals of two or three years; the fourteenth was still incomplete when Motoori died, and his followers added more of his jottings to complete it, as well as a fifteenth volume consisting of an index. There are more than a thousand jottings all together in the fourteen volumes.

The *katuma* of the title is a name for a tightly plaited bamboo basket; *tama* (jewel) is an ornamental, laudatory prefix. Motoori no doubt chose the title to suggest that the work was a sort of receptacle holding many items, but also because *tama-katuma* was an elegant word, belonging to the older language— it is used as a *makurakotoba* 枕 詞 in the *Man-yoo-syuu* 萬 葉 集.

Motoori-Norinaga (1730–1801) was one of the principal *kokugakusya* 國 學 者, or members of the Native-Learning school. He was born at Matuzaka 松 阪 in the Province of Ise 伊 勢. Although his father was a merchant, Motoori claimed that his ancestors had been samurai. In his youth he went to Kyooto 京 都 to study Confucianism and medicine and while there was impressed by the work of Keityuu 契 沖 (1640–1701) on ancient Japanese literature. When he returned to Matuzaka, where he set up as a medical man, he started at the same time to devote himself to *inisiemanabi* 古 學, or Learning about Old Times, i.e. more or less what is now usually called *kokugaku* 國 學, or Native Learning. His chief interest at first was the study of Heian 平 安 literature, but after meeting Kamo-Mabuti 賀 茂 眞 淵 (1697–1769), the most influential advocate of *inisiemanabi* and a poet in the *Man-yoo* style, he turned to studying the *Koziki*, the oldest extant book in Japanese. The outcome of this study, which occupied most of the rest of his life, was the commentary called the *Koziki-den* 古 事 記 傳, one of the greatest monuments of the *kokugaku* school. Motoori left altogether fifty-eight works on a wide range of subjects.

The style in which the *Tamakatuma* is written was known to those who affected it as *gabun* or *miyabibumi* 雅 文, elegant writing. It is a type of what is called *gikobun* 擬 古 文, writing imitating the past, archaistic writing. The *kokugakusya* of the Edo 江 戸 period (1603–1867) held that the Japanese

104

language had become progressively corrupt and vulgar, at least since the Heian period (794–1191), and that in order to appreciate the life and thought of earlier times it was necessary to write in the language of those times. In practice, it was largely Heian *kana* literature which they imitated; so far as possible they composed in the vocabulary, grammar, and *kana* spelling of that literature. This made for diffuseness, since they often had to set out at length what could have been expressed more concisely by using Sino-Japanese words, very few of which appeared in Heian *kana* literature. It also made for monotony. Motoori himself is very prolix; one wonders whether the habit grew out of anxiety lest his readers might not grasp his meaning if he said a thing only once, for he may have realized—even if only sub-consciously— that much of his vocabulary, if not radically imprecise, was likely to be unfamiliar. The translations here offered attempt to reproduce something of the style by avoiding words of Romance origin.

The text used is that of the *Motoori-Norinaga-zensyuu*, revised edition (1926), vol.8 (pp.93–5). There are translations by B. H. Chamberlain of some sections of *Tamakatuma*—dealing with art—in vol.XII (1885) of the TRANSACTIONS OF THE ASIATIC SOCIETY OF JAPAN.

F.J.D.

S.Y.

ひとむきにかたよることの論ひ

世の物しり人の、ヒト（他）のトキゴト（説）の

あしきをとがめず、ヒト（一）むきにかたよら

ず、これをもかれをもすてぬさまにアグツラ

ヒ（論）をなすは、多くはおのが思ひとりたる

趣をまげて、世の人の心に、あまねくかなへむ

とするものにて、まことにあらず、心ぎたなし、

たとひ世ノ人は、いかにそしるとも、わが思ふ

すぢをまげて、したがふべきとにはあらず、人

のほめそしりにはかゝはるまじきわざぞ、大

かた一むきにかたよりて、アダシトキゴト（他

説）をば、わろしととがむるを、心せばくよ

からぬとゝし、ひとむきにはかたよらず、アダ

シトキゴト（他説）をも、わろしとはいはぬを、

心ひろくおいらかにて、よしとするは、なべて

Hitomuki ni katayoru koto no ageturai

1 *hitomuki ni katayoru*. *Hitomuki*, as a noun, means '(facing in) one direction', and the phrase could be interpreted as 'lean (or incline) to one side'. But *hitomuki ni*, taken adverbially, means 'resolutely', 'in an unyielding way', which would give the phrase the sense rather of 'incline resolutely to one side'. Probably this comes nearer to the writer's intention. Either way, it seems that 'take sides' translates the phrase fairly adequately.

1 *ageturai*: discussion, argument. As with these English words, either a dispute between two persons may be referred to, or a setting-forth of the rights and wrongs of some topic. Here clearly it is the latter, and it may be imagined that Motoori used the word in the heading in order to suggest that it was to be taken in this sense in cols. 4–5 also.

2 *yo no;* of the world, of this world of ours. Here perhaps 'our' may pass as a translation.

2 *monosiribito = monosiri*.

2 *tokigoto:* an expressed opinion, a teaching (on some point).

2–3 *no asiki o = no warui* (or perhaps, rather, *matigatta*) *no o*.

4 *kare = are*.

5–6 *ono ga omoitoritaru omomuki:* ideas (or items of knowledge) which one's mind has seized on; one's own insights.

6 *kanaemu*, from *kanoo*, v.t., make [something] accord (with). The modern form of the verb would be *kanaeru*, although the modern *kanaeru* is hardly used in the same way. The object of the verb is *omomuki*.

7 *kokorogitanasi* (*kokoro ga kitanai*): despicable, mean-minded. Although similar compounds of *kokoro* with an adjective are still used (*kokorogurusii, kokorozuyoi*), this type of formation was more common in the Heian period than it is now: cf. *kokorosebaku* (*kokoro ga semaku*), cols. 12–13, and *kokorohiroku* (*kokoro ga hiroku*), col. 15.

の人の心なめれど、かならずそれさしもよき

事にもあらず、よるところ定りて、そを深く信

ずる心ならば、かならずひとむきにこそよる

べけれ、それにたがへるすぢをば、とるべきに

あらず、よしとしてよる所にコト（異）なるは、

みなあしきなり、これよければ、かれはかなら

ずあしきことわりぞかし、然るをこれもよし、

又かれもあしからずといふは、よるところさ

だまらず、信ずべきところを、深く信ぜざるも

の也、よるところさだまりて、そを信ずる心の

深ければ、それにとなるすぢのあしきとをば、

おのづからとがめざるとあたはず、これ信ず

るところを信ずるまめごゝろ也、人はいかに

おもふらむ、われは一むきにかたよりて、あだ

し説をばわろしとゝがむるも、かならずわろ

しとは思はずなむ、

8–9 *waga omoo suzi:* the line of one's thoughts; one's convictions; what one deems to be the way of things.

9 *ni wa arazu = de wa nai.*

10 *waza zo = koto (de aru) zo.*

10–11 *ookata* modifies *nabete no hito no kokoro nameredo,* cols. 15–16. The meaning here is much the same as that of *daitai* 大體.

11 *adasi-* (prefix): another ~ ; a ~ other than one's own.

12 *warosi:* older form of *warusi (= warui).*

15 *oiraka nite:* be seemly.

15–16 *nabete no hito:* men in general, the run of mankind.

16 *nameredo (< narumeredo) = de aroo ga.*

16 *sasimo,* a compound of *sa (= soo), si* (emphatic particle), and *mo;* roughly equivalent here to *sore hodo.*

17 *yoru tokoro:* the place (or point) one depends on, one's standing-ground.

18 *kokoro:* one's intention, how one is minded.

19 *tagaeru (< tagai aru) = tigatte iru.* (Do not confound with the modern transitive verb *tagaeru.*)

22 *kotowari zo kasi:* more or less equivalent to modern *doori* 道理 *na no da yo. Kasi* is an exclamatory particle which usually comes at the end of a sentence and gives a suggestion of sweet reasonableness on the part of the writer—*cf.* 39 *okasikaranu kata mo aru zo kasi.*

27–28 *kore sin-zuru tokoro o sin-zuru mamegokoro nari = kore ga zibun* 自分 *no sinnen* 信念 *o sin-zuru tyuuzitu-sa* 忠實さ *da.*

31 *namu:* emphatic particle, very similar to *zo,* but when at the end of a sentence a little less strong. (Do not confuse with *namu* after *MIZENKEI* of verb, which expresses desire.)

同じ人のトキゴト（説）の、こゝとかしこと
ゆきちがひて、ひとしからざるは、いづれによ
るべきぞと、まどはしくて、大かた其人の説、
すべてうきたるとなれ共、なほさしもあらず、はじ
めより終リまで、説のかはれることなきは、中
々におかしからぬかたもあるぞかし、はじめ
に定めおきつる事の、ほどへて後に、又ことな
るよき考への出來るは、つねにある事なれば、
はじめとかはれるとあることそよけれ、年をへ
てがくもむすゝみゆけば、説は必ズかはらで
かなはず、又おのがはじめの誤リを、後にしり
ながらは、つゝみかくさで、きよく改めたる
も、いとよき事也、殊にわが古學の道は、近き

Sakinoti to tokigoto no kawaru koto

32 *Sakinoti to* (modifies *kawaru*): between earlier and later, from earlier to later.

33–34 *koko to kasiko to yukitigaite:* disagree from this place to that, go here one way and there the other.

34 *hitosikarazaru:* conflicting with one another, being not alike.

35 *madowasikute = magirawasikute* (< *magirawasii*).

36 *ukitaru:* being frivolous or unreliable, lacking in weight.

36 *kokoti no seraruru:* one cannot help feeling that, you get the feeling that. *Seraruru* is the *RENTAIKEI* of the passive of *su* and is equivalent to a noun, so that the whole sentence has somewhat the force of an exclamation (what a feeling of . . . one gets!), though to attempt a translation on these lines would probably be making too much of this aspect. The passive form here gives a sense of inevitability—the feeling results naturally from a cause outside oneself.

36–37 *hitowatari = hitotoori.*

38–39 *nakanaka ni:* contrary to what might seem to be so; rather.

39 *okasikaranu kata mo aru zo kasi;* there is indeed an uninteresting aspect, there is indeed something dull. To bring out the force of *zo kasi* it may be better to translate as a rhetorical question, 'is there not something dull . . . ?'—cf. 22 *kotowari zo kasi.*

42 *hazime to kawareru koto aru koso yokere:* indeed, it is right that they should have shifted from what they were at the beginning.

43-44 *kawarade kanawazu:* it is not possible that they do not change, there must needs be a shift (in). The negative ending *-de* is thought to have been derived from *-zute*, in which the *-te* is the same as the normal *TE*-form ending.

44-45 ~ *o/ noti ni siri-nagara wa* seems to mean 'when one gets to know ~ afterwards, and while that state (of knowledge) continues', which amounts to ' ~ (which you) have become aware of afterwards'.

45 *kiyoku* = *isagiyoku.*

46 *waga inisiemanabi no miti.* Leaving aside for the moment the question whether *waga* applies to all the rest of the phrase or to *inisie* only, the sense of *miti* has to be determined. It seems almost certain that this is something like that of 'one's "line" (of business, etc.)', 'that which one has taken up or devoted oneself to'. Because of *hirakesometuru* in the next clause (*hirakeru* can be used of the being-opened-up of an actual road or pathway), there is a bare possibility that the root sense of *miti* may be called to mind, i.e. that the metaphor may come to life. But this is unlikely to occur because the metaphorical use is so firmly established. As regards the application of *waga*, i.e. the choice between 'our "line", (which is that) of the Learning about Old Times', and 'the "line" of learning about our [i.e. Japan's] past', the first seems on the whole to be the more likely. The translation suggested is 'the Learning about Old Times which we have made our business'.

ほどよりひらけそめつるとなれば、すみやか
にことぐ〵くは考へつくすべきにあらず、人
をへ年をへてこそ、つぎぐ〵くに明らかには成
リゆくべきわざなれば、一人のときごとの中
にも、さきなると後なると異るとは、もとより
あらではえあらぬわざ也、そは一人のイキ(生)
のかぎりのほどにも、つぎぐ〵くに明らかにな
りゆく也、さればそのさきのと後のとの中に
は、後の方をぞ、其人のさだまれる説とはすべ
かりける、但し又みづからこそ、初めのをばわ
ろしと思ひて、改めつれ、又のちに人の見るに
は、なほはじめのかたよろしくて、後のは中々
にわろきもなきにあらざれば、とにかくにえ
らびは、見む人のこゝろになむ、

46–47 *tikaki hodo = tikagoro.*

48 *kotogotoku wa kangaetukusubeki ni arazu:* everything cannot be thought out in full.
Kangaetukusu: think out completely; *-beki* here has the sense of 'possible', 'possibility'.

48–49 *hito o he:* (by) going through men. (Obviously, the idea is 'after more than one man
has done work on them'.)

52 *arade wa e-aranu waza nari = nakute wa naranai koto da.*

52 *So wa.* It is not altogether clear what *so* refers to, but it seems most likely to be 'the things'
or 'the teachings' (which undergo change). To take *so* as the subject of *nari* alone—not of
nariyuku nari—can only be made plausible by reading the *so wa* emphatically and giving
a longish pause after it; and although this would justify translating the *So wa . . . nari* as
'That is, . . .', which would sound well enough in English, it does not seem to be the most
natural way to take the Japanese.

54–55 *naka ni wa = naka de wa.*

57 *aratameture.* Although this form is necessitated by the occurrence of *koso* (col. 56), it has
here at the same time a concessive meaning, much as if it had been *aratameturedo mo.*

59 *tonikaku ni:* taking everything into consideration; after all.

60 *mimu hito no kokoro ni namu:* is (i.e. lies) in the way in which those who will regard them
are minded; lies in how they will seem to others. (One has to interpret 'lies in' in the sense
of 'depends on'.)

FROM
GOZYUU-NO-TOO
—chapters 31 and 32

THESE are two chapters from the novel *Gozyuu-no-too* 五重塔, published in 1891–2 in serial form by Kooda-Rohan 幸田露伴 (1867–1947). It deals with the struggle of 'Nossori' Zyuubei の つ そ り 十 兵 衞 to get himself recognized as a great architect.

It is planned to have a new five-storeyed pagoda built at the Kannoo 感 應 temple and it is expected that the contract will be awarded to the established master, Kawagoe no Genta 川 越 の 源 太. Zyuubei, however, by dint of great persistence, persuades not only the Abbot of the temple but also Genta to allow him to undertake the work. His methods arouse the hostility of the workmen, but he perseveres and finally the pagoda is completed. All admire it immensely and, alone among the buildings of Edo, it is undamaged by a great storm which arises. The author lays stress on the virtues of will power and devotion to art, common themes in his novels. The chapters selected are examples of his picturesque style.

The text used is that included in volume 8 of the GENDAI-NIHON-BUNGAKU-ZENSYUU, Tookyoo, 1927. As stated in the General Introduction, an English translation of the whole novel was published in Tookyoo in 1909 under the title *The Pagoda*.

J.B.
C.J.D.

15 　　　　10 　　　　5

肩を比すべき人も無く、八宗九宗の碩德達虎

重塔なれ、あら嬉しや、我等が賴む師は當世に

躍りあがつて歡喜び、これでこそ感應寺の五

忘れて讚歎すれば、圓道はじめ一山の僧徒も

門番までも初手のっそりを輕しめたる事は

未曾有ぢやまた（再）あるまじと爲右衞門より

つたる哉、あら快よき細工振りかな希有ぢや

ほ（嚴上）に突立ちたるごとく、天晴立派に建

六丈の姿を現じ坤軸動がす足ぶみしていは

と聳えしさま、金剛力士が魔軍を睥睨んで十

第々々に露るゝ一階一階また一階、五重巍然

の見事に出來上り、段々足場を取り除けば次

經營むなしからで、感應寺生雲塔いよ〳〵物

時は一月の末つ方、のっそり十兵衞が辛苦

Gozyuu-no-too

Chapter 31

2–56 *Toki wa . . . areidasinu.* The whole of this chapter consists of only one sentence. There are three passages of direct speech, the first from *appare* (8*) to *arumazi* (10), the second from *kore de* (13) to *ki-semu* (32) and the third from *hito no* (46) to *kae* (53). The remainder of the sentence has a major division at *hikikaete* (34). Up to this point the construction may be set out as follows: the clause up to *suetukata* (2) shows a characteristic absence of the copula, and a common way of indicating time; strictly speaking, this could be described as an independent sentence, but it is more convenient to think of it as a temporal adverbial expression. Then *dekiagari* (4), *gotoku* (8) and *santan sureba* (12) are co-ordinate to each other. *Munasikarade* (3) is linked with *dekiagari*, it being normal for the main co-ordinate divisions of a sentence (other than the last such division) to be indicated by conjunctive forms (REN-YOOKEI) such as *dekiagari*, and minor ones (other than the last) by *-TE* forms (among which the negative ending *-de* < *-zu-te* may be included). The construction of the passage from *dandan* (4) to *gotoku* (8) is that *sama* (6) is the subject of *gotoku*, the section from *dandan* to *gizen to* (5–6) being an adverbial phrase in three parts, which are, working backwards, *gizen to*, *gozyuu* (5) and the piece from *dandan* to *ikkai* (5) which describes the state of affairs as the scaffolding was gradually removed, and builds up to *gozyuu*. *Wasurete* (12) is linked with *santan sureba*. The construction of the clause preceding *gotoku* is clear—its appearance (*sama*) was like (*gotoku*) a *Kongoo-rikisi* showing . . . (*gen-zi*) and planting himself (*tuttatitaru*), with *nirande* linked with *gen-zi* and *asibumi site* with *tuttatitaru*. The *-EBA* form of *santan sureba* (12) is presumably temporal ('when . . .') but the temporal content is low and the

* numbers in brackets refer to columns in the text.

meaning is hardly different from that of a -*TE* form linked with *yorokobi* (13) which is co-ordinate with *katariaisi* (32). *Katariaisi wa* (colloquial, *katariatta koto wa*) is loosely attached to the clause which follows it; in contrast to (*hikikaete*) the fact that human feeling (*hito no zyoo*), which is not entirely moved by greed (*yoku nomi naranu*), is kind and praiseworthy (. . . *syusyoo naru*), [as we can see] by the fact that [they] talked to each other (*katariaisi wa*). After *hikikaete, hakarigataki . . . kokoro* (34) is parenthetical; expanded and put into colloquial it might be *hakarigatai no wa ten no kokoro de(su)*. *Hakarai to site* (35) is linked with *sakan naru* (35) in an adjectival clause qualifying *rakuseisiki-syugyoo* (35–6). *Sadamari* is co-ordinate with *narisi* (40). *Yurusi, hodokosi* (37) are best taken as co-ordinate with *syoo-suru* (38), *ippoo ni wa mata* (38) being equivalent to 'on the one hand . . . and in addition . . .'; *soo site* is then linked with *arubeki* (39). The passage from *Endoo* (34) to *narisi* (40) is now seen to qualify *saityuu*, with which it forms an adverbial clause. *Kumotte* (40) is co-ordinate with *kitanaku* (41), both depending on *kikoesi* (41) ('sounded muffled and . . . unpleasant'), *nitukazu* depending on *kitanaku*. *Ga* (41) is the normal co-ordinating *ga* (but, and) and connects *kikoesi* with *has-suru* (54), with which *narimasari* (45) is co-ordinate. *Hukiidasite* (42) and *naru* (44) are co-ordinate (as . . . started to blow . . . became sultry). *Monosugoku mo* (46) (which is equivalent to *monosugoi hodo ni*) modifies *has-suru* (54) and the whole passage from *Endoo* (34) to *has-suru* is made by *ya ina* (54) into an adverbial clause modifying the true main verb of the sentence, *areidasinu* (56), with which is linked *okotte* (54), the three kinds of *yasya* (55) being the subjects of *areidasinu*.

The first piece of speech (8–10) is a succession of statements; the third (46–53) is a succession of imperatives. The second (13–32) contains two difficult sentences. The first of these is from *warera* (14) to *nasi* (20). The three main co-ordinate verbs are *nite* (16–17), *nite* (18) and *nasi* (20), *naku* (15) being linked with the first *nite*. *Kohyoo-kakuro to* (15–16) is an adverbial expression modifying *sugure-tamaeru* (16). *Tatoeba sisi-oo kuzyaku-oo* (17) is not closely integrated into the sentence, but one can think of it as meaning 'if one were to make a comparison, he is . . .'. *Nara . . . sirazu* (18) is parenthetic. In the next sentence, which ends at *nari* (25), *bitoku* (22) and *tanomosisa* (24) are parallel and are the things which form the *kiinnen* and *myooinnen* (24–5). *Hiroiagerarete* (21) and *idasaresi* (22) are passives acting as honorifics. The rest of the construction should be clear.

2 *suetukata:* the end (of a month, etc.); *tu* is an old equivalent for *no*.

2 *Nossori:* here a nickname, 'Slowcoach'.

2 *ga* equals colloquial *no*, as often later in this text.

3–4 *mono no migoto ni:* used with expressions referring to some result achieved with difficulty; successfully, completely, admirably.

6 *Kongoo-rikisi:* the name of two gods, also known in Japan as *Nioo* (仁 王) and in Sanskrit as Vajrapāṇi. Their images are usually placed one on either side of a temple gateway, and they are customarily represented as semi-naked and of fearsome countenance; also known as Deva kings.

6 *magun:* army of demons, traditional enemies of Deva kings.

7 *konziku:* earth's axis.

8–9 *tattaru* = *tatitaru.*

9 *zya* = *da.*

10 *Tameemon:* name of the High Steward of the temple.

11 *karosimetaru* = *karonzita.*

12 *Endoo:* name of a priest at the temple.

12 *issan.* Temples have, in addition to any other name, one ending with -*san* 山, this referring to the whole group of buildings to be found within the temple enclosure, e.g. *Kooya-san* 高 野 山. *Issan:* the whole temple.

15 *kata o hi-subeki hito:* someone who could compare with him, *cf. kata o naraberu.*

15 *hassyuu kusyuu.* The eight sects referred to are the *Sanron* 三 論, *Hossoo* 法 相, *Kusya* 俱舍, *Zyoozitu* 成 實, *Ritu* 律, *Kegon* 華 嚴, *Tendai* 天 台, and *Singon* 眞 言; with the addition of the *Zen* 禪 sect they form the *kusyuu.*

113

豹鶴鷺と勝ぐれたまへる中にも絶類拔群に

て、譬へば獅子王孔雀王、我等が頼むこの寺の

塔も絶類拔群にて奈良や京都はいざ知らず

上野淺草芝山内、江戸にてこれ(此塔)に勝る

ものなし、殊更塵土に埋もれて光も放たず終

るべかりし男を拾ひあげられて心のたま(實

珠)の輝きを世にいだ(發出)されし師の美德、

困苦に撓まず知己に酬いて遂に仕遂げし十

兵衛が頼もしさ、おもしろくまた美はしき奇

因緣なり妙因緣なり、天の成せしか人の成せ

し歟將又諸天善神の蔭にて操り玉ひし歟、屋

を造るにたくみ(巧妙)なりし達膩伽尊者の噂

はあれど世尊在世の御時にもかく(如是)快き

事ありしを未だきかねばから(漢土)にもきか

ず、いで落成の式あらば、我偈を作らむ文を作

らむ、我歌をよみ詩を作して、頌せむ讃せむ詠

15–16 *kohyoo-hakuro to*. The holy men (*sekitoku-tati*) excel ordinary folk as do the tiger, leopard, crane and heron ordinary creatures. *Endoo* was as a king among them, as are the lion and peacock among the noble animals.

16 *zeturui-bakkun* (usually read *zeturui-batugun*) can be translated as 'supreme'.

17 *sisi-oo kuzyaku-oo*. See 15–16 *kohyoo-hakuro to*, above.

18 *iza sirazu* is more usually found as *isa sirazu*. It literally means 'Well, I don't know', and the expression *Nara wa iza sirazu* may be translated as 'I can't speak about Nara, but . . .', or 'however it may be with Nara'.

20 *zindo ni uzumorete*: buried in the dust.

24–25 *kiinnen, myooinnen*. *Ki-* and *myoo-* are adjectival to *innen*.

26 *syoten-zenzin*. *Zenzin* is the name given to the Buddhist tutelary gods. *Syoten* can refer either to all the gods or to the various heavens in which they reside; here the latter seems more probable—the benevolent gods in the various heavens.

27 *Tanika*: Sanskrit *Dhaniya*. He was a disciple of the Buddha, by whom he was rebuked for building a brick house and living in it.

28 *seson-zaise;* the world-honoured one's being in the world, i.e. the period of the Buddha's stay on this earth.

30 *ge*: equivalent to Sanskrit *gāthā*, a Buddhistic verse or hymn of praise frequently found in sutras, etc.

31 *si*: a Chinese poem, as opposed to an *uta*.

ぜむ記せむと各々互に語り合ひしは慾のみ

ならぬひと（人間）の情の、やさしくもまた殊

勝なるに引替へて、測り難きは天の心、圓道爲

成式執行の日も略定まり、其日は貴賤男女の

見物をゆるし貧者に剩れる金を施し、十兵衞

其他を犒らひ賞する一方にはまた伎樂を奏

して世に珍しき塔供養あるべき筈に支度と

りゞなりし最中、夜半の鐘の音の曇ってつ

ね（平日）には似つかず耳にきたなく聞えしが

そもゝゝ、漸々あやしき風吹き出して、眠れる

こども（兒童）も我知らず夜具踏み脱ぐほど時

候生暖かくなるにつれ雨戸のがたつく響き

烈しくなりまさり、闇に採まるゝ松柏の梢に

天魔の號びものすごくも、人の心の平和を奪

へ平和を奪へ、浮世の榮華に誇れる奴等の膽

右衞門二人が計らひとしていと盛んなる落

38 *gigaku* is a type of ancient dance in masks and with music.
39 *too-kuyoo:* service of dedication for the pagoda.
41 *kitanaku kikoesi:* sounded unpleasant.
42 *somosomo* suggests that what has gone before was only the beginning, and that what follows is the really important or startling part of the narrative.

115

を破れや睡りを攪せや、愚物の胸に血の濤打

たせよ、僞物の面の紅き色奪れ、斧持てる者斧

を揮へ、矛もてるもの矛を揮へ、汝等が銳き劍

は饑えたり汝等劍に食をあたへよ、人のあぶ

ら（膏血）はよき食なり汝等劍に飽まで喰はせ

よ、飽まで人のあぶら（膏膩）を餌へと、號令き

びしく發するや否、猛風一陣どっと起つて、斧

をもつ夜叉矛もてる夜叉饑えたる劍もてる

夜叉、皆一齊に暴れ出しぬ。

47–48 *kimo o yabure: cf. kimo o tubusu*, although there the subject is the owner of the *kimo*.
51–52 *abura:* grease or sweat, or, according to the characters with which it is written here, and which are normally read *kooketu*, sweat and blood. Here perhaps 'gross flesh' is the best translation.
55 *yasya* is a phonetic rendering of the Sanskrit *yakṣa*, in this context malevolent demons.

長夜の夢を覺まされて江戸四里四方の老

若男女、惡風來たりと驚き騒ぎ、雨戸の横ざる

（柄子）しつか（緊乎）と插せ、しんばり（辛張）棒

を強く張れと家々ごとに狼狽ゆるを、あはれ

（可愍）とも見ぬ飛天夜叉王、怒號の聲音たけ

だけしく。汝等人を憚るな、汝等ひと（人間）に

憚られよ、ひと（人間）は我等を輕んじたり、久

しく我等を賤みたり、我等に捧ぐべき筈の定

めの性を忘れたり、這ふ代りとしてたつて行

く狗、おごり（驕奢）の塒巣作れる禽、尻尾なき

猿、物言ふ蛇、露まこと（誠實）なき狐の子、け

がれ（汚穢）を知らざる豕の女、彼等に長く侮

られて遂に何時まで忍び得む。我等を長く侮

らせて彼等を何時まで誇らすべき、忍ぶべき

だけ忍びたり誇らすべきだけ誇らしたり、六

Chapter 32

58 *tyooya no yume* here suggests a double meaning, first the literal one, in that the people are wakened from their dreams, and secondly, in the metaphorical sense, that they were wakened from a long period of unthinking comfort and false security.

58 *Edo yo-ri-sihoo* apparently means the whole four league square of Edo.

59 *akuhuu*: evil wind.

59 *yokozaru*. A *saru* is a type of bolt fastened to the top or bottom of an *amado* and thrust into the lintel or threshold to hold the *amado* fast. A *yokozaru* is a similar bolt placed horizontally between two *amado* to hold them together and prevent movement.

62 *hiten* here means nothing more than *tenzin* 天人.

十四年は既に過ぎたり、我等を縛せし機運の

鐵鎖我等を囚へし慈忍のいはや（岩窟）は我が

神力にてちぎ（扯断）り棄てたりくずれ（崩潰）

させたり、汝等暴れよ今こそ暴れよ、何十年の

恨の毒氣を彼等に返せ一時に返せ、彼等がほ

こり（驕慢）の氣の臭さを鐵圍山外に擴んで捨

てよ、彼等の頭を地につかしめよ、無慈悲の斧

の刃味の好さを彼等が胸に試みよ、慘酷の矛

嗔恚の劍の刃糞と彼等をなし呉れよ、彼等が

喉に氷を與へて苦寒に怖れ顫かしめよ、彼等

が膽に針を與へて祕密の痛みに堪ざらしめ

よ、彼等が目前に彼等が生したるおほく（多

數）の奢侈の子孫を殺して、玩物の念を嗟歎の

灰の河に埋めよ、彼等は蠱兒の家を奪ひぬ汝

等彼等の家を奪へや、彼等は蠱兒の智慧を笑

ひぬ汝等彼等の智慧を讚せよ。すべて彼等の

73-74 *kiun no tessa:* the iron fetters of fate.

74 *zinin no iwaya. Zinin* has the double idea of *zihi* 慈悲, and *ninniku* 忍辱. These
virtues of compassion and forbearance are compared to a cave imprisoning the demons
and restraining them from their destructive activities.

78 *tetui-sange. Tetui-san,* the iron-encircling mountains, also read *tetui-sen* and *tetti-sen,*
Sanskrit cakravāla or cakravāḍa. In the Indian cosmology there were eight such concentric ranges encircling Mt. Sumeru, with eight seas in between, that of men being in
the seas between the seventh and eighth ranges. Thus *tetui-sange* is the space lying
outside the whole system, beyond the world's bounds.

80 *haazi:* the quality of your blades.

81 *hakuso* is the filth or rust that settles on the blade of a sword that has been used. The
sense is as though the order was *karera o hakuso ni nasi-kureyo,* make them the filth on
your blades.

82 *koori:* the icy steel of their weapons.

82 *kukan:* cold anguish.

85 *ganbutu no:* frivolous.

85-86 *satan no hai no kawa:* the ashy river of grief. There seems to be no reference here to
any particular tradition. The phrase is presumably an invention of the author's.

巧みとおもへる智慧を讃せよ大とおもへる

意を讃せよ、美しと自らおもへる情を讃せよ、

協へりとなす理を讃せよ、剛しとなせる力を

讃せよ、すべては我等の矛の餌なれば、劍の餌

なれば斧の餌なれば、讃して後にえもの（利

器）に餌ひ、よき餌をつくりし彼等を笑へ。嬲

らる、だけ彼等を嬲れ、急に屠るな嬲り殺せ、

活しながらに一枚一枚皮を剝ぎ取れ、肉を剝

ぎとれ、彼等がしん（心臓）を鞠として蹴よ、か

らたち（枳棘）をもて背を鞭てよ、歎息のいき

（呼氣）涙の水動悸の血の音悲鳴の聲、其等を

すべてひと（人間）より取れ。殘忍の外快樂な

し、酷烈ならずば汝等疾く死ね、暴れよ進めよ

無法に住して放逸無慚無理無體に暴れ立て

暴れ立て進め進め、神とも戰へ佛をもた、（擲）

け、道理を壞つて壞りすてなば天下は我等が

97–98 *karatati* is a type of thorny plant.

ものなるぞと、叱咤する度土石を飛ばして丑

の刻より寅の刻、卯となり辰となるまでもち

つと（毫）も止まず勵ましたつれば、數萬の眷

屬勇みをなし、水を渡るは波を蹴かへし、陸を

走るは沙を蹴かへし、天地をほこり（塵埃）に

黄ばまして日の光をもほとゝ掩ひ、斧を揮

つて數奇者が手入れ怠りなき松を冷笑ひつ

ゝほつきと斫るあり、矛を舞はして板屋根に

忽ち穴を穿つもあり、ゆさゝゝと怪力もて

さも堅固なる家を動かし橋を搖がすものも

あり。手ぬるし手ぬるし酷さが足らぬ、我に續

けと憤怒の牙嚙み鳴らしつゝ夜叉王の躍り

上つていらだて（焦躁）ば虚空に充ち滿ちたる

眷屬、をたけび銳くをめき叫んで遮に無に暴

威を揮ふほどに、神前寺内に立てる樹も、富家

の庭に養はれし樹も聲振り絞つて泣き悲み、

105 *doseki:* earth and stones.
107–108 *kenzoku:* minions.
108 *isami o nasi:* give rein to one's excitement, let oneself go.
109 *kekaesi:* kick up (backwards).
112 *hokki to* is much the same as *pokin to.*
113 *yusa-yusa-yusa to* (*cf. yurayura*) refers to the rocking motion imparted to the houses and bridges.
120 *huri-sibotte:* squeeze out, force out; *huri-* only adds vividness to the verb.

見る〳〵大地の髪の毛は恐怖に一々竪立な
し、柳は倒れ竹は割る〳〵折しも黒雲空に流れ
て樫の實よりも大きなる雨ばらり〳〵と降り
出せば、得たりとます〳〵暴る〳〵夜叉、垣を引
き捨て塀を蹴倒し門をもこは（破）し屋根をも
めくり軒場の瓦を踏み碎き、唯一ト採に屑屋
を飛ばし二タ採み採んでは二階を捻ぢ取り
三たび採んでは某寺を物の見事に潰し崩し、
どう〳〵どっと閧をあぐる其度毎に心を冷し
胸を騷がす人々の彼に氣づかひ此に案ずる
笑止の樣を見ては喜び、居所さへも無くされ
て悲むものを見ては喜び、いよ〳〵圖に乘り
狼藉のあらむ限りを逞しうすれば、八百八町
百萬の人みな生ける心地せず顔色さらにあ
らばこそ。中にも分けて驚きしは圓道爲右衛
門、折角僅に出來上りし五重塔は採まれ採ま

121–122 *zyuritu nasi:* stand on end.
123 *bararibarari* is like *barabara* and is used of rain falling in large drops.
126 *kuzuya.* In spite of the characters with which the word is written, this is presumably not a waste-paper merchant's shop, but 葛屋, thatched roof, or a house with a thatched roof; the former is probably intended here.
129 *doo-doo-dotto* is a lengthened form of *doodoo to.*
134–135 *araba koso. -ba koso* is like the modern colloquial *mon' ka;* 'if they had any colour at all (*sara ni*) in their faces I should be surprised', 'their faces were drained of all colour'.

れて、九輪は動ぎ、頂上の寶珠は空に得讀めぬ

字を書き、岩をも轉ばすべき風の突掛け來り、

楯をも貫くべき雨の打付り來る度撓むさま

（姿）、木の軋る音、復るさま（姿）、又撓むさま

（姿）、軋る音、今にもくつがへ（傾覆）らんず様

子に。あれ〳〵危し仕様は無きか、くつがへ（傾

覆）られては大事なり、止むる術も無き事か、

雨さへ加はり來りし上まはり（周圍）に樹木も

あらざれば未曾有の風にどだい（基礎）挾くて

丈のみ高き此塔の堪へむことの覺束なし、本

堂さへも此程に動けば塔は如何ばかりぞ、風

を止むる呪文はきかぬか、かく恐ろしき大あ

らし（暴風雨）に見無に來べき源太は見えぬ

歟、まだ新しき出入なりとて重々來では叶は

ざる十兵衛見えぬが寛怠なり、ひと（他）さへ

かほど（斯様）氣づかふに己が爲し塔氣にかけ

146 *take nomi takaki*. *Nomi* seems to have been moved from what might be considered its more normal place after *takaki*. The meaning is 'high in relation to its narrow base'.
150–151 *kode wa kanawazaru:* is unable not to come, is obliged to come.

ぬか、あれあれ危し又撓んだわ、誰か十兵衞
よ（招）びに行けといへども、天に瓦飛び板飛
び地上に砂利の舞ふ中を行かむといふもの
なく、漸くはうび（賞美）の金を飽かして掃除
人の七藏爺を出しやりぬ。

156 *hoobi no kane o akasite*. This is a variant of the expression *kane ni akasite*, regardless of expense—'gave him a lavish reward'.

PART II

TRANSCRIPTIONS
AND
TRANSLATIONS

Seimei o yobarete kusainagi o iarawasu monogatari

IMA wa mukasi, [ ]-no-kuni [ ]-no-koori ni aniototo hutari no otoko sumi-keri, ani wa hongoku ni arite asayuu ni kari suru o yaku to sikeri. Otooto wa miyako ni noborite miyazukae site, tokidoki zo hongoku [5]ni wa kikeru.

Sikaru aida sono ani nagatuki no simotuyami no koro, tomosi to yuu koto o site, ooki naru hayasi no atari o sugikeru ni, hayasi no naka ni karabitaru koe no kesiki kotonaru o motte, kono tomosi suru mono no seimei o yobi-kereba, ayasi to omoite [10]uma o osi-kaesite, sono yobu koe o yunde-zama ni nasite, hi o hogusi ni kakete yukikereba, sono toki ni wa yobazarikeri. Moto no gotoku mete ni nasite hi o te ni torite yuku toki ni wa kanarazu yobikeri. Sareba kamaete kore o iba ya to omoikeredo mo, mete nareba [15]irubeki yoo mo nakute, kayoo ni si-tutu yogoro o sugikeru hodo ni, kono koto o hito ni mo katarazarikeri.

Sikaru aida sono otooto miyako yori kudaritarikeru ni, ani sikazika no koto namu aru to katarikereba, otooto, 'Ito keu naru koto ni koso haberu nare, onore makarite kokoromimu' to [20]iite tomosi ni yukinikeri. Kano hayasi no atari o sugikeru ni, sono otooto no na oba yobazu site, moto no ani ga na o yobikereba, otooto sono yo wa sono koe o kikituru bakari nite kaerinikeri. Ani, 'Ika ni zo kiki-tamaitu ya' to toikereba, otooto, 'Ge ni sooraikeri, tadasi [25]esemono ni koso sooroomere. Sono yue wa makoto no onigami naraba onore ga na koso yobubeki ni, soko no on-na o koso nao yobisooraiture, sore o satoranu bakari no mono nareba, asu no yo makarite kanarazu iarawasite mise-tatematuramu' to iite sono yo wa akasinu. Mata no yo, yoobe no gotoku [30]yukite hi o tomosite soko o toorikeru ni, mete naru toki ni wa yobi, yunde naru toki ni wa yobazarikereba, uma yori orite kura o orosite, uma ni sakasama ni okite sakasama ni norite, yobu mono ni wa mete to omowasete, ware wa yunde ni nasite hi o hogusi ni kakete, ya o tugaimookete [35]sugikeru toki ni, mete to omoikeru ni ya, mae no gotoku ani ga na o yobikeru o, koe o osi-hakarite itarikereba, sirikotaetu to oboete, sono noti kura o tune no sama ni okinaosite uma ni norite, mete nite sugikeredo mo koe mo sezari-kereba, ie ni kaerinikeri.

[40]Ani, 'Ikani ka' to toikereba, otooto, 'Koe ni tukete isooraitureba siri-kotooru kokoti situ, akete koso wa atari atarazu wa yukite mimu' to iite, yo akekeru mama ni aniototo kaki-turete yukite mikereba, hayasi no naka ni ooki naru kusainagi ki ni itukerarete zo si-site [45]arikeru. Kayoo no mono no hito hakaramu to suru hodo ni, yosi naki inoti o horobosu nari. Kore otooto no omonpakari no arite iarawakasitaru nari tote zo hito homekeru to namu, kataritutaetaru to ya.

126

The story of the man who heard his name called and shot a wild boar, thus exposing its trickery

THERE were once two brothers who lived in the district of [ ] in the province of [ ]. The elder of the two stayed in his native province and spent all his time hunting, while the younger went up to the capital to serve in some nobleman's house, though he did return home from time to time.

Now one dark night towards the end of the ninth month, the elder brother was out hunting by the light of a flare when, as he was passing a large wood, he heard someone in it call out his name in a strange-sounding gruff voice. Puzzled, he turned his horse, and, placing the flare in its holder, rode back with the voice on his left, but this time no name was called. Whenever he took the flare in his hand and rode by with the voice, as at first, on his right, his name was called. 'Somehow I must shoot this thing,' he thought; but he could not shoot it when it was on his right. This went on for several days, but he said nothing to anybody of what had happened.

Meanwhile the younger brother came down from the capital, and when his brother told him about the affair, he said, 'What a queer business! I'll go and see what I can do,' and went out to hunt. As he passed the wood a voice called out, not his own name, but that of his brother, as before, and having heard the voice, he did no more that night, but went home. 'Well, did you hear it?' said his brother. 'Yes, it was there', he replied, 'but it must be a fraud, for if it had been a real demon, it would have been my name that it called, but it still called yours. It hasn't even enough sense for that, so I'll go out tomorrow night and shoot it – then I'll show you what it is.' He did no more that night, but the next night he went out and rode along past the place with a flare, as he had done the night before. When he was right-side on, the voice called; when he was left-side on, it was silent. Dismounting from his horse, therefore, he took off the saddle, reversed it and remounted back to front, so that the thing calling him would think him right-side on, whereas he had it on his left; then, putting his flare into the holder, he fitted an arrow to his bow and rode past. The thing must have thought him right-side on, for it called out his brother's name, as before. Judging where the voice was coming from, he shot an arrow and sensed that it had hit the mark. Then he replaced the saddle in its normal position, remounted and rode past with the thing on his right; but this time no voice was heard and so he went back home.

'Well, what happened?' asked his brother, and he said, 'I shot in the direction of the voice and I had the feeling I had scored a hit. When it's light, let's go and see whether I did or not.' As soon as dawn came, the brothers went out together and found a large wild boar dead in the wood, pinned to a tree by an arrow. Creatures like this, in trying to trick people, throw away their lives. The story goes that the younger brother was much praised for having the resourcefulness to shoot this one and expose its trickery.

127

Oomi-no-kuni no Sinohara no tukaana ni iru otoko no monogatari

IMA wa mukasi, Mino-no-kuni no kata e yukikeru gesu-otoko no, Oomi-no-kuni no Sinohara to yuu tokoro o toorikeru hodo ni, sora kurakute ame hurikereba, tati-yadorinubeki tokoro ya aru [5]to mimawasikeru ni, hitoge tooki nonaka nareba tati-yorubeki tokoro nakarikeru ni, tukaana no arikeru o mitukete, sore ni haiirite sibaraku arikeru hodo ni, hi mo kurete kuraku narinikeri. Ame wa yamazu hurikereba, kon-ya bakari wa kono tukaana nite yo o akasamu [10]to omoite, oku-zama o miru ni hirokarikereba, ito yoku uti-yasumite yoriitaru ni, yo uti-hukuru hodo ni kiku ni, mono no irikitaru oto su. Kurakereba nanimono to mo miezu, tada oto bakari nareba kore wa oni ni koso wa arame, hayoo oni no sumikeru tukaana o sirazu site [15]tati-irite, kon-ya inoti o usinaitemuzuru koto o kokoro ni omoinagekikeru hodo ni, kono kitaru mono tada kitari ni irikitareba, otoko osorosi to omoo koto kagiri nasi. Saredo mo nogarubeki kata nakereba, katawara ni yorite oto mo sede kagamariitareba, kono mono tikaku kite, mazu mono o hata [20]to orosioku nari. Tugi ni sayasaya to naru mono o oku, sono noti ni inuru oto su. Kore hito no kesiki nari.

Kono otoko gesu naredo mo siryoo ari kokoro kasikokarikeru yatu nite, kore o omoimegurasu ni, kore wa hito no mono [25]e yukikeru ga, ame mo huru higure waga irituru yoo ni, kono tukaana ni irite saki ni okituru wa moti-tarikeru mono o hata to okituru oto nameri. Tugi ni wa mino o nugite oku oto no sarasara to kikoeturu nameri to omoedo mo, nao kore wa kono tukaana ni sumu oni nameri [30]to omoeba, tada oto mo sede mimi o tatete kikiitaru ni, kono ima kitaru mono otoko ni ya aramu, hoosi ni ya aramu, warawabe ni ya aramu, sirazu. Hito no koe nite yuu yoo, 'Kono tukaana ni wa mosi sumi-tamoo kami nado ya owasuru, sareba kore kikosimese, onore wa mono e makarituru [35]mono no koko o toorituru aida ni, ame wa itoo huru, yo wa hukenureba, kon-ya bakari to omoite, kono tukaana ni irite sooroo nari' to iite, mono o maturu yoo ni site okeba, moto no otoko sono toki ni zo sukosi kokoro otiite, sareba koso to omoiawasekeru.

[40]Sate sono okituru mono o tikaki hodo nareba, hisoka ni nani zo to omoite te o sasiyarite sagureba, tiisaki moti o sanmai okitari. Sareba moto no otoko makoto no hito no miti o yukikeru ga, motitaru mono o maturu ni koso arikere to kokoroete, miti wa yuki-koo-zite mono no hosikarikeru [45]mama ni, kono moti o torite hisoka ni kuitu. Ima no mono sibasi arite kono okituru moti o sagurikeru ni nasi.

Sono toki ni ge ni oni no arite kuitekeru nameri to omoikeru ni ya, otoko niwaka ni tatihasiru mama ni, motitarituru [50]mono o mo torazu, mino kasa o mo sutete hasiriide ininu. Mi no naramu yoo mo sirazu nigete inikereba,

The story of the man who went into a burial-cave at Sinohara in the province of Oomi

A MAN of humble station was once on his way to the province of Mino, and while he was passing through a place called Sinohara in the province of Oomi, the sky was very overcast and it was raining, so he looked about to see if there was any place where he might shelter. But it was an extremely lonely spot out in the open country, and there was no house for him to go to. However, noticing a burial-cave, he crawled into that and, after he had been there for some time, evening came and it grew dark. As it continued to rain, he decided to spend all that night in the cave; further in, he found it quite roomy, and he settled down up against the wall, resting very comfortably. It was already well into the night when suddenly he heard the sound of something entering the cave. It was so dark that he could not see what it was, but could only hear a noise. 'It must be a demon. I have rushed into this cave not knowing that a demon lived here, and now tonight I shall lose my life,' he thought sorrowfully. Meanwhile the thing which had entered came further and further in, and he was utterly panic-stricken. However, there was no way of escape, and so he crouched down by the wall of the cave without making a sound. The thing came close to him and put down something with a bump, next it put down something which made a rustling noise, then he heard it sit down. All this seemed to indicate a human being.

Our man was only of humble station but he had plenty of common sense and intelligence, and he decided that it was a person on his way somewhere who had come into this burial-cave, as he himself had done, since it was a wet night. The noise of something being put down must have been the bump as he put down things he was carrying. Next, the rustling he had heard must have been the noise of him taking off his straw cape and putting it down. He reflected, however, that it might yet be a demon who lived in this burial-cave, and so he remained listening intently and not making a sound. Then the newcomer—man, priest or boy, whatever he was—spoke in a human voice. 'If there is some deity living in this cave, deign to accept of this. I was on my way somewhere, and as I was passing this place, it was raining hard and it was already late, so I came into this cave, just for this one night.' With these words he put down some things as if making an offering. Now the first man felt a little calmer, for he realized that he had been right.

The things which had been put down were near him, and wondering what they were he stealthily put out his hand and groped for them, whereupon he found three small rice-cakes. Tired after his journey and hungry, he took the rice-cakes and furtively ate them. After a while the other man groped for the rice-cakes he had put down, and found them gone.

At this he must have thought that there was indeed a demon there who had eaten them, for he suddenly got up and ran, and, not stopping to pick up the things he had had with him, or his straw cape and hat, rushed out of the cave.

129

moto no otoko sa wa koso hito no kitarikeru ga, moti o kuitaru ni osorete
nigenuru narikeri. Yoku kuitekeru to omoite, kono sutesarinuru mono [55]o
sagureba, mono hitamono iritaru hukuro o sika no kawa o motte tutumitari,
mata mino kasa ari. Mino no atari yori noborikeru yatu narikeri to omoite,
mosi ukagai mo zo suru to omoikereba, mada yo no uti ni sono hukuro kaki-
oite, sono mino kasa o uti-kite tukaana o idete yukikeru hodo ni, mosi
[60]arituru yatu ya hitozato ni yukite, kono koto o katarite hito nado o gu-site
kinuramu to omoikereba, haruka ni hitobanaretaru tokoro ni yama no naka
ni yukite, sibaraku arikeru hodo ni yo mo akenikeri.

Sono toki ni sono hukuro o akete mikereba, kinumono, wata [65]nado o
hitamono iretarikeri. Omoigakenu koto nareba, ten no sarubekute tamaeru
to omoite, yorokobite sore yori namu yukikeru tokoro e wa yukinikeru.
Omowanu syotoku sitaru yatu kana. Ima no yatu wa niguru mottomo kotowari nari kasi. Ge ni tare mo nigenamu. Moto no otoko no kokoro ito [70]muku-
tukesi.

Kono koto wa moto no otoko no oi no hate ni, tumako no mae ni katarikeru
o kikitutaetaru nari. Ima no yatu wa tui ni tare to mo sirade yaminikeri.

Sareba kokorosakasiki yatu wa gesu naredo mo, kakaru [75]toki ni mo
yorozu o kokoroete, yoku hurumaite omoigakenu syotoku o mo suru narikeri.
Saru nite mo moto no otoko moti o kuite, ima no yatu no nigenikeru o, ikani
okasi to omoikemu. Keu no koto nareba, kaku namu kataritutaetaru to ya.

He dashed blindly away, and the first man said to himself, 'Just as I thought, some person came in, and then ran off in a panic when his rice-cakes were eaten. What a good thing I ate them!' When he searched for what the other had left behind, he found a bag stuffed full of things and wrapped up in deer-skin, as well as a straw cape and hat. It occurred to him that this man must have come up from Mino; and, being afraid that he might come and investigate, the first man left the cave while it was still dark and went off carrying the bag on his back and wearing the cape and hat. Then, for fear that the other might have gone to some village and told people about what had happened, and might bring some of them along with him, he went to a spot in the mountains far from any human habitation; and, after he had been there for a while, dawn broke.

Then he opened the bag and found it full of silk and cotton-wool. It was so unexpected a gain that he felt it had been given him by Heaven as his rightful due, and, very pleased with himself, he left the place and continued on to where he had been going. What an unexpected windfall it was for him! No wonder the second man ran away. Indeed, anybody would have done so. The first man was utterly despicable.

This story has been passed on by someone who heard the first man tell it in his old age to his wife and children. No-one ever found out who the second man was.

So we see how a quick-witted fellow, however humble his station, makes an unexpected gain even at a time like this, if he knows what's what and goes the right way about things. How funny, though, the first man must have thought it when he ate the rice-cakes and the other ran away. It is because it is so unusual that this story has been passed on.

Hanazakura oru syoosyoo

Tuki ni hakararete, yo hukaku okinikeru mo, omooramu tokoro itoosikeredo, tati-kaeramu mo tooki hodo nareba, yooyoo yuku ni, koie nado ni rei otonoo [-5]mono mo kikoezu, kumanaki tuki ni, tokorodokoro no hana no kidomo mo, hitoe ni magainubeku kasumitari. Ima-sukosi sugite mituru tokoro yori mo, omosiroku sugigataki kokoti site,

Sonata e to / yuki mo yararezu / hanazakura /
[10]nioo kokage ni / tati-yorare-tutu

to uti-zunzite, hayaku koko ni mono iisi hito ari to, omoiidete tati-yasuroo ni, tuizi no kuzure yori, siroki mono no, itoo siwabuki-tutu izumeri. Awarege ni are, hitoge naki tokoro nareba, koko kasiko nozokedo togamuru [-15]hito nasi. Kono arituru mono o yobite, 'Koko ni sumi-tamaisi hito wa imada owasu ya, yamabito ni mono kikoemu to yuu hito ari, to monoseyo' to ieba, 'Sono on-kata wa koko ni mo owasimasazu, nani to ka yuu tokoro ni namu sumase-tamoo' to kikoetureba, aware [-20]no koto ya, ama nado ni ya naritaruramu to, usirometakute, 'Kano Mitutoo ni awazi ya' nado, hohoemite notamoo hodo ni, tumado o yawara kai-hanatu oto su nari. Otokodomo sukosi yarite, suigai no turanaru murasusuki no sigeki-sita ni kakurete mireba, 'Syoonagon-no-kimi koso ake [-25]ya sinurame, idete mi-tamae' to yuu. Yoki hodo naru warawa no, yoodai okasige naru, itoo naesugite, tonoi-sugata naru suoo ni ya aramu, tuyayaka naru akome ni, uti-sukitaru kami no suso, koutigi ni haete namamekasi. Tuki no akaki kata ni, oogi o sasikakusite, 'Tuki to [30]hana to o' to kutizusamite, hana no kata e ayumikuru ni odoro-kasamahosikeredo, sibasi mireba, otonasiki hito no, 'Suemitu wa nado ka ima made okinu zo, Ben-no-kimi koso koko narituru, mairi-tamae' to yuu wa, mono e moozuru narubesi. Arituru warawa wa tomaru narubesi. [-35]'Wabi-siku koso oboyure. Sabare tada on-tomo ni mairite, tikakaramu tokoro ni ite, on-yasiro e wa mairazi' nado ieba, 'Monoguruosi ya' nado yuu. Mina sitatete gorokunin zo aru. Oruru hodo mo ito nayamasige ni, kore zo aruzi naruramu to miyuru o, yoku mireba, kinu nugikaketaru [-40]yoodai, sasayaka ni imizyuu komeitari. Mono iitaru mo, rootaki mono no yueyuesiku kikoyu. Uresiku mo mituru kana to omoo ni, yooyoo akureba kaeri-tamainu. Hizasi agaru hodo ni oki-tamaite, yobe no tokoro ni humi kaki-tamoo. 'Imizyuu [-45]hukoo haberituru mo, kotowari narubeki mi-kesiki ni ide-haberinuru wa, turasa mo

The Minor Captain who plucked the cherry-blossom

DECEIVED by the moonlight, he had risen in the depth of night, but though he pitied her for what she would be thinking, it would have been too far to go back; so he kept on his way. The usual noises were not to be heard from the small dwellings nearby, and in the pervasive moonlight the cherry-trees all around gave the complete illusion of a mist. Finding this more pleasing than the scenes he had just passed, he felt loth to go further. So he lingered, reciting,

> 'I cannot pass by this spot, being drawn to the shade of the
> trees bright with cherry-blossom,'

and recollected that a person with whom he had once had an affair had lived here. And then, from where the earth-bank had crumbled, he saw a white figure appear, coughing noisily. The spot was a wretchedly desolate and lonely one; and, though he peered in all directions, there was none to challenge him. Calling this person who had appeared, he said, 'Is the lady who used to live in this place still here? Tell her there is someone who says he would like to talk to the hermit.' 'That lady is not here. It is at so-and-so that she is living,' was the reply. 'How sad!' he thought uneasily; 'Could she have become—perhaps a nun?';—and then, smiling, he suggested that she might have met Mitutoo. At that moment there came the creak of a door being gently opened.

Sending his men a little way off, he hid among some thick clumps of *susuki* grass beside the open-work fence and watched. Then someone said, 'Mistress Syoonagon! Go out and see if it is daylight yet.' Then he saw a girl of marriageable age, with attractive features—a graceful picture, with the lower ends of her combed-out hair set off against her *koutigi*, under which was a beautiful *akome*, apparently a dark-red one that she wore for attendance at night, since its stiffness was all worn out of it. With her fan held up to keep off the moonlight, she was humming 'The Moonlight and the Blossom'. As she walked up to the flowers, he felt a desire to surprise her, but he remained watching for a while, and then an adult voice said, 'Why is Suemitu not up yet? So you were here, mistress Ben! Come along to the shrine'; which suggested that they were going to worship somewhere. This girl who had appeared was presumably to stay behind, for she exclaimed, 'How dull!' and said something about going all the same, simply as an attendant, and waiting somewhere nearby without going into the shrine; but was told she was talking nonsense. When they were all ready there were five or six people. Looking carefully at one of them who seemed very frail as she came down the steps and was evidently the mistress of the house, he noticed how the set of the collar revealed the nape of her neck and how small and very girlish she was. Her voice, too, was charming, yet with a note of dignity. 'How glad I am to have seen her,' he thought, as with the approach of daylight he returned home.

He rose when the sun was already high and wrote a letter to the place he had

ikabakari' nado, aoki usu-yoo ni yanagi ni tukete,

> Sirazarisi / inisie yori mo / aoyagi no
> itodo zo kesa wa / omoimidaruru

[50]tote yari-tamaeri. Kaerigoto meyasuku miyu.

> Kakezarisi / kata ni zo haesi / ito nareba
> toku to misi ma ni / mata midare-tutu

to aru o mi-tamoo hodo ni, Gen-tyuuzyoo, hyooe-no-suke, koyumi motasete owasitari. 'Yobe wa izuku ni kakure-tamaerisi [55]zo, uti ni gyoyuu arite mesisikado mo, mituke-tatematurade koso' to notamaeba, 'Koko ni koso haberisika, ayasikarikeru koto kana' to notamoo. Hana no kidomo no saki-midaretaru, ito ooku tiru o mite,

> Akade tiru / hana miru ori wa / hitamiti ni
[60]to areba, suke,
> waga mi ni katu wa / yowarinisi kana

to notamoo. Tyuuzyoo-no-kimi, 'Saraba kai naku ya' tote,

> Tiru hana o / osimitomete mo / kimi nakuba
> tare ni ka misemu / yado no sakura o

[65]to notamoo. Tawabure-tutu morotomo ni izu. Kano mituru tokoro tazuneba ya to obosu. Yuugata tono ni moode-tamaite, kureyuku hodo no sora, itoo kasumikomete, hana no ito omosiroku tirimidaruru yuubae o, mi-su makiagete nagameide-tamaeru on-katati iwamu kata [70]naku, hikari mitite, hana no nioi mo muge ni keosaruru kokoti zo suru. Biwa o ooziki-tyoo ni sirabete, ito nodoyaka ni okasiku hiki-tamoo on-tetuki nado, kagiri naki onna mo kaku wa e-arazi to miyu. Kono kata no hitobito mesiidete, samazama uti-awase-tutu [75]asobi-tamoo. Mitusue, 'Ikaga onna no mede-tatematurazaramu. Konoe no mi-kado watari nite koso, medetaku hiku hito are. Nanigoto ni mo ito yue-zukite zo miyuru' to, onogadoti yuu o kiki-tamaite, 'Izure, kono sakura ookute, aretaru yado, wara wa ikade ka misi, [80]ware ni kikaseyo' to notamaeba, 'Nao tayori arite, makaritarisi ni namu' to mooseba, 'Saru tokoro wa misi zo, komaka ni katare' to notamoo. Kano misi warawa ni monoyuu narikeri. 'Ko-Gen-tyuunagon no musume ni namu. Makoto ni okasige ni zo haberu naru. Kano on-ozi no taisyoo namu, [85]mukaete uti ni tatematuramu to moosu naru' to mooseba, 'Sarazaramu saki ni, nao tabakare' to notamoo. 'Sa omoi-haberedo, ikade ka' tote tatinu. Yuusari, kano warawa wa, mono ito yoku

visited the night before: 'Though it was still dead of night, at the hint in your looks I left you, and oh! how hard it was!', with more to the same effect, and on thin green *torinoko*, attached to a sprig of willow, he sent this poem:

'Even of old my thoughts were troubled, when I knew you not;
but still more tangled are they now, like tresses of green willow.'

Her reply was written in a beautiful hand:

'Those tresses grew where you had not set your heart, so as soon
as they seem smoothed out, they are again entangled.'

As he was reading this, the Minamoto Middle Captain and the Assistant Captain of the Military Guards arrived with servants carrying small bows. 'Where were you hiding last night?' they said; 'There was a concert at the Palace and you were sent for, but we didn't find you.' 'How strange!' he said; 'I was here at home.' The cherry-trees were covered with blossom and seeing that a great many petals were falling, one of them composed the lines:

'When I see the flowers falling before I have gazed my fill at them,
how keenly I feel that . . .'

and the Assistant Captain added:

'In the same way I too have withered and faded.'

'That won't do!' said the Middle Captain, and recited:

'Though I should try to keep the flowers from falling, to whom could
I show them, the cherries at my house—with you not there?'

The two departed, still in playful mood. 'If only I could visit that place I saw!' he thought. In the early evening he paid a visit to the Hall. Rolling up the bamboo blind, he gazed out at the sunset glow in the haze-covered westering sky, where blossom fell in delightful confusion; his face was so beautiful that one felt it entirely outshone even the loveliness of the flowers. Tuning his *biwa* to the *ooziki* mode, he played quietly and charmingly, and the movements of his hands seemed to be such as even the most beautiful woman could scarcely equal. He summoned several other performers and amused himself by playing various tunes with them. Hearing Mitusue say in conversation with his companions, 'How could any woman fail to love him? There's someone who lives near the Konoe Gate who is a fine player. She seems to be very accomplished in every way,' the Minor Captain asked, 'Where? In that dilapidated house with all the cherry-trees? Tell me how you come to have seen it.' 'I just went there on some errand,' he replied. 'I have seen the place you mention; tell me about it,' said the Minor Captain. It happened that Mitusue was the lover of the servant girl whom the Minor Captain had seen there. He replied, 'The lady of the house is the daughter of the late Minamoto Middle Counsellor, and is indeed very beautiful. They say her uncle the Major Captain has become her guardian and is going to procure her an appointment at Court.' 'You must just arrange something before that occurs,' said the Minor Captain. 'I agree, sir, but how?' he said, as he went off.

One evening the servant girl, who had a very ready flow of talk, was

yuu mono nite, kotoyoku kataroo. 'Taisyoo-dono no tune ni wazurawasiku kikoe-tamaeba, $^{-90}$hito no on-humi tutooru koto dani, oba-ue imiziku notamoo mono o' to, onazi tokoro nite medetakaramu koto nado notamoo koro, koto ni semureba, wakaki hito no omoiyari sukunaki ni ya, 'Yoki ori araba ima' to yuu. On-humi wa kotosara ni, kesiki misezi tote tutaezu. $^{-95}$Mitusue mairite, 'Iiomomukete haberu. Koyoi zo yoku haberubeki' to mooseba, yorokobi-tamaite, sukosi yo hukete owasu. Mitusue ga kuruma nite owasinu. Warawa kesiki miarikite ire-tatematuritu. Hi wa mono no usiro e toriyaritareba honoka naru ni, moya ni ^{100}ito tiisayaka nite uti-husi-tamaeru o, kaki-idakite nose-tatematuri-tamaite, kuruma o isogite yaru ni, 'Ko wa na zo na zo' tote, kokoroezu asamasyuu obosaru. Tyuuzyoo-no-menoto kiki-tamaite, 'Oba-ue no usirometagari-tamaite, husi-tamaeru ni namu, moto yori tiisaku $^{-105}$owasikeru o, oi-tamaite, hoosi ni sae nari-tamaeba, kasira samukute, on-zo o hikikazukite husi-tamaeru namu, sore to oboekeru mo kotowari nari.' Kuruma yosuru hodo ni hurubitaru koe nite, 'Ina ya, ko wa tare zo' to notamoo. Sono noti ikaga okogamasyuu $^{-110}$koso. On-katati wa kagiri nakarikeredo.

chatting away freely to Mitusue. 'Oh, but her aunt makes a great fuss even about the passing on of a letter, because the Major Captain is always so particular,' she said. When the coming auspicious event was being discussed there, he urged her more strongly than ever, and she, probably because she was young and rather thoughtless, said, 'As soon as there's a good opportunity.' But she deliberately did not pass on the Minor Captain's letter, so as not to reveal what was afoot. When Mitusue presented himself and said, 'I have persuaded her; tonight should be the best time,' the Minor Captain was overjoyed and, after the night had drawn on a little, set off, travelling in Mitusue's carriage. The girl went and had a look round and then let him in. It was rather dim inside because the light had been screened, but he gathered up the tiny figure of someone who was lying asleep in the main room and, putting her into the carriage, hurriedly drove off. In her bewildered amazement she cried, 'What's this? What's happening?' Tyuuzyoo, the nurse, when she heard of the matter, thought to herself, 'It was her aunt sleeping there because she was uneasy about her. It's no wonder he thought her to be the one. For of course she is small; and then, she's old, and what's more, a nun, so that she must have felt her head cold and been sleeping with her robe pulled up over her head.' When the carriage arrived, an aged voice exclaimed, 'Oh dear! Who is it?' What an absurd situation he found himself in then! She was very good-looking, but apart from that . . .

Ootoo-no-miya Kumano-oti no koto

OOTOO-NO-MIYA nihon-sinnoo wa, Kasagi no siro no anpi o kikosimesaren tame ni, sibaraku nanto no Hannya-zi ni sinonde goza arikeru ga, Kasagi no siro sude ni otite, syuzyoo torawaresase-tamainu [-5]to kikoesikaba, tora-no-o o humu osore on-minoue ni semarite, tenti hirosi to iedo mo on-mi o kakusarubeki tokoro nasi, zitugetu akiraka nari to iedo mo tyooya ni mayoeru kokoti site, hiru wa nohara no kusa ni kakurete, tuyu ni husu uzura no toko ni on-namida o arasoi, yoru wa koson no tuzi [10]ni tatazumite, hito o togamuru sato no inu ni on-kokoro o nayamasare, izuku tote mo on-kokoro yasukarubeki tokoro nakarikereba, kakute mo sibasi wa to obosimesarekeru tokoro ni, Itizyoo-in no koonin Azeti-hoogen-Koosen, ikani site kikitariken, gohyakuyo-ki o sos-site, bimei ni Hannya-zi e zo yosetarikeru. [-15]Orihusi miya ni tuki-tatematuritaru hito itinin mo nakarikereba, hitohusegi husegite otisasetamoobeki yoo mo nakarikeru ue, sukima mo naku, tuwamono sude ni zinai ni uti-iritareba, magirete on-ide arubeki kata mo nasi. Saraba yosi zigai sen to obosimesite, sude ni osi-hadanugase-tamaitarikeru [-20]ga, kotokanawazaran go ni nozonde, hara o kiran koto wa ito yasukarubesi. Mosi ya to kakurete miba ya to obosimesikaesite, butuden no kata o goran-zuru ni, hito no yomikakete okitaru dai-hannya no karoodo mitu ari. Hutatu no hitu wa imada huta o akezu, [-25]hitotu no hitu wa on-kyoo o nakaba-sugi toriidasite huta o mo sezarikeri. Kono huta o aketaru hitu no naka e, on-mi o tizimete husase-tamai, sono ue ni on-kyoo o hikikazukite, ongyoo no zyu o on-kokoro no uti ni tonaete zo owasikeru. Mosi sagasiidasareba, yagate tukitaten [30]to obosimesite, koori no gotoku naru katana o nuite, on-hara ni sasiatete, tuwamono, 'Koko ni koso' to iwanzuru hitokoto o matase-tamaikeru on-kokoro no uti, osihakaru mo nao asakarubesi. Saru hodo ni tuwamono butuden ni midareitte, butudan no sita tenzyoo no ue made mo nokoru tokoro naku sagasikeru [35]ga, amari ni motomekanete, 'Kore-tei no mono koso ayasikere. Ano dai-hannya no hitu o akete miyo' tote, huta sitaru hitu hutatu o hiraite, on-kyoo o toriidasi, soko o hirugaesite mikeredo mo owasezu, huta akitaru hitu wa miru made mo nasi tote, tuwamono mina zityuu o idesarinu. Miya wa [40]husigi no on-inoti o tugase-tamai, yume ni mitiyuku kokoti site, nao hitu no uti ni owasikeru ga, mosi mata tuwamono tati-kaeri, kuwasiku sagasu koto mo ya aranzuran to go-sian atte, yagate saki ni tuwamono no sagasimitarituru hitu ni, irikawarase-tamaite zo owasikeru. An no gotoku

Ootoo-no-miya's flight to Kumano

OOTOO-NO-MIYA, Imperial prince of the Second order, had for some time been secretly at the Hannya Temple in the Southern Capital to learn how it fared with the fortress at Kasagi and, when he heard that the fortress at Kasagi had fallen and the Emperor been taken prisoner, the fear oppressed him as of one who treads upon a tiger's tail; how wide soever the heavens and the earth, there would be for him no place in which to conceal himself; how bright soever the sun and the moon, it would be to him as a long night through which he wandered lost—by day to hide among the grasses of the open moor, his tears outvying where the quails couch in their beds of dew—at night to stand at the crossroads of solitary hamlets, his heart plagued by the village curs which give challenge to strangers—there was no place, he thought, where he might feel at ease, nor for a time would things be otherwise: where-upon it came about that Azeti-Koosen, of *hoogen* rank, Lay-Priest Adminis-trator at the Itizyoo Seminary, having in some unknown manner received news, bore down upon the Hannya Temple before daybreak at the head of over five hundred horsemen. None of those attached to the prince being present at the time, there was no chance of flight under cover of a defensive action; nor, since warriors had already penetrated to every corner of the temple precincts, was it possible to steal out unobserved. Be it so then! he would put an end to himself; and in this resolve he had already bared the upper part of his body, when he had second thoughts: it would be quite simple to cut his belly as soon as matters became desperate; might he not hide himself, hoping against all odds for a favourable outcome? And, looking towards the Buddha Hall, he saw three Chinese chests of the Mahā-prajñā which someone had been reading. Two of the chests had their lids on; one had been emptied of more than half of the sutra volumes in it, and its lid had not been replaced. He squeezed into the open chest and crouched down, drawing volumes of the sutra over him to cover himself, and remained there, silently repeating the spell to produce invisibility. It is quite impossible adequately to appreciate his state of mind as, resolved to deliver the thrust the instant he was discovered, he drew his ice-cold blade and, placing its point against his belly, waited for a warrior to utter the single phrase, 'Here he is'. Warriors now burst into the Buddha Hall and searched everywhere, even under the altar and in the roof, but with such ill success that someone said, 'The things here indeed are of a sort to arouse suspicion; try opening those Mahā-prajñā chests'; and the two chests which had their lids on were opened, emptied of the sutra volumes in them, and turned upside down, but he was not found. All the warriors, thinking it unnecessary to look at the open-lidded chest, went out of the temple. The prince's life, of a marvel, had been preserved. He remained in the chest with the feeling that he was passing through a dream, but, re-flecting that the warriors might return and search more thoroughly, he

tuwamonodomo [45]mata butuden ni tati-kaeri, 'Saki ni huta no akitaru o mizarituru ga obotukanasi' tote, on-kyoo o mina uti-utusite mikeru ga, karakara to uti-waroote, 'Dai-hannya no hitu no naka o yokuyoku sagasi-tareba, Ootoo-no-miya wa irase-tamawade Oo-Too no Genzoo-Sanzoo koso owasikere' to tawaburekereba, [-50]tuwamono mina itidoo ni waroote mongai e zo idenikeru. Kore hitoe ni Marisi-ten no myoo-oo, mata wa zyuuroku-zenzin no oogo ni yoru inoti nari to, sinzin kimo ni mei-zi kanrui on-sode o uruoseri. Kakute wa nanto-hen no on-kakurega mo kanaigatakereba, suna-wati Hannya-zi o on-ide arite, Kumano no kata [55]e zo otisase-tamaikeru. On-tomo no syuu ni wa, Koorin-boo-Genson, Akamatu-rissi-Sokuyuu, Kidera-Sagami, Okamoto-no-Mikawa-boo, Musasi-boo, Murakami-Hiko-siroo, Kataoka-Hatiroo, Yata-Hikositi, Hiraga-no-Saburoo, karekore izyoo kunin nari. Miya o hazime-tatematurite, on-tomo no mono made mo mina kaki no koromo ni oi o kake, tokin mayu-nakaba ni [60]seme, sono uti ni tosi tyoo-zeru o sen-dati ni tukuritate, inaka-yamabusi no Kumano-sankei suru tei ni zo misetarikeru. Kono kimi moto yori ryuuroo-hooketu no uti ni hitotonarase-tamaite, kaken-koosya no hoka o idesase-tamawanu on-koto nareba, go-hokoo no tyooto wa sadamete kanawase-tamawazi to, on-tomo [65]no hitobito kanete wa kokorogurusiku omoikeru ni, an ni sooi site, itu narawase-tamaitaru on-koto naranedo mo ayasige naru tabi habaki warazi o mesite, sukosi mo kutabiretaru go-kisyoku mo naku, yasiro-yasiro no hoohei, yado-yado no on-tutome okotarase-tamawazarikereba, rozi ni yukiaikeru [-70]doosya mo, gonzyu o tumeru sen-dati mo mitogamuru koto nakarikeri. Yura no minato o miwataseba oki kogu hune no kazio tae, ura no hamayuu ikue to mo, siranu namizi ni naku tidori, Ki-no-zi no tooyama byoobyoo to, Huzisiro no matu ni kakareru iso no nami, Waka Hukiage o yoso ni mite, tuki ni migakeru Tamatusima, [-75]hikari mo ima wa sarade dani, tyootei kyokuho no tabi no miti, kokoro o kudaku narai naru ni, ame o hukumeru koson no ki, yuube o okuru enzi no kane, aware o moyoosu toki si mo are, Kirime no Oozi ni tuki-tamoo.

quickly transferred himself into one of the chests the warriors had searched before. Sure enough, the warriors came again to the Buddha Hall and, expressing uneasiness at not having previously examined the open chest, shifted all the sutra volumes, when one of them, laughing loudly, said in jest: 'After all our looking into the Mahā-prajñā chests, we have found, not Ootoo-no-miya, but *Oo-too no Genzoo-Sanzoo* (Hsüan-tsang, Tripitaka, of the Great T'ang)'; and all the warriors went laughing together out of the gateway. Believing that in all this he owed his life entirely to the favour of Marīci, or else to the protection of the Sixteen Beneficent Deities, the prince's faith was redoubled, and he wetted his sleeve with tears of gratitude. No hiding-place in the vicinity of the Southern Capital being likely to be adequate, he left the Hannya Temple forthwith and fled in the direction of Kumano. In his train were 'Genson' of the Koorin Cloister and Master-of-Buddhist-Asceticism Akamatu-'Sokuyuu', Kidera-Sagami and the monk of the Mikawa Cloister in Okamoto, the monk of the Musasi Cloister and Murakami-Hikoziroo, with Kataoka-Hatiroo, Yata-Hikositi, and Hiraga-no-Saburoo, making nine all together. Prince and followers, one and all, travel-boxes slung over persimmon robes, and priests' caps pulled down over their eyes, with the oldest among them made to appear their leader, assumed the guise of itinerant priests from the country going to worship at Kumano. His followers had been apprehensive: 'My lord's circumstances', said one, 'have been such from the start that amidst Dragon Galleries and Phoenix Towers he has grown to manhood, and only in a Flowery Chariot or Scented Carriage ever gone abroad; doubtless, then, he will not be equal to a long journey on foot'; but, against all expectation, although he had had no particular experience, clad in his coarse-looking foot-coverings, leg-cloths, and straw sandals, and showing no slightest sign of fatigue, he failed not to make offerings at every shrine, to do services at every inn, so that neither pilgrims met upon the road nor senior priests with long training in austerities eyed him with suspicion. O'er Yura roadstead as the gaze is bent, rowed offshore, a boat, the helm-thong snapped; sea-edge amaryllis, course on course untold's the wave-way where sea-birds cry; Kii's distant hills seen vaguely vast: at Huzisiro, draped about the pine-trees, shore-line waves; to Waka, Hukiage, unresponsive; moonlight-polished Island-of-the-Jewel; even if the light shone now less brightly, by long coast road and winding shoreway, unease of heart were wonted; but withal, solitary hamlet's rain-drenched trees, far-off temple's eve-dismissing bell—then is the time indeed of utter sadness: and so Oozi in Kirime is reached.

Sazareisi

ZINMU-TENNOO yori zyuu-nidai Seimu-tennoo to moosi-tatematuru wa, kagirinaku medetaki mi-yo nari. Kono mikado ni otokomiko, himemiya sanzyuu-hatinin no oozi owasikeru. Sanzyuu-hatinin-me wa [5]himemiya nite watarase-tamoo. Kazu mo siranu hodo no oozi-tati no mi-sue nareba tote, sono mi-na o Sazareisi-no-miya to zo moosikeru. On-katati yo ni sugurete medetaku owasikereba, amata no on-naka ni mo koete, go-tyooai nanome-narazu itukikasizuki-tamaikeru. Saru hodo [-10]ni on-tosi zyuu-si nite, Sessyoo dono no kita no mandokoro ni utusi-mairase-tamoo. Medetaki on-oboe, itten-sikai no uti ni ue kosu hito koso nakarikeri.

Sazareisi-no-miya, seken no ui-tenpen no kotowari o, tukuzuku obosimesi-yorite, sore butudoo o negoo ni, [15]zyoodo wa zip-poo ni ari to kikedo mo, naka ni mo medetaki zyoodo wa, tooboo-Zyooruri-sekai ni siku wa nasi to obositorite, tune ni okotarazu, Yakusi no go-myoogoo, namu Yakusi-rurikoo-nyorai to tonae-tamoo. Aru yuugure no koto naru ni, tuki no izuru yamanoha uti-nagame-tamai, waga [20]umaren zyoodo wa sonata zo to obosimesi, hitori tatazumi-tamoo ni, on-mae ni kokuu yori kogane no tenkan o hitai ni atetaru kannin hitori mairi, Sazareisi-no-miya ni ruri no tubo o sasage-moosikereba, Yakusi-nyorai no on-tukawasime, Konpira-taisyoo nari to zo moosikeru.

[26]Kono tubo ni myooyaku ari, kore sunawati huroo-husi no kusuri nari. Kore o kikosimesareba, on-tosi mo yori-tamawazu, wazurawasiki mi-kokoti mo naku, itu mo kawaranu mi-sugata nite, on-inoti no owari mo naku, itu made mo medetaku [-30]sakae-tamawan tote, kakikesu yoo ni usenikeri. Sazareisi-no-miya, kono tubo o uketorase-tamai, ara arigata ya, tosituki negai-tatematuru sirusi kana tote, sando rai-si, rooyaku name-tamoo ni, amata aziwai yuu bakari nasi. Aoki tubo ni siroki mozi ari, yomite [-35]goran-zureba, uta nari.

Kimi ga yo wa / ti-yo ni yati-yo ni / sazareisi no
iwao to narite / koke no musu made

to ari. Kore sunawati Yakusi-nyorai no go-eika narubesi. Sore yori mi-na o hiki-kaete, Iwao-no-miya [40]to zo moosikeru.

Sono noti tosituki o okuri-tamoo ni, isasaka mono no kanasiki koto mo naku, itu mo tokiwa no mi-sugata nite, eiga ni hokori-tamoo. On-inoti nagaku watarase-tamoo koto wa, subete happyaku-yo-sai nari. Seimu-tennoo, Tyuuai-tennoo, Zingoo-koogoo, Oozin-tennoo, [-45]Nintoku-tennoo, Rityuu-tennoo, Hansei-tennoo, Ingyoo-tennoo, Ankoo-tennoo, Yuuryaku-tennoo, Seinei-tennoo, zyuu-itidai no aida, itu mo kawaranu mi-sugata nite, sakaesase-tamoo nari. Sazareisi-no-miya, aru yomosugara tomosibi o kakage,

Pebble

THE reign of the emperor Seimu, twelfth in the line from the emperor Zinmu, was one of unbounded happiness. This emperor had thirty-eight Imperial children, princes and princesses. The thirty-eighth was a princess. Since she was the last of the innumerable Imperial children, she was named Princess Pebble. Her beauty was so extraordinary that the Emperor loved her exceedingly and bestowed on her care and attention above all the rest. And then, in her fourteenth calendar year, he made her the wife of the Regent. There was no-one between the four seas under the one sky who enjoyed more of the Imperial favour.

Princess Pebble gave deep thought to the principle of worldly mutability; now, on enquiring about the Way of Buddha, one learns that there are pure lands in all the ten directions, yet, of them all, she concluded, none surpasses in happiness the Pure Beryl Realm in the east, and she repeated unremittingly the invocation to Bhaiṣajyaguru: Hail, Bhaiṣajyaguru of Beryl Light, Tathā-gata! It happened one evening that, unaccompanied, she had stopped to gaze at the ridge of the mountains where the moon was rising, thinking ' 'Tis there, the pure land into which I shall be born'; when before her, out of empty air, there came an official with a golden head-dress about his brows, who, offering a beryl jar to Princess Pebble, said that he was the General Kumbhīra, a messenger of the tathāgata Bhaiṣajyaguru.

'This jar', he said, 'contains a marvellous balsam, even the elixir of life. Partake of this, and, without age coming upon you or your experiencing any vexation, you will remain ever unchanged in appearance; your life will be without end, and you will enjoy prosperity for ever'; whereupon he vanished. Princess Pebble received the jar, saying 'Ah, how thankful I am for it—the response to my years of prayer!' and made obeisance three times; and, tasting the efficacious medicine, she found that its numerous flavours defied description. On the green jar were white characters which, reading, she saw to be a poem.

As for your life, / a thousand, eight thousand, ages; / till pebble is
changed to rock, / and moss has grown.

This must be the composition of the tathāgata Bhaiṣajyaguru. From this time forward, changing her name, she was called Princess Rock.

Thereafter, although time passed for her, nothing occurred to cause her the slightest sadness; constantly the same in appearance, she lived in splendour and magnificence. The length of her life was, in all, more than eight hundred years. So it was that, ever unchanged in appearance, she prospered during eleven reigns, those of the emperors Seimu and Tyuuai, of the empress Zingoo, of the emperors Oozin, Nintoku, and Rityuu, Hansei, Ingyoo, and Ankoo, Yuuryaku and Seinei. Once, during an all-night vigil, Princess Pebble was keeping a lamp burning and meditating on the mantra of Bhaiṣajyaguru,

Yakusi-singon o nen-zi owasikeru ni, katazikenaku mo Yakusi-nyorai, $^{-50}$ito mo tattoki mi-sugata nite, Iwao-no-miya ni mukai notamoo wa, nanzi wa itu made kono sekai ni aran, ningen no tanosimi wa wazuka no koto nari, sore Zyooruri-sekai no ti wa, sunawati ruri nari, nanzi o utusan zyoodo wa, sippoo no renge no ue ni tama no hooden o tatete, kogane ^{55}no tobira o narabe, tama no sudare o kake, yuka ni wa nisiki no sitone o siki, ryoora syoogon o motte mi o kazaritaru, su-sen-nin no nyokan, zizi-kokkoku ni syugo o kuwae, hyakumi no onziki o sasaguru koto hima mo nasi, kono sekai nite tigirihukaki hito wa, menomae ni namii-tutu, nanigoto mo kokoro no mama $^{-60}$no gokuraku nareba, sa nomi wa ikade hakku no sekai ni aran tote, Iwao-no-miya o tooboo-Zyooruri-sekai ni mitibiki-tamoo. Sono mi o mo kaezu site zyoobutu si-tamoo koto, kitai-husigi no tamesi to ka ya. Zyoodai mo matudai mo kakaru medetaki tamesi nasi. Ima wa masse no koto, $^{-65}$ka hodo ni koso wa owasezu to mo, kami ya hotoke o nen-zuru hito wa, yawaka sono sirusi no nakarubeki. Namu Yakusi-rurikoo-nyorai namu Yakusi-rurikoo-nyorai, on korokoro sendari matooki sowaka on korokoro sendari matooki sowaka.

when, in his graciousness, the tathāgata Bhaiṣajyaguru, very noble in appearance, spoke to Princess Rock, saying: 'How long will you remain in this realm? Human joys are paltry; now, in the Pure Beryl Realm the ground itself is of beryl; in the pure land to which I will transfer you, on a lotus flower of the Seven Treasures I will build a Treasure Hall, and set hinged doors of gold one beside another, and put up bejewelled hanging screens, and spread brocaded cushions on its floor; ladies-in-waiting in thousands, attired in all the beauty and dignity of patterned stuffs and gauzes, shall keep guard over you from moment to moment and never cease from offering you, to eat and drink, all manner of delicacies; and, with those for whom you have a deep attachment in this present realm ranged before you, it will be perfect bliss, with everything accordant to your heart's desire: Why, then, remain thus in the Realm of the Eight Afflictions?'—and, so saying, he led Princess Pebble to the east, to the Pure Beryl Realm. What a strange and wonderful experience to attain to buddhahood without rebirth in another form! Neither in early nor in later ages is there another example of such a happy event. Though, since we are now in the Latter Days, such things as this do not occur, yet how can those who meditate on the gods and buddhas fail to obtain their reward? Hail, Bhaiṣajyaguru of Beryl Light, Tathāgata! Hail, Bhaiṣajyaguru of Beryl Light, Tathāgata! *Oṃ huluhulu caṇḍāli mātaṃgī svāhā! Oṃ huluhulu caṇḍāli mātaṃgī svāhā!*

Huzi no hu

Ranran

HUZI wa Hinomoto no Hoorai-san nari. Mukasi, Koorei gonen, yama hazi-mete gen-zu. Zyohuku mo kono yama ni noborite sen-yaku o motome, [-5]Kaguya-hime mo kami to ke-site koko ni rei o todomu. Mine wa hatiyoo ni warete ne wa sisyuu ni matagaru. Dooro wa mikuti yori noborite, ti-suzi ni wakare, susono wa toozai ni nagoo site, hyaku-ri ni turanaru. Katati kezuritaru ga gotoku, takaki koto hokuto ni tikasi. Yain ni asahi o kagayakasi, katen ni yuki [10]o itadaku. Sankan ni umi o tatae, sanzyoo wa masago o yozu. Wakoku ityoo rui-suru mono naku, sangoku meizan to syoo-site, Giso-rokuzyoo ni hanahada hometari. Yamatodake-no-mikoto wa, tooi o tairagete, Kusanagi no na o aratame, u-daisyoo Yoritomo wa, mononohu o atumete, makigari o karu. Narusawa-no-ike wa, Syunzei [-15]no adana o tori, Hitoana no oku wa, Nitta ga muhunbetu soo nari. Zyuuroo no miya, Goroo no yasiro, Saigyoo wa go-mozi o suekane, Tan-yuu wa sumiiro ni agumu. Keburi wa Kokin no zyo ni, niryuu ni yomare, kumo wa kaisen ni osorete, issyaku-hassun no goo o todomu. Zenzyoo no hito wa, hookan ni kasira o tutumi, [-20]gekoodoo wa, kosode no suna o huruu. Zettyoo no konosiro, hanpuku no suzume, sudaka wa oo-kokoro ni site, Iyo no Matuyama ni otosi, mizutori no haoto ni wa, okubyoo ni natte, miyako no kata ni nogaru. Huzi-nori, huzi-bai, huzi-kanzoo, huzi-ooki, kuri, kaki, matu, hinoki no tagui, ookan wa Take-nosita-goe, Nebara-goe. [-25]Seki wa Asigara-no-seki, Yokobasiri-no-seki, Arai no tokoo, Sayo no yamagoe, umi o hedate, mine o kasanu. Miho, Seikenzi no mikosi, Hakone, Kamakura no sugata, Nihon, Ryoogoku no kyoozyoo ni wa, bazyoo no hito no koobe o megurasi, Akasaka Surugadai ni wa, norimono no mado ni manaziri o saku. Tooku wa Asama-yama o kagiri, [-30]tikaku wa, Hara Yosiwara no atari narubesi. Suwa no umi ni wa, sakasima no kage o hitasi, Koo-syuu no hu ni wa mitumine ni miete, oogi no e wa koko narubesi. Mukasi yori, siika renpai no ku-kazu, awasete kore o tumamaba (*sic*), ookata kono yama no takasa ni wa hi-semu. Saredo kokon no aida, tada [35]issyu hiidetaru mono wa, Akahito no sirotae narubesi. Sono yo wa kono yama ni tai-site, man-ga-iti ni mo oyobazu. Waga okina, Huzi-Yosino no ku, issyoo nasi to ka ya. Azuma-zi ni omomuku hito wa, kaku narigataki Huzi no ei ni,

Prose poem on Huzi

Ranran

HUZI is the Mount P'êng-lai of Japan. Long ago, in the fifth year of Koorei, the mountain first appears. Hsü Fu ascends this mountain in search of the elixir of the Immortals; and Princess Kaguya, transformed into a deity, still has her spirit here. Its peak is split into eight petals; its roots bestride four provinces. Roads climb from three approaches and branch into a thousand paths; the plain at its base stretches east and west, on and on for a hundred leagues. It is shaped as if whittled; it is nearly as high as the Great Bear. In the dark it causes the rising sun to shine; under the summer sky it wears a cap of snow. Held in its folds are lakes; on it one clambers up fine sand. It has no parallel in Yamato or foreign realms; described as a mountain famed in the Three Lands, it is highly praised in the Six Books of I-ch'u. Yamatodake-no-mikoto, after quelling the Eastern Barbarians, renames Herbage-mower; Yoritomo, General of the Right, assembles warriors and holds a battue. From the pool of Narusawa, Syunzei takes his nickname, and, in the recesses of Hitoana, Nitta, it seems, confronts reality. The shrine to Zyuuroo, the Goroo chapel; Saigyoo failing to find the acceptable first line, Tan-yuu giving up black pigment in despair. Its smoke is written of in two ways in the *Kokin* preface; its cloud, dreaded by the cargo-boats, is still called One-foot-eight. Mountain-cult devotees, heads wrapped in jewel-crown hoods, on their way back shake the grit from their gowns. *Konosiro* at the summit, sparrows of the middle slopes; young-caught hawks, spirited enough to strike at Matuyama in Iyo; the sound of waterfowls' wings causing cowardice, and flight towards the capital. Huzi waterweed, Huzi censer-ash, Huzi liquorice, Huzi sneeze-wort; its various trees—chestnut, persimmon, pine, and cypress—; the high-ways, at the Takenosita Pass and the Nebara Pass; the barriers, the Asigara Guardhouse and the Yokobasiri Guardhouse; the ferry at Arai and the mountain-pass of Sayo—the sea between, and range on range of hills. Huzi viewed from Miho and from Seikenzi, the appearance it has from Hakone and from Kamakura; on the Nihon and Ryoogoku bridges mounted men glance back, and at Akasaka and Surugadai, through the windows of palanquins, eyes strain for a glimpse. From afar the limit is Asama-yama; the best near view, perhaps, is from around Hara and Yosiwara. In the lake of Suwa is immersed its inverted image; from the capital of Kai it appears triple-peaked —this must be the view which is depicted on fans. Such, from times of old, has been the number of its Chinese poems and its *uta*, of its linked-verses of both serious and lighter sorts, that, were they all piled one on another, they would almost rival this mountain in height. And yet, surely, throughout the ages the only one to attain excellence has been Akahito's 'white splendour'. For the rest, they do not even begin to do this mountain justice. Our Master, so they say, had not a verse on Huzi or on Yosino his whole life through. He who takes the road to the East and racks his brains over composing verses to

147

sinryoku o tuiyasi, mata Azuma-zi ni omomukanu hito wa, kaku arigataki Huzi o [40]mizu site, issyoo o owaru mo, tomo ni nokoriooki koto narubesi.

Minomusi no setu

Sodoo

MINOMUSI minomusi, koe no obotukanaki o awarebu. Titiyo titiyo to naku wa, koo ni moppara naru mono ka. Ikani [-5]tutaete oni no ko naruran. Sei-zyo ga hude no saganasi ya. Yosi oni nari to mo Kosoo o titi to site Syun ari. Nanzi wa musi no Syun naran ka.

Minomusi minomusi, koe no obotukanakute, katu munoo naru o awarebu. Matumusi wa koe no bi naru ga tame ni, rootyuu [-10]ni hanano o naki, kuwako wa ito o haku ni yori, karoozite sizu no te ni si-su.

Minomusi minomusi, munoo ni site sizuka naru o awarebu. Kotyoo wa hana ni isogasiku, hati wa mitu o itonamu ni yori, oorai odayaka narazu. Taga tame ni kore o [15]amaku suru ya.

Minomusi, minomusi, katati no sukosiki naru o awarebu. Wazuka ni itteki o ureba, sono mi o uruosi, itiyoo o ureba, kore ga sumika to nareri. Ryooda no ikioi aru mo, ooku wa hito no tame ni mi o sokonoo. Sikazi [20]nanzi ga sukosiki naru ni wa.

Minomusi minomusi, gyohu ga issi o tazusaetaru ni onazi. Gyohu wa uo o wasurezu, huuha ni taezu. Ikutabi ka kore o tokite, sake ni atemu to suru. Taikoo sura Bunnoo o turu no sosiri ari. Siryoo mo Kannoo ni itimi no kan o samatageraru.

[26]Minomusi minomusi, tamamusi yue ni sode nurasikemu, Tamino-no-sima no na ni kakurezu ya. Ikeru mono tare ka kono madoi nakaran. Tori wa mite takaku agari, uo wa mite hukaku iru. Henzyoo ga mino o siborisi mo, huruzuma o [30]nao wasurezaru nari.

Minomusi minomusi, haru wa yanagi no tukisomesi yori, sakura ga tiri ni sugarite, Teika no kokoro o okosi, aki wa ogi huku kaze ni ne o soete, Zyakuren ni kan o susumu. Kogarasi no noti wa, utusemi ni mi o naroo ya, kara mo mi mo tomo ni suturu [35]ya.

148

this so intractable Huzi, and he who does not take the road to the East and ends his days without seeing this so delectable Huzi—what regret they both must feel!

On the mantle-grub

Sodoo

MANTLE-GRUB, mantle-grub, I exclaim at the feebleness of your voice. With your cry of 'titiyo titiyo' (Father, Father), you must be filial piety itself. How came you to be known as a devil's child? The lady Sei's description wronged you. Devil's child though you be, Shun there was who was Ku Sou's son. Are you not the Shun of insects?

Mantle-grub, mantle-grub, as well as at your feeble voice I exclaim at your lack of ability. Caged for the beauty of its voice the pine-insect weeps for the flowery fields; for the silk it spins the mulberry-insect finally dies in low-born hands.

Mantle-grub, mantle-grub, I exclaim at your inability and the calmness it brings. The butterfly is busy at the flower, the bee works at her honey, and hence they know no peace as they hasten to and fro. Who benefits from this sweetness that they make?

Mantle-grub, mantle-grub, I exclaim at your smallness. With one mere droplet you nourish yourself; one leaf, and there is your dwelling. Dragons and serpents, for all their power, most often suffer harm at the hand of man. Better far to be small like you!

Mantle-grub, mantle-grub, you are like a fisherman holding a line in his hand. The fisherman has his mind upon fish, but, unable to withstand the wind and the waves, takes off his mantle again and again and tries to put it to *sake*. It is maliciously reported that T'ai Kung Wang hooked Wên Wang, and Tzǔ Ling had his moment of leisure spoiled by the king of Han.

Mantle-grub, mantle-grub, for the jewel-insect's sake, it seems, you wet your sleeve—like Mantle Island, perhaps, without cover from your name. Who of living creatures is spared this distraction? Seeing his mate, a bird flies high, a fish plunges deep; and Henzyoo's drenching his mantle with tears, too, was that he was yet mindful of his wife of old.

Mantle-grub, mantle-grub, after beginning on the willow in spring, you cling to the falling cherry-petals, so rousing Teika's sensibility. In autumn you join your note to the wind blowing through the reeds and stir Zyakuren's emotions. After winter's blasts, following perhaps the fashion of the cicada, do you cast off your skin and life together?

149

Mata otoko-mozi o motte kohuu o nobu

Minomusi minomusi / otite sootyuu ni iru
Issi taen to hossu / sun sin tomo ni munasi
Goona no katati ni nite / tityuu no takumi nasi
Hakuro kuti ni amaku / seitai mi o yoso-oo
Syooyoo to site ame o okasi / hyoozen to site kaze ni zyoo-zu
Seia tuibamu koto nakare / kadoo muragaru o kin-zu
[40]Ten wa yurusu in o nasu koto o / ware wa awaremu oo to syoo-suru
koto o
Sai o das-si saraba / tare ka sono owari o siran

150

Or, to express it in the old style, using a man's words:

> Mantle grub, mantle grub, / you drop in through the window:
> Your thread will break, / but your tiny body and mind are quite unperturbed.
> In shape you are like the hermit-crab; / you have not the spider's skill.
> The white dew is sweet to your lips; / the green moss adorns your body.
> Calmly you brave the rain; / carefree you ride on the wind.
> Let not the homing crows peck you; / see that the children harass you not.
> Providence allows you to build a retreat; / I am amused to call you old man.
> When you take off your mantle and go away, / who knows what becomes of you?

Tuuhuu-Ise-monogatari

Iba-Kasyoo saku
Torii-Kiyonaga ga

Koko ni sake-syoobai o sesi Iseya-Tokuemon to yuu [5]mono ari. Tikaki koro yori dandan sinsyoo sidasi, kunimoto yori nenki-kodomo hutari yobi-yose, tokui o mawarase, nitiniti hanzyoo sesi nari.

"Kore Tokukiti me o samase. Ware mo Koosuke to issyo ni yu ni de mo itte koi. Ano obi no sizama [10]o mi-sassyare."

"Are goroo-zimase. Koosuke mo Tokukiti mo onazi tosi-kakkoo naredo mo, Koosuke-me wa maiban yu ni de mo yuki, kami mo kotti kara iwanu saki ni saisoku site yuimasu ni, Tokukiti wa eri mo mimi mo makkuro ni site, tada inemuri [15]ga etemono sa."

Sate mo Tokuemon-kata no hutari no go-yoo wa, nitiniti tokui o aruki, mukasi to tigai imadoki wa, 'Go-yoo wa yoo gozarimasu ka' to wa iwazu, taga mae e de mo hutokorode o site, nosorinosori to nozoku bakari, sore de mo yoo wa tariru [20]nari. Koosuke wa kinzyo no kami-sama ya sibumuketa musume nado ni, 'Ee ko da kara, ii sake o hayaku motte kite kur'ya' to iware, ii sake wa wasurete mo, ee ko to iwareta ga nani yori uresiku, tatimati motte kuru yoo na ki-date nareba, hudan kara [25]site siri o hasyori, uti o dete mo kinzyo o hanareru to siri o orosite, tada asuko no kamiyuidoko, koko no zisinban no en-bana e yokotaosi ni natte, asuko no nyooboo wa iki dano, koko no musume wa zatsu dano to, yuu yoo na hanasi ga omosiroku, tatimati konogoro wa, siokara de mo kutta [30]yoo na koe ni narinu.

Sore ni hikikae, Tokukiti wa asa kara ban made, uti e hyakudo-mairi site yoo o tasi, kami mo hudan susuhaki no yoo ni site, mimi mo eri mo makkuro ni natte aruki, kinzyo no kodomo ga gorokunin mukuronzi o moti, hukimuku [35]o sitari, aruiwa keteatta o torite asobu o tukuzuku mite, omosiroku nari, doo de mo ore mo site mitai to omoedo mo, mukuronzi mo naku, nisanniti mo kokorogake, toori no mise-sita nite mukuronge syoorongе o hazime, siawase to hitotu no [40]muku ga muttu nanatu ni nari, yo wa taisetu ni nuno-kosiage no naka e osikomi, neru ni mo osaete neru hodo ni daizi ni site, mata hutatu hue mittu hue, noti ni wa nisanzyuu ni mo narikeri. Kore yori waruku kakegoto ni mi no iru mono nari. Tokukiti wa tada motode hitotu de mo, sei [45]dasite hitotu o taisetu ni site kasegeba ribai suru koto ni kokorogake,

A modern Ise-monogatari

modelled on The-Man-Who-Once-Upon-A-Time

Written by Iba-Kasyoo
Illustrated by Torii-Kiyonaga

HERE we have Iseya-Tokuemon, a wine merchant. Of late, he has been acquiring an ever-growing fortune, has sent to his home province for two articled lads whom he sends round to his customers, and daily grows more prosperous.

> 'Hey, Tokukiti, wake up! Go along with Koosuke and have a bath or something. I say, look at the way that waistband's tied!'
>
> 'Look at 'em! Koosuke and Tokukiti may be much the same age, but while that brat Koosuke's off every night for a bath, for instance, and suggests having his hair done even before we tell him to, Tokukiti has his neck and ears absolutely black—all he's good at is dozing!'

Well now, these two errand-boys at Tokuemon's make a round of the customers every day; but instead of saying, as in the past, 'Is there anything you require, madam?' you now have your arms stuffed inside your kimono whoever you approach and just stare up in a lumpish way—which does duty nevertheless. Koosuke is the sort who, if some housewife or not unattractive girl of the neighbourhood were to say to him 'Hurry up and fetch me some best rice-wine, there's a nice boy', might forget she had said 'best rice-wine' but would be so overjoyed at being called 'nice boy' that he would bring it at once; and always, though his kimono skirts might be tucked up on his leaving the shop, it has been his way to let them down again when clear of the neighbourhood and to stretch himself out on the edge of the veranda at a hairdresser's over here or a street-watchman's box over there for the pleasure of a talk about how the wife at one place is smart and the girl at another is no class; and now, all of a sudden, his voice has come to sound as if he has been eating pickled fish.

By contrast, Tokukiti does his duties in a fervour of to-ing and fro-ing from the shop from morning till night, and has his hair like a kitchen broom all the time and his ears and neck all black wherever he goes; and after watching intently five or six of the neighbours' children playing at pitch-the-berry or *keteatta* with soap-berries, he becomes interested and wishes he could somehow have a try himself, but, not having any berries, he keeps the matter in mind for two or three days and, getting started with a 'spurter' under the shop front, is lucky enough to have the one berry become six or seven, which he carefully stuffs away into the waist-pleat of his kimono, treasuring them so much that he keeps a hand over them even in his sleep; and, increasing by twos and threes, they finally amount to no less than twenty or thirty. This is how people start who become viciously addicted to gambling. Tokukiti never forgets that even a little capital grows by accumulation of profits if you work

153

akekure oyakata no tyoomen-san-yoo suru soba nite, ikura mo ri ari to yuu koto omosiroku, noti ni wa Tokuemon ga sironezumi wa kono Tokukiti narubesi.

Sono noti kooin ya no gotosi to itte wa, doo ka [50]katakiuti-meite katakurosii kara hirattaku, kodomo no nobiru wa takenoko no gotoku, Koosuke Tokukiti wa haya zyuu-gorokusai ni nari, oni-waka-syu de wa mukasi-meite warui to, Tokuemon-huuhu wa sewa o yaki, hutari-tomo genbuku sase, Koosuke wa negai nite, 'Yahari Koosuke ga yorosii' to yuu [55]yue sono mama oki, sate Tokukiti wa Tokubee to na o aratame, Koosuke to wa tosi hitotu otorisi ga, mise no koto mo yoku nomikomi banzi midokoro ari tote, mazu bantoo-sita-zi ni site, Tokuemon ga kutimane mo sasekeru.

Tokubee wa wakai mono ni narisi yue, moo kodomo de [60]wa naku, sukosi no sioti mo ima made to wa tigatte omoku naru doori to, iyoiyo kokoro o tukete tutomesi ni, Koosuke wa norakuramono no kuse ni, tosisita na Tokubee ni tyoomen o sare, sukosi kuyasiku wa omoedo mo, Tokubee ga mimoti no mane wa naranu to akirame, iyoiyo [65]otokoburi o migakikereba, ittai umaretuki yokobutori nite sugata ga hirattaku, Tokubee to wa otokoburi mo otorisi ga, temae no ki nite wa, ano Toku-me wa tonda yabo na nari da to, yappari unu ga hoo kara otoko ga ee to kokoroe, atama mo Hyakusuke ga kuko to yuu [-70]tokoro de, bin wa kirigirisukago no yoo ni site, osii mayuge o iiwake no tame ni sukosi nokosite sorituke, syozi kinkin-mekasi ooki ni kaburu.

> Tokuu* "Koosuke koko e dero. Ware ga kami no huu wa nan da. Soo site konogoro mireba tohoo mo nai, sansyoo no [75]tenugui o motte yu ni yuki hutatoki hodo no nagayu da. Sore sono kiseru wa nan da. Gan-kubi mo suikuti no ana mo onazi yoo da."
>
> Koo "Hai hai, kono kiseru no na wa oo-tububari to moosite, tikagoro daibun hayarimasu."
>
> [80]Toku "Kyookoo, kami no huu mo naosasemasu kara gomen nasarete tukawasaremase."

Koosuke wa nan de mo hitotu to site waga ki ni iraneba, naroo nara oyakata mo Tokubee mo tatakidasite simaitakeredo mo, sono kabu wa nasi. Syosen kakeoti site [85]hara-ippai ni kinkin to irootoko ni kosirae, seken no onna ni ki o momasete tanosimimasyoo to, kinsu hyaku-ryoo nusumidasi kubi ni kake, zuitokuzi to dekakeru.

> Koo "Ima made wa hito no atama ya kimono no mihaba made, doo dano koo dano to ooki ni o-sewa. Doitu [90]mo doitu mo issyoo

---

hard and cherish that little and, day in, day out, while his master does the books, he is by his side, taking pleasure in the magnitude of the profits. It is surely our Tokukiti who will one day be Tokuemon's right-hand man.

Then the two heavenly luminaries, in arrow-like flight—but that sounds painfully stiff, somehow, as though this were a blood-feud story, so, more simply, children shoot up like bamboos, and Koosuke and Tokukiti are already fifteen or so. Tokuemon and his wife, holding it nasty and old-fashioned for them to be long-haired louts, arrange for the two of them to go through the coming-of-age ceremony and, since Koosuke says 'Koosuke is all right when all is said and done', his name is, as he wishes, left unchanged. But Tokukiti is now renamed Tokubee and, although a little younger than Koosuke, is, as a first step, on the grounds of his good grasp of the business and the all-round promise he shows, made Tokuemon's assistant-to-be, and is even allowed to speak as if he were Tokuemon himself.

While Tokubee, now that he has become a young man, is more con-scientious than ever about his work, telling himself that, as he is no longer a child, what would earlier have been a slight lapse would now be something serious, Koosuke, idler though he is, feels somewhat resentful at having Tokubee, who is the younger, in charge of the books; but he resigns himself to it with the thought that there can be no emulating Tokubee's conduct for him, and he goes on making more and more improvements to his manly appearance so that, although in fact his natural tubbiness gives him such a squat figure that he is Tokubee's inferior in manly looks too, in his own humble opinion that blighter Toku cuts an awfully outlandish figure, and he makes bold to believe that, when all is said, *he* is a nice-looking chap; and for his hair, it's nothing less than Hyakusuke's box-thorn oil, and, what with doing his side-whiskers like the bars of a cricket's cage and shaving off all his precious eyebrows except a little left as an apology, everything has the 'flash' touch, and he puts it on in a big way.

> Tokuu: 'Come here, Koosuke. What's this way you're doing your hair? And I've noticed lately—it's preposterous—you go off to the bath-house with a *sansyoo*-pattern towel and spend about four hours over your bath. What ever's that pipe you've got there? The bowl looks the same size as the hole in the mouthpiece.'
>
> Koo: 'Yes, sir, certainly! This is what's called an *oo-tubu*-style pipe—it's all the go lately.'
>
> Toku: 'Please excuse him, sir. I will see that he does his hair and things properly in future.'

Finding not a single thing to please him, Koosuke would like to send both his master and Tokubee packing if he could, but he's in no position to do that. In the end he thinks he will decamp, get himself up as a ladies' man as 'flash' as he's a mind to, and enjoy himself setting all the women's hearts a-flutter; so he purloins the sum of a hundred *ryoo*, which he slings from his neck, and is off like a shot.

> Koo: 'It's none of their business, all this fuss they've been making, about a chap's hair and the cut of his clothes even. I suppose what'll happen is, the whole lot of the blighters'll go on looking sights all

henteko de kutihateru no de aroo, ki-no-doku na koto da. Ee inu made yabo da, ki no kikanee. Sizuka ni hoero si! si!"

Tokuemon-uti nite wa, itu mo no toori asa okitaru tokoro, kanebako no hikidasi e oitaru hyaku-ryoo no kane miezu. [95]Kagi wa hako no soba ni sutete ari. Saredo mo Koosuke ga kakeoti nite hoka e utagai mo kakarazu, yanuti kimo o tubusu.

Koosuke wa syuzin no kane o nusumitori, sukosi no sirube nite Yanaka-hen e isooroo to nari, waga omoiire ni irui o kosirae, nani ga sate [100]yokobiroi otoko de, hikizuru yoo na kuro-nanako no awasebaori ni ko-mon-tirimen, kawari-hatizyoo to yuu tokoro o hurikasane, samezaya ippon otosizasi, obi wa kuro-zyusu ni aka-ito de kikuzyu o orikomi, uratuki wa hungurikaesu yoo na no o haki, hudan Asakusa, Yamasita, Ryoogoku, sono ta, Mukoozima wa [105]motiron Edo-zyuu o aruku ni, doo mo bukakkoo ni hirattai nari no otoko to, hito no me ni tuki, asuko no musume koko no nyooboo, tya-ya-onna made NARIHIRA NARIHIRA to, adana o iikeru o ee to kikituke, 'Mukasi no Narihira wa o-kuge de atta soo da ga, ooku no onna no kokoro o kakerareta [110]irootoko soo na. Ore mo otoko ga ee kara sore de Narihira to yuu to miete, kore wa kaku adana o tuketa ka. Sikasi Edo-zyuu no onna ni horerareru ni wa yowatta su' to, unubore wa masumasu zootyoo suru. Sono noti Koosuke wa, doko e dete mo toori no mono, masite onna [115]to na no tuita hodo no mono wa mehiki-sodehiki warau o, mina ore ni horeta to kokoroe, kono hiroi Edo-zyuu no onna ni horerarete, hyotto hitori no onna ni ee henzi o site omoi o kanaetaraba, sihoo happoo kara urami oroo si, dore mo dore mo sukosi-zutu kanaete [120]yatte wa, maa karada ga tuzukanu kara, sari to wa tumi da ga, koko o koraete mazu yoozyoo-gui o sen-iti to site, dai-zyoobu to natte, seken no onna no hyaku-bu-iti mo kanaete yaroo to omoi, narutake sei no tuku mono o konomu.

[125]Sore kara Koosuke wa, tonda ki no nagai no ka hananosita no nagai no ka, gorokunen ni naredo mo, nitiniti unagi ya suppon ottosei, sono hoka kan ni ireba arayuru neri-yaku o motii, sore de mo uti ni oru koto wa narazu, orihusi dete mireba, konogoro Narihira ga mienanda ga, are mukoo [130]o

156

their lives till they rot away. Can't help feeling sorry for 'em. Why, the dog's as bad as they are—no common sense! Bark quietly, ssh, ssh!'

At Tokuemon's, when they get up as usual in the morning, the hundred *ryoo* they had put in the drawer of the money-box is nowhere to be seen. The key has been left beside the box. But it is Koosuke who has decamped and no one else is even suspected; the whole household is aghast.

Having stolen his master's money, Koosuke, on the strength of a slight acquaintance, makes himself at home with someone in the Yanaka district, and has clothes made, as many as he likes: with a lined *haori* of black silk which, as there's no denying the squatness of his figure, seems as if it would sweep the ground, goes nothing less than small-patterned crêpe de chine and exclusive-dyed Hatizyoo silk, one garment on top of another, and, wearing a shark-skin scabbard stuck in straight up-and-down, a waist-band of black satin with chrysanthemums and lucky characters woven into it in red, and thick-soled sandals which look like capsizing him, he continually walks about Asakusa, Yamasita, Ryoogoku, etc.—and Mukoozima, of course—and all the rest of Edo, but he strikes people as such an ungainly, dumpy figure of a man that girls and housewives at one place and another, and even the women at tea-houses, call out 'Narihira! Narihira!' ('Dumpy! Dumpy!'[1]), giving him a nickname which sounds to him as if they are being nice. 'Narihira was a court noble long ago, so they say, a ladies' man who had a lot of women in love with him. I'm another chap with nice looks—which seems to be why anyone gets called Narihira—so they've given me this nickname, eh? It's a bit of a facer, though, having all the women in Edo crazy about me'—and his conceit grows even more overweening. After this, Koosuke feels sure that the glances and sleeve-pullings among the passers-by—above all, those worth calling women —which are smilingly exchanged wherever he walks abroad, mean that they are all crazy about him. 'With the women in all parts of this vast Edo crazy about me', he thinks, 'if I should respond nicely to one of them and comply with her desires, it would no doubt cause ill-feeling all round; on the other hand, to be compliant to all and sundry, share and share alike, why, the strain would be too great, so though it may be held against me, I'll practise self-restraint for the time being and first of all concern myself solely with taking nourishing food; then, after I've grown very strong, from among them all I'll oblige one woman in every hundred'; and he goes in for the most invigorating fare he can get.

And now, for Koosuke, who must be either extraordinarily patient or extraordinarily amorous, it's eels and turtle and seal-meat day after day, though it should go on for five or six years, and in addition to these, as soon as the cold period sets in, he uses every possible electuary; and when, despite everything, he is unable to remain in the house and does occasionally venture out, he finds that he is the talk of the town—'Narihira's not put in an appearance lately—but look! he's going by on the other side'; 'He's just gone towards Asakusa'; 'Yesterday he was in the Peacock tea-house'—and so he pampers himself more than ever. 'Another ten years or so of nourishment and

---

[1] Punning on the name 'Narihira', as if it were *nari*, 'figure' and *hira* 'flat', 'squat'.

tooru no, ima Asakusa no hoo e itta no, kinoo wa Kuzyaku-tya-ya e haitta no to yuu hyooban nareba, iyoiyo mi o daizi ni site, 'Moo zyuu-nen mo yoozyoo o site, sore kara hara-ippai tanosiman' to yuu o, hari no ue o tooru nezumi ga warau mo mottomo nari. Soosoo [135]hito no sewa ni natte mo irarezu, osiiredana o karite, hitorigurasi to wa nattaredo mo, itu nandoki de mo nyooboo o motitakereba, gohyaku-nin motoo ga sen-nin motoo ga, suki na koto to osamete iru.

[140]Ima-Narihira to adana sarete, ore mo yohodo no irootoko to omou ma ni haya sannen ni nari, moo sukosi-zutu irogoto o hazimeyoo to wa omoedo mo, hazimeta to itta naraba, seken de onnadomo ga asayu no kuguri ga aita yoo ni, dorodoro to osikakete kuru de [145]aroo. Doozo tirahora onna no horeru yoo ni sitai mono to omoi, Asakusa no Inga-Zizoo e gan o kakeru.

> Koo "Watakusi wa onna ni ookuho rerarete komarimasu. Doozo gonin ka zyuu-nin gurai de todomarimasu yoo ni, o-mamori [150]kudasarimase, namu Zizoo-bosatu."

Koosuke wa gan wa kakeru, moo yosi to omoi, Umamiti-hen o toorisi ni, aru koosi-zukuri no uti yori, gezyo to miete ko-girei naru onna, sibuutiwa ni too-nasu no heta yara tanegara o nosete, sute ni idesi o, kore [155]mo ore wa horete waza to sute ni deta to kokoroe, yaniwa ni usiro yori dakitukisi o, onna wa kimo o tubusi hurikitte nigeru.

Hikaru Genzi naraba, utiwa e noseta too-nasu de kosiore to yuu tokoro da ga, kono Narihira wa uta o yomu huu de nakereba, [160]hanauta de kono ba o kaeru.

> Koo "Hate na koo yuu hazu de wa nai ga, kinoo Zizoo-sama e o-negai moosita no de horenu to mieru."

Sore yori Koosuke wa, asuko-koko no onna ni kamatte mite mo, tokoro-dokoro nite terasare, waga nagaya no ooya no [165]kami-sama wa doo ka kite iru yoosu, kore wa daizyoobu dekiru to, iyami o iikakesi ni, tune no toori kami-sama mo hanbun naburu ki nite sukosi ayanasita tokoroga, hon no koto ni narisoo na anbai yue, hazusite kinzyo e deru.

> [170]Onna "Koosuke-san ee tokoro e kinasutta. Titto no uti-rusu o tanomimasu yo."
> Koo "Koitu mo ikenu wae. Zizoo-sama ga amari kikisugite hitori mo dekinu."

Koosuke tukuzuku kangaete miru ni, tokaku ore ga [175]otoko ga yosugiru yue, onnadomo rikimi ga atte, hitotu mo soodan ga dekinu to mieta. Isso zi-iro wa omoikitte, zyoroo-kai to deyoo to omoituki, Yosiwara nite na-aru

then I'll take my fill of pleasure', he says—the rats running across the rafters may well laugh to hear him. As he cannot go on getting free hospitality for ever, he rents a cubby-hole of a place and, although it has come to living on his own, he disposes of the matter with the thought that, should he at any time whatever wish to take a wife, he could have five hundred or a thousand women at will.

It being now three years since he acquired the nickname of the modern Narihira and took to regarding himself as another such regular ladies' man, he thinks he will now gradually set about his love-making. But if it got about that he had made a start, all the women would no doubt come thronging round with a clatter like that when the bath-house door is opened in the morning. He offers up a prayer to the Inga-Zizoo in Asakusa, wishing to have things arranged, please, so that just a woman here and there may become enamoured.

> Koo: 'I've got too many women crazy about me. Do please keep me safe and not let their number go above about five or ten. Hail, Zizoo-bosatu!'

The prayer has been offered up, all is now well, thinks Koosuke; and, as he makes his way along by the Uma-miti, quite a trim-looking woman, a servant by the look of her, comes out of a house with a latticed entrance to throw away the stalk and seed-waste of a pumpkin which she carries on a kitchen fan, whereupon Koosuke, taking it that this is one of his admirers come out to throw the things away of set purpose, promptly crushes her to him from behind; but this terrifies the woman, who wrenches herself free and escapes.

Had it been Hikaru Genzi, he would have made it an occasion for some piece of broken-backed verse about the pumpkin she was carrying on the fan, but, as composing poetry isn't in our Narihira's line, he makes his exit humming to himself.

> Koo: 'Well! I didn't expect that, I must say. It looks as though she isn't in love with me, because of my prayer to Zizoo yesterday.'

After that, Koosuke tries making advances to women at various places but meets with nothing but rebuffs; somehow, the landlady at the tenements where he lives seems forthcoming, and when he makes some doubtful remarks to her with the idea that this time he's on to a certainty, the usual thing happens; the woman, having half a mind to trifle with somebody, leads him on a bit until it looks as if he means business and then slips off out somewhere.

> Woman: 'It's nice you've come just now, Koosuke. I'm sure you won't mind minding the house for a bit while I'm out.'
>
> Koo: 'Another flop! This Zizoo stuff's working too well—I can't get even one.'

Koosuke does some hard thinking and, as he sees it, one way and another he is so excessively good-looking that women are affected too violently for it to be at all possible to come to terms. It occurs to him to give up the idea of amateur love-affairs altogether—he'll start patronizing the brothels; and he engages

159

zyoroo o asuko-koko nite kaedo mo, tokaku omou yoo ni saki kara horeta yoosu wa miezu, su-nen [180]koraeta hodo no omosiromi wa naku, iroiro ki o momu.

Koosuke wa sono noti mo syosyo nite asobisi ga, doko de mo omosiro-okasiku sareru bakari de, nekkara saenu yue, tito basyo o kaete asoban to Sinagawa to dekake, aru uti nite O-Kiku to yuu mawari-zyoroo o agesi ni, [185]yokuyoku no bu-ikimono to miete, tonda yoku sesi yue, hazimete onna wa koo sita mono to yuu koto o siri, saa yuku hodo ni, metta-musyoo ni kayoisi yue, oyakata Tokuemon-kata nite nusumisi kane mo, yoozyoo-gui sono hoka tana-tin ni nakusita ue, sukosi no nokori [190]o Hokkoku nite tukaitirasi, kanzin omosiroku asobu dan ni natta tokoro de binboo ni nari, sukosi wa atta irui mo butikorosi, konogoro wa hito no mono o karigi site no zyoroo-kai to narisi wa, hakanasi.

Hito no mi no nariyuki wa azi na mono nite, syuzin no [195]me o kuramasi, omoire zyosyoku no miti o syuugyoo suru kokoro nite yoozyoo-gui o si, saraba to omotta toki wa saki no omowaku ga tigai, yooyoo Sinagawa no hate nite onna ni omoitukare, omosiroi to omou to otibureru ga it-toki nite, ima wa mi no okidokoro sae naku, komo itimai o hatizyoo [200]to mo sima-tirimen to mo omoi, mi ni matoi-nagara mo yappari unubore wa yamazu, mukasi no Huziya-Izaemon wa, Yuugiri to yuu onna ni kingin o tukaisute, kamiko itimai to natte sono na o nokosita to yara, ware wa sono ue o itte, komo o kaburu to yuu mo, Izaemon yori wa irootoko nari [205]to, kore bakari o honmoo to akiramete, yukiki no hito ni issen nisen o morai yo o okurikeru. Mata Tokuemon ga kata nite wa, Tokubee o yoosi to site ie o yuzuri, huuhu wa inkyo site, ima wa Tokubee no sindai to nari, aru toki Asakusa-Kanzeon e mairisi kaeri ni, izen no hoobai Koosuke [210]ni meguriai, mazu sewa o site yaran tote turekaerikeri.

Tokuemon (sic) wa Koosuke o turekaeri, iroiro to iken site, inkyo e mo wabigoto iite, 'Sukosi motode o tukawasi, sewa itasitaki' to negaikereba, inkyo-huuhu [215]mo Tokubee ga zinsin ni men-zi, 'Doo nari to mo seyo' to yurusesi yue, kane o atae dootyoo e mise o dasase, sioya o sasesi ni, Koosuke mo ima ni natte waga mi no tawake o kuyami kasegisikaba, wazuka no aida ni ri-gai site, dandan to hanzyoo sikeru. [220]Makoto ni hutari-nagara turedatite, hanattarasi no zibun Ise yori Edo e kite mo, hito no kokoro wa kitui tigai na

public women of note at various houses in the Yosiwara, but, since his companions show no sign of the infatuation for which he is hoping, and the pleasure he gets is not in proportion to his long years of self-denial, it all leaves him very disturbed.

Koosuke still goes on frequenting various houses, but, meeting with nothing but ridicule wherever he goes, he finds it no fun at all, so he thinks he will change his haunt a bit and sets out for Sinagawa. At one of the houses there he calls in a low-class prostitute named O-Kiku, who, though in appearance the very reverse of smart, so gratifies him that now at last he knows what woman is. But ah!—the more he goes, the more recklessly does he make his visits, with the result that even the money he stole from the place of his master Tokuemon has gone on nourishing foods, and also rent, and the little that remained has been squandered in the North-land,[2] bringing him to poverty just as he reaches the all-important stage of getting pleasure from his dissipations; so he pawns or sells what few clothes he has, and recently—what a sorry state!—he has come to whoring in borrowed clothes.

The fortunes of men are unpredictable: he hoodwinks his master, feeds himself up in a resolve to dedicate himself to venery to his heart's content, but finds, when he thinks the time has come, that the other party has other ideas; and when, at last, a woman away out at Sinagawa does take a liking to him, he no sooner begins to enjoy himself than ruin comes in no time at all, and now, with nowhere to call his own, and for all that he is wrapped in a straw mat, which seems to him like Hatizyoo silk and striped crêpe de chine, he still fancies himself as much as ever: 'It's said that the name of Huziya-Izaemon has come down from the past because he threw his money away on a woman called Yuugiri and was reduced to a single paper kimono. I've gone one better in wearing a straw mat over my head, and that itself shows that I'm more of a ladies' man than Izaemon', he tells himself, and, accepting this as the realization of his hopes, he lives on the few coppers he receives from passers-by. Meanwhile, at Tokuemon's, they have adopted Tokubee and transferred the business to him, and, the husband and wife having retired, Tokubee now owns the family property. One day, on his way back from a visit to the Kannon temple in Asakusa, he has run across his old companion Koosuke and, telling himself that the first thing is to do something for him, has brought him home with him.

Having brought Koosuke home and given him a good talking to, Tokubee also apologizes for him to Tokuemon and asks for his agreement, saying 'What I'd like to do is to help him with a small capital sum'. The retired couple thereupon pardon him, yielding to Tokubee's kindness of heart, and say 'Do whatever you like about it'; so he gives him some money to enable him to set up shop as a salt-dealer in the same ward. As Koosuke is by this time regretting his foolish behaviour and working hard too, in a short time he is doing business at a profit and has gradually become prosperous. The two of them did indeed come from Ise to Edo together in their snotty-nosed days, but people differ extremely: to commit a crime and decamp in defiance of one's obligations to one's master is as different from becoming one's master's son

---

[2] *Hokkoku;* another name for the Yosiwara brothel quarter. See n. to col. 190.

mono nite, akuzi o nasi syuzin no on o sute kakeoti sitaru to, syuzin no ko to nari ie o tugu to wa, geta to yaki-miso hodo no tigai naredo mo, sue ni hanzyoo sesi [225]ga husigi. Kore mo yokusin de sezu tada koosyoku nomi yue, kami no megumi to mietari.

Sono noti Tokubee mo sinrui-uti yori nyooboo o yobi, sono tuide ni mata inkyo e negai, Koosuke ni mo sewa site O-Kiku o sowase, ryooke tomo ni hanzyoo hi ni masi, Tokubee-huuhu [230]wa inkyo Tokuemon-huuhu e kookoo o tukusi, medetaki haru o mukae kagyoo sakaekeru. Kono medetai tuide ni, tumaranu hutari no Ise-monogatari no go-hyooban mo, tada yoi yoi to go-hiiki o negai-mairasesooroo kasiku.

and succeeding him in the headship as clogs are from bean-paste—strange, then, that he should nevertheless prosper in the end! A blessing by the gods, it seems, because he was not moved by greed, but only by a liking for venery.

Tokubee later summons a wife from a family to which he is related and takes the opportunity to again ask Tokuemon to agree to his helping Koosuke so that he may marry O-Kiku; and, with both families increasing daily in prosperity, the Tokubees treat the retired Tokuemon and his wife with the utmost filial devotion as they welcome in the glad New Year with the family business flourishing. We should like to take advantage of this happy state of affairs to beg the favour of your unqualified praise for this unworthy tale of the two who came from Ise, to oblige

Yours faithfully.

Muoo no rigyo

MUKASI Entyoo no koro / Mii-dera ni Koogi to yuu soo arikeri / E ni takumi naru o mote na o yo ni yurusarekeri / Tune ni egaku tokoro / butuzoo sansui katyoo o koto to sezu / [5]Zimu no itoma aru hi wa umi ni kobune o ukabete / abiki turi suru ama ni zeni o atae / etaru uo o moto no e ni hanatite / sono uo no asobu o mite wa egakikeru hodo ni / tosi o hete kuwasiki ni itarikeri / Aru toki wa e ni kokoro [10]o korasite neburi o sasoeba / yume no uti ni e ni irite / sabakari no uo to tomo ni asobu / Samureba yagate mituru mama o egakite kabe ni osi / mizukara yobite muoo no rigyo to nazukekeri / Sono e no tae naru o medete / koimotomuru mono tuide [-15]o arasoeba / tada katyoo sansui wa koo ni makasete atae / rigyo no e wa anagati ni osimite / hito-goto ni tawaburete yuu / 'Syoo o korosi azarakeki o kuroo bonzoku no hito ni / hoosi no yasinoo uo kanarazu si mo ataezu' to nan / Sono e to wazagoto to tomo ni ame-ga-sita [-20]ni kikoekeri /

Hitotose yamai ni kakarite / nanoka o hete tatimati ni manako o tozi iki taete munasiku narinu / Totei tomodoti atumarite nagekiosimikeru ga / tada mune no atari no sukosi atataka naru ni zo / mosi ya to imegurite [-25]mamoritu mo mikka o henikeru ni / teasi sukosi ugokiizuru yoo narisi ga / tatimati tameiki o hakite / me o hiraki / sametaru ga gotoku ni okiagarite / hitobito ni mukai 'Ware ninzi o wasurete sude ni hisasi / Iku-niti o ka sugosiken' / Syuu-tei-ra yuu / 'Si mikka [-30]saki ni iki tae-tamainu / Zityuu no hitobito o hazime / higoro mutumaziku katari-tamoo tonobara mo moode-tamaite hoomuri no koto o mo hakari-tamainuredo tada si ga mune no atataka naru o mite / hitugi ni mo osamede kaku mamori-haberisi ni / ima ya yomigaeri-tamoo ni tukite / kasikoku mo monosezarisi [-35]yo to yorokobiaeri' Koogi unazukite yuu / 'Tare ni mo are hitori danke no Taira-no-suke no tono no mi-tati ni mairite moosan wa / hoosi koso husigi ni iki-habere / Kimi ima sake o kumi azarakeki namasu o tukurasime-tamoo / Sibaraku en o yamete tera ni moodesase-tamae / Keu [40]no monogatari kikoe-mairasen tote / kano hitobito no aru sama o miyo / waga kotoba ni tuyu tagawazi' to yuu / Tukai ayasimi-nagara kano mi-tati ni yukite sono yosi o ii-irete ukagaimiru ni / aruzi no suke o hazime / otooto no Zyuuroo / ienoko kamori nado imegurite [-45]sake o kumiitaru / Si ga kotoba no tagawanu o ayasi to su / Suke no mi-tati no

The dream carp

LONG ago during the Entyoo era (923–30) there lived in the Mii-dera Temple a priest named Koogi, whose skill in painting was widely acknowledged. Generally, for the subjects of his paintings, his chief interest was not in Buddhist portraits, or landscapes, or studies of birds and flowers. On days when he was free from temple duties he would go out in a small boat on Lake Biwa where fishermen were fishing with net and line, and, giving them money, throw back into the lake the fish they had caught, and paint these as he watched them leaping and darting. As the years went by he became very skilled. One day he was so absorbed in his painting that he became sleepy, and dreamt that he plunged into the lake and sported with fish of all sizes. As soon as he woke up he painted what he had seen and put the picture up on the wall. He himself gave it the title of 'The Dream Carp'. Many people admired the extraordinary beauty of the picture and vied with each other to obtain it. But although Koogi gave away as many of his landscapes and bird studies as were asked for, he had the strangest reluctance to parting with his carp pictures, telling everybody jokingly, 'I, a priest, could never give away my pet carps to you lay folk who kill living things and eat their flesh.' These pictures and the joke both became famous throughout the land.

One year Koogi fell ill, and after seven days his eyes suddenly closed, his breathing stopped, and he ceased to live. His disciples and friends came together, lamenting his loss; only, there was a slight warmth around his heart, so they kept watch round him, just in case. After three days his hands and feet stirred, then suddenly he heaved a sigh, opened his eyes, and sat up as though he had just woken from sleep. He turned to those present: 'I have been unconscious for a long time. How many days have gone by?' 'Three days ago, sir, you ceased to breathe. The question of the funeral was discussed by us of the temple, and also by the gentlemen you have been so friendly with, who had come here. However, noticing the warmth around your heart, sir, we left you uncoffined, and have been keeping watch like this. We are all overjoyed, for what a miracle, now that you have come to life again, that we did not do anything!' replied his disciples. Koogi nodded and said: 'One of you go to the mansion of my lord Taira-no-Suke, the patron of this temple, and say to him, "Wonderful to relate, our master is alive. Although you are at this moment, my lord, drinking wine, and having a dish of finely chopped fish prepared, leave your banquet for a while, I pray, and come to the temple, and our master will tell you a strange story." Observe the scene, and you will see that everything is exactly as I have said.' Greatly mystified, the messenger went off to the mansion and sent in the message. He had a look, and saw to his astonishment that Suke, the master of the house, his younger brother Zyuuroo, a retainer, and a servant were sitting around, drinking rice-wine exactly as his master had said. When they heard the

165

hito-bito kono koto o kikite ooi ni ayasimi / mazu hasi o tomete / Zyuuroo, kamori o mo mesi-gu-site tera ni itaru /

Koogi makura o agete rozi no wazurai o katazikenoo $^{-50}$sureba / suke mo yomigaeri no kotobuki o nobu / Koogi mazu toite yuu / 'Kimi kokoromi ni waga yuu koto o kikase-tamae / Kano gyohu Bunsi ni uo o aturae-tamoo koto ari ya' / Suke odorokite / 'Makoto ni saru koto ari ika ni site sirase-tamoo ya' / Koogi / 'Kano ^{55}gyohu mitake-amari no uo o ko ni irete kimi ga mon ni iru / Kimi wa kentei to minamiomote no tokoro ni go o kakomite owasu / Kamori katawara ni haberite momo no mi no ooi naru o kui-tutu eki no syudan o miru / Gyohu ga mana o tazusaekitaru o yorokobite / takatuki ni moritaru momo o atae / $^{-60}$mata sakazuki o tamoote sankon nomasime-tamoo / Kasiwabito sitarigao ni uo o toriidete namasu ni sesi made / hoosi ga yuu tokoro tagawade zo arurame' to yuu ni / suke no hitobito kono koto o kikite / aru wa ayasimi / aru wa kokoti madoite / kaku tubara naru koto no ^{65}yosi o sikiri ni tazunuru ni / Koogi katarite yuu /

'Ware konogoro yamai ni kurusimite taegataki amari / sono si-sitaru o mo sirazu / atuki kokoti sukosi samasan mono o to / tue ni tasukerarete mon o izureba / yamai mo yaya wasuretaru yoo nite ko no tori no kumoi ni kaeru $^{-70}$kokoti su / Yama to naku sato to naku yuki-yukite / mata e no hotori ni izu / Kosui no midori naru o miru yori / ututu naki kokoro ni abite asobinan tote / soko ni koromo o nugisutete mi o odorasite hukaki ni tobiiritu mo / otikoti ni oyogimeguru ni / wakaki $^{-75}$yori mizu ni naretaru ni mo aranu ga / omoo ni makasete tawaburekeri / Ima omoeba oroka naru yumegokoro narisi / Saredomo hito no mizu ni ukabu wa uo no kokoroyoki ni wa sikazu / Koko nite mata uo no asobi o urayamu kokoro okorinu katawara ni hitotu no mana ^{80}arite yuu / "Si no negoo koto ito yasusi / Matase-tamae" tote / haruka no soko ni yuku to misi ni / sibasi site / kamuri soozoku sitaru hito no / saki no mana ni matagarite / amata no urokuzu o hikiite ukabikitari ware ni mukaite yuu / "Watazumi no ^{85}mikotonori ari / Roosoo kanete hoozyoo no kudoku oosi / Ima e ni irite uo no asobi o negoo / Kari ni kinri ga huku o sazukete suihu no tanosimi o sesase-tamoo / Tada e no kanbasiki ni kurama-sarete / turi no ito ni kakari mi o usinoo koto nakare" to iite sarite miezu narinu / Husigi $^{-90}$no amari ni ono ga mi o kaerimireba / itu no ma ni uroko kinkoo o sonaete hitotu no rigyo to ke-sinu /

Ayasi to mo omowade / o o huri hire o ugokasite kokoro no mama ni syooyoo su / Mazu Nagara no yamaorosi / tatiiru $^{-95}$nami ni mi o nosete / Siga no Oowada no migiwa ni asobeba / katibito no mo no suso nurasu

message, the people of the house were amazed; the meal was immediately abandoned, and Suke went to the temple, accompanied by Zyuuroo and a servant.

Koogi raised his head from the pillow, and thanked them for taking the trouble to come. Suke in turn congratulated him on his return to life. Koogi then asked, 'Just listen, my lord, to what I have to say—Did you order some fish from Bunsi the fisherman?' 'Indeed I did. How do you come to know of it?', answered Suke in surprise. 'He came to your house with a fish more than three feet long in a basket', Koogi went on; 'You were sitting in the south room, playing *go* with your brother. Your servant was in attendance near by, eating a large peach as he watched the game. You were very pleased when the fisherman brought in his great fish, and gave him some peaches piled up on a fruit-dish, and three cups of rice-wine to drink. Then the cook, with a triumphant air, took the fish out of its basket, and made it into a dish of chopped raw fish. All that I have said is surely quite correct, to this last detail'. At this story, Suke and his companions were some of them astonished, and some of them bewildered, and they all plied Koogi with questions as to how he came to know this in such detail.

'A few days ago,' answered Koogi, 'I was suffering so grievously from my illness that, without realizing that I had died, I walked out of the gate with the help of a stick, longing only to cool my burning fever a little. I then seemed to become less conscious of my illness, and felt like a caged bird returning to the skies. On and on I went, over hills and through villages, until I arrived once more at the shores of the lake. As soon as I saw its green waters, I thought, as if in a dream, that I would bathe in it; taking off my clothes, I flung them down and, with a leap, dived into the depths. I swam here and there, just as my fancy led me—I, who from my earliest days had never been used to the water. I realize now that I was in a foolish, dream-like state. But men can never find so much pleasure in swimming as fish do—and hereupon I began to feel envious of the way the fish were sporting in the water. There happened to be a large fish near by who said, "Your wish is very easy to grant, sir. Please be so good as to wait." I saw it go far down into the depths, and then before long a man in court dress swam up astride the same fish, at the head of a great number of other fishes. He said to me, "Hear the words of the Sea-God. In the past, venerable priest, you have acquired much merit by liberating living things from captivity. Now you have entered the lake, and wish to sport in it like a fish, and the Sea-God is graciously pleased to offer you temporarily the apparel of a golden carp and bid you partake of the joys of his city under the waters. But take care lest you be deceived by the sweetness of a bait and lose your life by getting caught on a fishing line." With these words he disappeared from view. Wondering, I looked around at my body, and found that, without realizing it, I had been transformed into a carp, arrayed in glittering golden scales.

'I did not think this particularly strange, and swam about wherever my fancy led me, flicking my tail and flapping my fins. First, letting myself be borne on the waves raised by the wind blowing down from Mount Nagara, I disported myself by the shore of Siga-no-Oowada, where I was startled by the people walking to and fro along the shore and trailing the hems of their

yukikai ni odosarete / Hira no takayama kage uturu / hukaki minasoko ni kazuku to suredo / kakure-Katada no isaribi ni yoru zo ututu naki / Nubatama no yonaka no kata ni yadoru $^{-100}$tuki wa / Kagami-no-yama no mine ni sumite / yaso no minato no yasokuma mo nakute omosiro / Oki-tu-simayama / Tikubu-sima / nami ni uturoo ake no kaki koso odorokarure / Sasimo Ibuki no yamakaze ni / Asazuma-bune mo kogiizureba / asima no yume o samasare / Yabase no watari suru hito no minarezao o nogarete $^{-105}$wa / Seta no hasimori ni ikuso-tabi ka owarenu / Hi atataka nareba ukabi / kaze araki toki wa ti-hiro no soko ni asobu /

Niwaka ni mo uete monohosige naru ni / otikoti ni asariezu site kuruiyuku hodo ^{110}ni / tatimati Bunsi ga turi o taruru ni oo / Sono e hanahada kanbasi / Kokoro mata kawagami no imasime o mamorite omoo / Ware wa hotoke no mi-desi nari / Sibasi mono o motomeezu to mo / nazo mo asamasiku uo no e o nomubeki tote soko o saru / Sibasi arite ue masumasu hanahadasikereba / ^{115}kasanete omoo ni / ima wa taegatasi / tatoe kono e o nomu to mo oko ni torawaren ya wa / Moto yori kare wa ai-siru mono nareba / nan no habakari ka aran tote tui ni e o nomu / Bunsi hayaku ito o osamete ware o toroo / Ko wa ika ni suru zo to sakebinuredo ^{120}mo / kare katute kikazu-gao ni motenasite / nawa o mote waga agito o turanuki / asima ni hune o tunagi / ware o ko ni osiirete kimi ga mon ni susumiiru / Kimi wa kentei to omote no ma ni eki-site asobase-tamoo Kamori katawara ni haberite konomi o kuroo / Bunsi ga mote-kosi mana $^{-125}$o mite hitobito ooi ni medesase-tamoo / Ware sono toki hitobito ni mukai koe o hariagete / "Katagata-ra wa Koogi o wasure-tamoo ka / yuru-sase-tamae / tera ni kaesase-tamae" to sikiri ni sakebinuredo / hitobito siranu sama ni motenasite / tada te o utte yorokobi-tamoo / Kasiwabito naru mono ^{130}mazu waga ryoogan o hidari no oyubi nite tuyoku torae / migiri ni togi-sumasesi katana o torite manaita ni nobosi / sude ni kirubekarisi toki / ware kurusisa no amari ni oo-goe o agete / Butu-desi o gai-suru tamesi ya aru, ware o tasukeyo tasukeyo to nakisakebinuredo $^{-135}$kikiirezu / Tui ni kiraruru to oboete yume sametari' to kataru / Hitobito ooi ni medeayasimi / 'Si ga mono-gatari ni tukite omoo ni / sono tabi-goto ni uo no kuti no ugoku o miredo / sara ni koe o dasu koto nasi / Kakaru koto ma-no-atari ni misi koso $^{-140}$ito husigi nare' tote / zusa o ie ni hasirasimete nokoreru namasu o umi ni sute-sasekeri / Koogi kore yori yamai iete haruka no noti yowai o mote makarikeru / Sono owari ni nozomite egaku tokoro no rigyo suu-mai o torite umi ni tiraseba/

garments in the water, but, dive as I would down to the depths, in which the lofty mount of Hira was reflected, I yet found myself approaching the fishing-fires at Katada—senselessly, for there would be no hiding there. How fascinating to see the moon, dweller on midnight shores, shine, mirror-clear, over the peak of Mount Kagami, bathing countless inlets in brilliant light! Okitusimayama, Tikubu-sima—and the wonder of the red shrine-fences reflected in the waves! I was awakened from my dreams among the reeds when the boats of Asazuma ferry set sail in the wind from famed Mount Ibuki. I dodged the boat-pole of the Yabase ferryman, only to be chased away time and again by the keeper of the bridge at Seta. When the sun was warm, I would float on the surface; when the wind was rough, I would sport on the bottom, countless fathoms deep.

'Suddenly I realized that I was hungry and in need of food. I hunted everywhere for food, but in vain, and was swimming about frantically, when I suddenly came across Bunsi fishing. The bait smelled very good. But I was mindful of the River-God's warning, and told myself that I was a disciple of Buddha. Even if I was short of food for the time being, how could I possibly so demean myself as to swallow a fish's bait. So I swam away from the place. After a while, however, my hunger became still more intense, and I had second thoughts. I could bear it no longer. Even if I did swallow the bait, I would surely not be foolish enough to let myself be captured. Bunsi and I of course knew each other, so why should I hesitate? With these thoughts I finally swallowed the bait. Bunsi quickly drew up the line and caught me. "Hey, what's this you're doing?" I shouted, but Bunsi looked as if he had not heard me at all. He put a cord through my gills, moored his boat among the reeds, and, thrusting me into a basket, went off to your house. You were playing *go* with your brother in the south room. A servant in attendance was eating fruit. When you saw the great fish that Bunsi had brought, you all admired it greatly. I shouted at you then at the top of my voice; "Gentlemen!" I called again and again, "Have you forgotten Koogi? Spare me! Let me go back to the temple!" but all you did was to clap your hands in delight, without taking any notice. The cook at once grasped me firmly by my two eyes with the fingers of his left hand and, seizing a well sharpened knife in his right hand, put me up on a chopping-board. Just as he was going to cut me, I cried out in anguish. "It is unheard of to do violence to a disciple of Buddha," I shouted; "Save me! Save me!" but you would not listen. With the realization that the moment had come when I was to be cut up, I woke from my dream.' At this tale everyone was filled with wonder and amazement, and they said, 'Now that you say so, sir, we remember seeing the fish's mouth move on each of the occasions you have mentioned, but it never gave any sound at all. How extraordinary that we should have witnessed such a thing with our own eyes!' They thereupon despatched a retainer to the house to throw what remained of the dish of chopped fish into the lake. After this Koogi recovered from his illness, and it was long afterwards, when full of years, that he died. When his end was imminent, several of his carp pictures were taken and scattered on the lake, whereupon the painted fish left their paper and silk and sported in the water. This is the reason why these paintings of Koogi's have not come down to us, though his mastery was handed on to his pupil Narimitu, who was very

egakeru uo siken [145]o hanarete mizu ni yuuge su / Koko o mote Koogi ga e yo
ni tutawarazu / Sono desi Narimitu naru mono / Koogi ga sinmyoo o tutaete
toki ni na ari / Kan-in no tono no syoozi ni niwatori o egakisi ni / ikeru tori
kono e o mite ketaru yosi o / huruki monogatari ni nosetari /

famous in his time. An old story tells how, on a sliding screen in the palace of Kan-in, he once painted a cock, and how a real bird, seeing it, kicked at the picture.

Hitomuki ni katayoru koto no ageturai

Yo no monosiribito no / hito no tokigoto no asiki o togamezu / hitomuki ni katayorazu / kore o mo kare o mo sutenu sama ni ageturai [-5]o nasu wa / ooku wa ono ga omoitoritaru omomuki o magete / yo no hito no kokoro ni / amaneku kanaemu to suru mono nite / makoto ni arazu / kokorogitanasi / Tatoi yo no hito wa / ikani sosiru to mo / waga omou suzi o magete / sitagoobeki koto ni wa arazu / Hito [10]no homesosiri ni wa kakawarumaziki waza zo / Ookata hitomuki ni katayorite / adasi-tokigoto oba / warosi to togamuru oba / kokorosebaku yokaranu koto to si / hitomuki ni wa katayorazu / adasi-tokigoto o mo / warosi to wa iwanu o / [15]kokorohiroku oiraka nite / yosi to suru wa / nabete no hito no kokoro nameredo / kanarazu sore sasimo yoki koto ni mo arazu / Yoru tokoro sadamarite / so o hukaku sin-zuru kokoro naraba / kanarazu hitomuki ni koso yorubekere / sore ni tagaeru suzi oba / torubeki ni [20]arazu / Yosi to site yoru tokoro ni kotonaru wa / mina asiki nari / kore yokereba / kare wa kanarazu asiki kotowari zo kasi / Sikaru o kore mo yosi / mata kare mo asikarazu to yuu wa / yoru tokoro sadamarazu / sin-zubeki tokoro o hukaku sin-zezaru mono [-25]nari / Yoru tokoro sadamarite / so o sin-zuru kokoro no hukakereba / sore ni kotonaru suzi no asiki koto oba / onozukara togamezaru koto atawazu / kore sin-zuru tokoro o sin-zuru mamegokoro nari / Hito wa ikani omooramu / ware wa hitomuki ni katayorite / adasi-tokigoto [-30]oba warosi to togamuru mo / kanarazu warosi to wa omowazu namu /

Sakinoti to tokigoto no kawaru koto

Onazi hito no tokigoto no / koko to kasiko to yukitigaite / hitosikarazaru wa / izure ni yorubeki [-35]zo to / madowasikute / ookata sono hito no tokigoto / subete ukitaru kokoti no seraruru / So wa hitowatari wa saru koto naredo mo / nao sasimo arazu / Hazime yori owari made / tokigoto no kawareru koto naki wa / nakanaka n iokasikaranu kata mo aru zo kasi / Hazime [40]ni sadameokituru koto no / hodo hete noti ni / mata kotonaru yoki kangae no dekiru wa / tune ni aru koto nareba / hazime to kawareru koto aru koso yokere / Tosi o

172

The rights and wrongs of taking sides

THE way our learned men set forth the rights and wrongs of things, without speaking out against the mistaken teachings of others or taking sides, and so throwing out neither this nor that, is more often than not a warping of their own insights so as to make them to the liking of everybody, and is unstraight-forward and mean-minded. However ill the world may speak of you, it is not right to fall into line by warping what you deem to be the way of things. Indeed, it should not be any of your business how others speak of you, whether well or ill. Although mostly, it seems, the run of mankind are so minded as to hold it narrow-minded and wrong if, taking sides, you speak out against some other teaching as mistaken, but broad-minded and seemly, and so, right, if you do not take sides or call even a teaching which is other than yours mistaken, yet this need not everyway be right. If your standing-ground is settled, and you are minded to believe it strongly, it must needs be right to lean one way, and you will be wrong to take a line of thought that goes against this. Everything is wrong that is not the same as what you stand upon as right: Is it not the true way of things that, this being right, that must needs be wrong? On the other hand, calling both this right and that also not wrong means that your standing-ground is unsettled, and that you do not believe strongly what you ought to believe. When your standing-ground is settled, and you are strongly minded to believe this, it follows that you cannot but speak out against the mistakenness of any other line of thought; this is the true-heartedness of believing what you believe. What do others think, I wonder?—for myself, I do not think it must needs be wrongful to take sides and speak out against some other teaching as mistaken.

Shifts between earlier and later teachings

WHEN the same man's teachings are not alike but go here one way and there the other, you are at a loss which to trust in, and you most often get the feeling that all his teachings lack weight. Although, off-hand, this may seem right enough, it is not truly so. Rather, is there not something dull about teachings which from beginning to end have undergone no shift? For, indeed, it is right that they should have shifted from what they were at the beginning, since it is a wonted thing to make up your mind and then, some time after, have some other happy thought. Through the years, as your scholarship goes

173

hete gakumomu susumiyukeba / tokigoto wa kanarazu kawarade kanawazu /
mata ono ga hazime no ayamari o / noti ni siri-nagara [-45]wa / tutumikakusade /
kiyoku aratametaru mo / ito yoki koto nari / Koto ni waga inisiemanabi no
miti wa / tikaki hodo yori hirakesometuru koto nareba / sumiyaka ni kotogotoku wa kangaetukusubeki ni arazu / hito o he tosi o hete koso / tugitugi ni
akiraka ni wa nariyukubeki [-50]waza nareba / hitori no tokigoto no naka ni mo /
saki naru to noti naru to kotonaru koto wa / moto yori arade wa e-aranu waza
nari / So wa hitori no iki no kagiri no hodo ni mo / tugitugi ni akiraka ni
nariyuku nari / Sareba sono saki no to noti no to no naka ni [55]wa / noti no
kata o zo / sono hito no sadamareru tokigoto to wa subekarikeru / Tadasi
mata mizukara koso / hazime no oba warosi to omoite / aratameture / mata
noti ni hito no miru ni wa / nao hazime no kata yorosikute / noti no wa nakanaka ni waroki mo naki ni arazareba / to ni kaku ni erabi wa / [-60]mimu hito
no kokoro ni namu /

174

on making headway, there must needs be a shift in your teachings, and it is a very good thing to have put right, readily and without hiding anything, blunders you made at the beginning and have become aware of afterwards. Least of all in the Learning about Old Times which we have made our business, since it is but lately that it was opened up, can everything quickly be thought out in full; it is, as hardly needs saying, by going through men and through years that things come, one by one, to be seen in a right light, and so there cannot but be shifts between earlier and later even in the teachings of one man. Even within the span of one man's lifetime, first one thing and then another comes to be seen in a right light. And so, of an earlier and a later, it is the later that ought to be taken as a man's settled teaching. But, then again, you yourself may think the earlier to be mistaken and put it right, only to have it happen afterwards, as it sometimes does, that to the eyes of others the earlier one seems to be the better and the later one to be mistaken; and so, after all, the taking of one rather than another lies in how they will seem to others.

Gozyuu-no-too

Sono sanzyuu-iti

Toki wa itigatu no suetukata, Nossori Zyuubei ga sinku-keiei munasikarade, Kannoo-zi Syooun-too iyoiyo mono no migoto ni dekiagari, dandan asiba o torinozokeba sidai-sidai −5ni arawaruru ikkai ikkai mata ikkai, gozyuu gizen to sobiesi sama, Kongoo-rikisi ga magun o nirande zyuu-rokuzyoo no sugata o gen-zi konziku yurugasu asibumi site iwao ni tuttatitaru gotoku, appare rippa ni tattaru kana, ara kokoroyoki saiku-buri kana keu zya ¹⁰misou zya mata arumazi to Tameemon yori monban made mo syo-te Nossori o karo-simetaru koto wa wasurete santan sureba, Endoo hazime issan no sooto mo odoriagatte yorokobi, kore de koso Kannoo-zi no gozyuu-no-too nare, ara uresi ya, warera ga tanomu si wa toosei ni ¹⁵kata o hi-subeki hito mo naku, hassyuu-kusyuu no sekitoku-tati kohyoo-kakuro to sugure-tamaeru naka ni mo zeturui-bakkun nite, tatoeba sisi-oo kuzyaku-oo, warera ga tanomu kono tera no too mo zeturui-bakkun nite Nara ya Kyooto wa iza sirazu Ueno Asakusa Siba-sannai, Edo nite kore ni masaru ²⁰mono nasi, kotosara zindo ni uzumorete hikari mo hanatazu owarubekarisi otoko o hiroiagerarete kokoro no tama no kagayaki o yo ni idasaresi si no bitoku, konku ni tayumazu tiki ni mukuite tui ni sitogesi Zyuubei ga tanomosisa, omosiroku mata uruwasiki kiinnen −²⁵nari myooinnen nari, ten no nasesi ka hito no nasesi ka hatamata syoten-zenzin no kage nite ayaturi-tamaisi ka, oku o tukuru ni takumi narisi Tanika-sonzya no uwasa wa aredo seson-zaise no on-toki ni mo kaku kokoro-yoki koto arisi o imada kikaneba Kara ni mo kikazu, −³⁰ide rakusei no siki araba, ware ge o tukuramu bun o tukuramu, ware uta o yomi si o nasite, syoo-semu san-semu ei-zemu ki-semu to onoono tagai ni katariaisi wa yoku nomi naranu hito no zyoo no, yasasiku mo mata syusyoo naru ni hikikaete, hakarigataki wa ten no kokoro, Endoo Tameemon −³⁵ninin ga hakarai to site ito sakan naru rakuseisiki-syugyoo no hi mo hobo sadamari, sono hi wa kisen-nannyo no kenbutu o yurusi hinzya ni amareru kane o hodokosi, Zyuubei sono ta o negirai-syoo-suru ippoo ni wa mata gigaku o soo-site yo ni mezura-siki too-kuyoo arubeki hazu ni sitaku toridori −⁴⁰narisi saityuu, yohan no kane no ne no kumotte tune ni wa nitukazu mimi ni kitanaku kikoesi ga

The pagoda

Chapter 31

THE close of the first month—and Slowcoach Zyuubei's toil and planning had not been in vain, for at last the Kannoo temple's Syooun pagoda was most admirably completed; as piece by piece the scaffolding was taken down, roof after roof and yet another were in turn revealed, and there it stretched skywards, five-storeyed and lofty, as one might see a Deva king, glaring at the demon host and towering sixteen times human height, where with a stamp of his foot enough to shake the earth on its axis he has planted himself upon a rock. All, from Tameemon to the porter, were full of praises for Slowcoach—'How finely it stands there!', 'What delightful workmanship!', 'It's unprecedented', 'It's unique', 'There could never be another like it'—their first contempt for him being now forgotten; and all the priests of the temple too, from Endoo downwards, danced with joy—'Here indeed is a pagoda worthy of the Kannoo temple. What joy is ours! Our master in whose charge we are is unmatched in the world today and stands pre-eminent even among the holy men of the eight sects, the nine sects, who themselves surpass other men as the tiger and leopard, heron and crane, do other creatures, but he surpasses them as if he were the lion, king of beasts, or the peacock, king of fowls; so too does the pagoda of this temple in whose charge we are excel all others, for, though I cannot speak of Nara or Kyooto, nothing have we to match it in Edo, whether at Ueno or Asakusa or in the precincts of Siba. What a fine and wonderful stroke of fate it was, what a strange destiny, that linked the nobility of our master and the trustiness of Zyuubei; the one stretching out his hand to raise up this man who would have ended his days buried in the dust, his light unseen, and bringing forth for all to see the jewel-like lustre of his mind, the other, undaunted amid hardship, repaying friendship with final achievement! Is this the work of Providence, is it the work of man, or again has it been effected secretly by the beneficent gods of all the heavens? Tales are told, it is true, of the revered Tanika who was skilled in building, yet to this day we have not heard of such a glad event even in the time of the Buddha, nor yet in ancient China. Why! when the inauguration ceremony is held, I shall compose a hymn of praise, I shall write an essay; I shall write an *uta* or make a poem, eulogizing it, singing of it, chronicling it . . .'—thus one spoke to another; yet in contrast to the kind-hearted and praiseworthy and not entirely selfish sentiments of men, how unpredictable is the will of Heaven! When, under the direction of Endoo and Tameemon, everything, even to the fixing of an approximate date, had been decided upon for the performance of a most magnificent inauguration ceremony, on which day a truly remarkable service of dedication for the pagoda was to be held, with men and women, high and low alike, allowed to be present as sightseers, money unspent distributed to the poor, Zyuubei and his helpers fêted and honoured, and in addition a performance of *gigaku*,—just as all these preparations were at their height, the

177

somosomo, zenzen ayasiki kaze hukiidasite, nemureru kodomo mo ware sirazu yagu huminugu hodo zikoo nama-atatakaku naru ni ture amado no gatatuku hibiki [45]hagesiku narimasari, yami ni momaruru matu-kasi no kozue ni tenma no sakebi monosugoku mo, hito no kokoro no heiwa o ubae heiwa o ubae, ukiyo no eiga ni hokoreru yatura no kimo o yabure ya nemuri o midase ya, gubutu no mune ni ti no nami utaseyo, gibutu no omote no akaki iro tore, ono moteru mono ono [50]o hurue, hoko moteru mono hoko o hurue, nanzira ga toki turugi wa uetari nanzira turugi ni syoku o ataeyo, hito no abura wa yoki syoku nari nanzira turugi ni aku made kuwaseyo, aku made hito no abura o kae to, goorei kibisiku has-suru ya ina, moohuu itizin dotto okotte, ono [55]o motu yasya hoko moteru yasya uetaru turugi moteru yasya, mina issei ni areidasinu.

SONO SANZYUU-NI

Tyooya no yume o samasarete Edo yo-ri-sihoo no roonyaku-nannyo, akuhuu kitari to odorokisawagi, amado no yokozaru [-60]sikka to sase, sinbari-boo o tuyoku hare to ie-ie-goto ni urotayuru o, aware to mo minu hiten-yasya-oo, dogoo no kowane takedakesiku. Nanzira hito o habakaru-na, nanzira hito ni habakarareyo, hito wa warera o karonzitari, hisasiku [-65]warera o iyasimitari, warera ni sasagubeki hazu no sadame no nie o wasuretari, hoo kawari to site tatte yuku inu, ogori no negurasu tukureru tori, sirio naki saru, mono yuu hebi, tuyu makoto naki kitune no ko, kegare o sirazaru inoko no me, karera ni nagaku anadorarete [-70]tui ni itu made sinobiemu. Warera o nagaku anadorasete karera o itu made hokorasubeki, sinobubeki dake sinobitari hokorasubeki dake hokorasitari, rokuzyuu-yo-nen wa sude ni sugitari, warera o baku-sesi kiun no tessa warera o toraesi zinin no iwaya wa waga [75]sinriki nite tigirisutetari kuzuresasetari, nanzira areyo ima koso areyo, nan-zyuu-nen no urami no dokki o karera ni kaese itizi ni kaese, karera ga hokori no ke no kusasa o tetui-sange ni tukande suteyo, karera no koobe o ti ni tukasimeyo, muzihi no ono [80]no haazi no yosa o karera ga mune ni koko-romiyo, zankoku no hoko sin-i no turugi no hakuso to karera o nasi kureyo, karera ga nondo ni koori o ataete kukan ni osorewananakasimeyo, karera ga kimo ni hari o ataete himitu no itami ni taezarasimeyo, karera ga mesaki ni karera ga nasitaru ooku [-85]no syasi no sison o korosite, ganbutu no nen o satan no hai no kawa ni uzumeyo, karera wa kaiko no ie o ubainu nanzira karera no uti o ubae ya, karera wa kaiko no tie o warainu nanzira karera no tie o san-seyo. Subete karera no takumi to omoeru tie o san-seyo dai to omoeru [90]kokoro o san-seyo, uruwasi to mizukara omoeru zyoo o san-seyo, kanaeri to

midnight bell one night had a muffled sound, which fell on the ear with a quite unwonted unpleasantness; this was but the beginning, for a strange wind got up, and the air grew so sultry that sleeping children unconsciously kicked off their bedclothes, while the rattling of the sliding doors grew more and more violent, and in the topmost branches of the pines and oak trees tossing in the dark was heard the dread voice of the arch-fiend crying: 'Pluck out the peace in the hearts of men! Snatch it away! Strike terror into the bosoms of these wretches who glory in the vanities of the world; break up their slumbers! These blockheads! Make waves of blood pound in their breasts; these im-postors! turn pale their ruddy countenances. Ye with axes, wield your axes! Ye with spears, wield your spears! Your sharp swords are famished—give them to eat! The gross flesh of men makes fine food—feed your swords to the full, let them eat their fill of men's flesh!'—no sooner had he uttered the strict command than, of a sudden, a tempest sprang up, and demons with axes, demons with spears, and demons with hungry swords all at once began to run amok.

Chapter 32

AWAKENED from their comfortable dreams, all, young and old, male and female, over the whole seventy square miles of Edo, were thrown into alarm and uproar to find this evil wind come upon them, and every house rang with confused cries of 'Bolt the sliding doors tightly!' 'Put up the bars firmly!'; yet, quite unmoved, the heavenly arch-fiend, his enraged cries fiercely resounding, urged on his minions: 'Stand ye not in awe of men—let them stand in awe of you! Men have slighted us; long have they held us in contempt and forgotten the sacrifices lawfully due to us as offerings. Dogs that walk upright instead of on all fours, birds that build nests of proud luxury, tailless monkeys, snakes with speech, sons of foxes crammed with guile, sows that recognize not their own filth!—long have we let them mock us. How much longer shall we bear it? Long have we let them mock us. How much longer shall we leave them to their arrogance? We have forborne to the limits of forbearance; we have endured to the limits of endurance. Thus four-and-sixty years have passed, but by my divine power I have burst asunder and cast off the iron fetters of fate that bound us, and have smashed open the cave of compassion and forgiveness that held us captive. Rage on then—now, now is your time! Fling back at them the baneful malice of countless decades—fling it back all at once! Seize their stinking pride and fling it beyond the world's bounds! Bow their heads to the ground! Try out the excellence of your ruthless battle-axes on their breasts! Let them sully the blades of your cruel spears, your angry swords! Strike at their throats with your icy blades and make them shrink and tremble in cold anguish! Pierce their livers with needles till they can no longer bear their secret suffering! Strike dead before their eyes the many pampered children they have engendered, and bury their frivolous thoughts in the ashy stream of their grief! They have robbed silkworms of their homes—rob them then of theirs! They have mocked at the silkworm's skill—bepraise ye their skill! Bepraise all this skill they have held so apt; bepraise the will they have held so great; bepraise the feelings that have seemed to them so fine; bepraise the

179

nasu ri o san-seyo, tuyosi to naseru tikara o san-seyo, subete wa warera no hoko no e nareba, turugi no e nareba ono no e nareba, san-site noti ni emono ni kai, yoki e o tukurisi karera o warae. Naburaruru [-95]dake karera o nabure, kyuu ni hohuru-na naburikorose, ikasi-nagara ni itimai itimai kawa o hagitore, niku o hagitore, karera ga sin o mari to site keyo, karatati o mote se o ute yo, tansoku no iki namida no mizu dooki no ti no oto himei no koe, sorera o [100]subete hito yori tore. Zannin no hoka keraku nasi, kokuretu narazuba nanzira toku sine, areyo susume yo muhoo ni zyuu-site hooitu muzan muri-mutai ni aretate aretate susume susume, kami to mo tatakae butu o mo tatake, doori o yabutte yaburisutenaba tenka wa warera ga [105]mono naru zo to, sitta suru tabi doseki o tobasite usi no koku yori tora no koku, u to nari tatu to naru made mo titto mo yamazu hagemasitatureba, su-man no kenzoku isami o nasi, mizu o wataru wa nami o kekaesi, oka o hasiru wa suna o kekaesi, tenti o hokori ni [110]kibamasite hi no hikari o mo hotohoto ooi, ono o hurutte suki-mono ga teire okotari-naki matu o azawarai-tutu hokki to kiru ari, hoko o mawasite itayane ni tatimati ana o ugatu mo ari, yusa-yusa-yusa to kairyoku mote samo kengo naru ie o ugokasi hasi o yurugasu mono mo [115]ari. Tenurusi tenurusi mugosa ga taranu, ware ni tuzuke to hunnu no kiba kaminarasi-tutu yasya-oo no odoriagatte iradateba kokuu ni miti-mititaru kenzoku, otakebi surudoku omekisakende syani-muni booi o huruu hodo ni, sinzen zinai ni tateru ki mo, huuka [120]no niwa ni yasinawaresi ki mo koe hurisibotte naki-kanasimi, mirumiru daiti no kaminoke wa kyoohu ni itiiti zyuritu nasi, yanagi wa taore take wa waruru orisimo kurokumo sora ni nagarete kasi no mi yori mo ooki naru ame bararibarari to huriidaseba, etari to masumasu aruru yasya, kaki o hikisute [-125]hei o ketaosi mon o mo kowasi yane o mo mekuri nokiba no kawara o humikudaki, tada hitomomi ni kuzuya o tobasi hutamomi monde wa nikai o nezitori mitabi monde wa nanigasi-dera o mono no migoto ni tuiyasi-kuzusi, doo-doo-dotto toki o aguru sono tabi-goto ni kokoro o hiyasi [130]mune o sawagasu hitobito no are ni ki-zukai kore ni an-zuru syoosi no sama o mite wa yorokobi, idokoro sae mo naku sarete kanasimu mono o mite wa yorokobi, iyoiyo zu ni nori roozeki no aramu kagiri o takumasyuu sureba, happyaku-ya-tyoo hyaku-man no hito mina ikeru kokoti sezu gansyoku sara ni araba [-135]koso. Naka ni mo wakete odorokisi wa Endoo Tameemon, sekkaku wazuka ni dekiagarisi gozyuu-no-too wa momare-momarete, kurin wa yuragi, tyoozyoo no hoozyu wa sora ni e-yomenu zi o kaki, iwa o mo korobasubeki kaze no tukkakekitari, tate o mo turanukubeki ame no butukarikuru tabi tawamu sama, [-140]ki no kisiru oto, modoru sama, mata tawamu sama, kisiru

principles they have held so sound; bepraise the power they have held so mighty! All are food for your spears, food for your swords, food for your axes —bepraise them therefore, and then feed them to your weapons, and mock them that have furnished such good meat! Deride them to the limit of derision! Do not slaughter them at once, but torment them to death—peel layer by layer their living skin and strip off their flesh! Make of their hearts footballs and kick them about! Lash their backs with thorns! Sighs, tear-drops, heartbeats, cries of anguish—deprive men of them all! There is no pleasure save brutality; soon would ye die without cruelty. Run riot then! On! On! All laws cast aside, abandoned and unrelenting, carrying all before you, rage on! Rage on! On, on! Strive with the gods! Smite down the buddhas! Destroy right, destroy it and fling it aside, and the world is ours!' At each exhortation he set up a hail of earth and stones; from the hour of the Ox to the hour of the Tiger, to the Hare and on to the Dragon, ever unceasingly he urged them on. His minions in their tens of thousands gave rein to their excitement; some, crossing the waters, kicked up waves; others, rushing overland, kicked up sand. Heaven and earth they yellowed with dust, and almost blotted out even the rays of the sun. Some wielded their axes and with scornful laughter threw down the pine-trees so lovingly and painstakingly tended by the man of taste; others again, brandishing their spears, drove sudden holes in shingle roofs; yet others, by mighty feats of strength, made solid-seeming houses sway and bridges rock. 'Sluggards! Sluggards! You still lack in fierceness. Follow me!' cried the arch-fiend, clashing his fangs in rage and dancing with impatience, at which his followers who thronged the air all round gave vent to a great piercing cry and wantonly raged about. Trees standing before shrines and in temple grounds, trees cosseted in rich men's gardens, all alike forced out cries of lamentation; in an instant the earth's locks rose each on end in terror, willows crashed and bamboos split asunder. Now black clouds filled the sky and rain-drops began to pour down larger than acorns. The demons seized their chance to commit yet greater outrages, and tore away fences, kicked down walls, shattered gateways, ripped off roofs, and trod to pieces the tiles of the eaves. With only one onslaught, they sent thatched roofs flying; with two, upper storeys were wrenched away; while with three attacks they succeeded in demolishing a temple. They rejoiced to see the pitiable way in which men, chilled with fear and shaken with foreboding as each great battle-roar went up, turned their attention first this way, then that, and they rejoiced to see them in their grief deprived even of their homes and, as, ever more flushed with success, they abandoned themselves to the very extremes of violence, all the million inhabitants of the eight hundred and eight streets of Edo gave themselves up for lost, and their faces were drained of all colour. Nor were any to be found more terror-stricken than Endoo and Tameemon. The pagoda, so recently completed and with so much effort, was receiving buffeting after buffeting. Its spire was swaying, the topmost ball writing indecipherable letters against the sky. Each time the pagoda was struck by a wind of a strength to overturn rocks, and lashed by rain such as might well pierce a shield, it swayed with a creaking of timber, righted itself, then swayed and creaked again, and seemed about to crash to the ground at any moment. Seeing this, people set up a cry of 'Look! It's not safe! Can't anything be done?

oto, ima ni mo kutugaeranzu yoosu ni. Are are ayausi si-yoo wa naki ka, kutu-gaerarete wa daizi nari, todomuru sube mo naki koto ka, ame sae kuwawari-kitarisi ue mawari ni zyumoku mo [145]arazareba misou no kaze ni dodai semakute take nomi takaki kono too no koraemu koto no obotukanasi, hondoo sae mo kore hodo ni ugokeba too wa ikabakari zo, kaze o todomuru zyumon wa kikanu ka, kaku osorosiki oo-arasi ni mimai ni kubeki Genta wa mienu [150]ka, mada atarasiki deiri nari tote zyuuzyuu kode wa kanawazaru Zyuubei mienu ga kantai nari, hito sae kahodo ki-zukoo ni ono ga sesi too ki ni kakenu ka, are are ayausi mata tawanda wa, tare ka Zyuubei yobi ni yuke to iedo mo, ten ni kawara tobi ita tobi [-155]tizyoo ni zyari no moo naka o yukamu to yuu mono naku, yooyaku hoobi no kane o akasite soozinin no Sitizoo-zizi o idasiyarinu.

It would be terrible if it were blown down. Surely there's some means of preventing it! What's worse, the rain's started, and there aren't any trees around either, so what a small chance the pagoda has of standing up to such a dreadful wind when it's got such a small base for its height! Look! When the Main Hall's shaking so much, what about the pagoda? Wouldn't a spell to stop the wind be of avail? Genta ought to have come to see how things are in such a terrible storm—isn't he here? And Zyuubei, new as he is in his association with the temple, he's under a definite obligation to come, so it's very remiss of him not to be here. Doesn't he care about his own pagoda, when even other people are so worried? Look! It's not safe! It's swaying again! Somebody go and fetch Zyuubei!' But there was no-one who would venture out into the midst of the flying tiles and flying planks, and the gravel swirling up from the earth; in the end they gave old Sitizoo the sweeper a handsome reward and got him to go.